Hospitality and the Other

FAITH MEETS FAITH

An Orbis Series in Interreligious Dialogue
William R. Burrows, General Editor
Editorial Advisors
John Berthrong
Diana Eck
Karl-Josef Kuschel
Lamin Sanneh
George E. Tinker
Felix Wilfred

In the contemporary world, the many religions and spiritualities stand in need of greater communication and cooperation. More than ever before, they must speak to, learn from, and work with each other in order to maintain their vital identities and to contribute to fashioning a better world.

The FAITH MEETS FAITH Series seeks to promote interreligious dialogue by providing an open forum for exchange among followers of different religious paths. While the Series wants to encourage creative and bold responses to questions arising from contemporary appreciations of religious plurality, it also recognizes the multiplicity of basic perspectives concerning the methods and content of interreligious dialogue.

Although rooted in a Christian theological perspective, the Series does not limit itself to endorsing any single school of thought or approach. By making available to both the scholarly community and the general public works that represent a variety of religious and methodological viewpoints, FAITH MEETS FAITH seeks to foster an encounter among followers of the religions of the world on matters of common concern.

FAITH MEETS FAITH SERIES

Hospitality and the Other

Pentecost, Christian Practices, and the Neighbor

Amos Yong

ORBIS BOOKS

Maryknoll, New York 10545

Founded in 1970, Orbis Books endeavors to publish works that enlighten the mind, nourish the spirit, and challenge the conscience. The publishing arm of the Maryknoll Fathers and Brothers, Orbis seeks to explore the global dimensions of the Christian faith and mission, to invite dialogue with diverse cultures and religious traditions, and to serve the cause of reconciliation and peace. The books published reflect the opinions of their authors and are not meant to represent the official position of the Maryknoll Society. To obtain more information about Maryknoll and Orbis Books, please visit our website at www.maryknoll.org.

Library of Congress Cataloging in Publication Data

Yong, Amos.
    Hospitality and the other : Pentecost, Christian practices, and the neighbor / Amos Yong.
        p. cm. — (Faith meets faith series)
    Includes bibliographical references and index.
    ISBN 978-1-57075-772-3
    1. Hospitality—Religious aspects—Christianity. I. Title.
    BV4647.H67Y66 2008
    241'.671—dc22
                                                    2007036513

To Anna

Contents

vii

Preface

The initial occasion for this book was an invitation to deliver the William W. Menzies Annual Lectures at Asia Pacific Theological Seminary (APTS) in Baguio City, Philippines, in January 2007. I am grateful to Won-suk Ma, former academic dean of APTS, who laid the groundwork for my coming, and to Paul Lewis, current dean, for seeing me through the week of lectures. Thanks also to David Hymes, who shouldered the bulk of the organizational work that made my visit possible and my stay pleasant and enjoyable. I also appreciate the hospitality shown to me by APTS faculty members Roli de la Cruz, A. Kay Fountain, Melvin T. Johnson, Galen Hertwick, Joseph R. L. Suico, Tham Wan Yee, and their families. The food was delicious, and my first visit to the Philippines was spiced up with invigorating theological conversation. Last but not least, thanks to the many students who were bold enough to ask questions, and who also welcomed "home" to Asia with open arms this Malaysian-born Chinese whose family immigrated to the United States when he was ten. I left Baguio enriched by the hospitality shown to me, and all the more convinced that the practice of hospitality holds one of the keys to life in a global context of the twenty-first century.

I am also indebted to many colleagues and friends who gave me essential feedback on the manuscript. My discussion of the interreligious situation in Sri Lanka benefited from critical comments by Ajith Fernando and G. P. V. Somaratna, while the section on Nigeria is now improved because of the suggestions of Bramwell Osula, Samuel Zalanga, Ogbu Kalu, and Jan H. Boer. Having never visited either country, I was dependent primarily on the published literature in the English language. Their comments, informed by firsthand experiences of the interreligious issues in these nations, have been invaluable.

I am also grateful to Frank D. Macchia, Thomas E. Reynolds, Gerald R. McDermott, and Doc Hughes for reading through the entire manuscript. Frank has long been an esteemed dialogue partner in matters related to pneumatological theology, but in this case his influence—communicated in part through a long conversation at a hotel room at this past Society for Pentecostal Studies annual meeting (March 2007) at Lee University in Cleveland, Tennessee—covers the entire book. Tom's expertise in theology of religions and interest in theology of hospitality helped sharpen my arguments at various places throughout the manuscript. Gerry's very helpful, critical feedback came in at the last minute as I was sending the manuscript to the publisher. Although I have not had as much time to rewrite in various places as I would have wished, he has been, nevertheless, a mentor, friend, and indispensable dialogue partner to me in the task of evangelical theology today. Doc has served as my graduate assistant this past year, and his careful reading of the manuscript has made it, in turn, more readable. Finally, Bradford McCall, my current graduate assistant, helped me develop the indexes and also saved me from a few grammatical and typographic errors. Of course, none of these named individuals should be held responsible for the errors of fact or interpretation that remain in the pages of this book.

Since writing my dissertation on theology of religions almost ten years ago, I have desired to be published in Orbis Books' Faith Meets Faith series. My thanks to Paul Knitter for encouraging me in various ways over the years. Thanks also to Bill Burrows, who has become more than just an editor, but also a friend. As an editor, he has given me both guidance and freedom—the former resulting in a more clearly articulated work, the latter allowing me to retain the more extensive documentation I think important for some of my readers. As a friend, I have come to appreciate Bill's missionary vision, his catholic and ecumenical spirit, and his theological acumen.

My wife, Alma, remains the steadfast inspiration behind my life and scholarship. She has been a more loving companion than I deserve. Words cannot express my gratitude to her.

I dedicate this book to my youngest daughter, Annalisa Nicholle. While on the verge of her teenage years as this book goes to press, she is already the epitome of hospitality with her friendliness, compassion, and kindness toward others. At this point in her life, she says she wants to be an international ambassador when she grows up! If the skills she is developing as negotiator, adjudicator, and peacemaker among her school and neighborhood friends is any indication, she will make a fine ambassador. Nan, I love you!

Introduction

There are three strands interwoven in this book. The first, connecting theology of hospitality with theology of religions, occurred to me initially during my work in 2003-2004 as a member of the World Council of Churches consultation process on religious plurality and Christian self-understanding launched jointly by Faith and Order, the Commission on World Mission and Evangelism, and Office of Interreligious Relations and Dialogue.[1] The central theme that emerged in our discussions was that of hospitality in a world of many faiths.[2] The genesis of this book's main idea can be traced to the many stimulating conversations we members of the consultation had together.

The second strand emerged for me in thinking through the implications of the first motif. If hospitality plays a central role for revisioning Christian theology of religions today, then the result is not only a set of ideas but a central virtue with a correlative set of practices. I began to sense that all Christian theologies of religions similarly either assumed and emerged out of a set of practices or preferred and recommended some kinds of interreligious attitudes, postures, and practices rather than others. I also saw that my observation was not one "out of season" in that the connection between beliefs and practices was a live one in the present theological climate. In this book, I explore the possibilities for thinking about the relationship between Christian theology of religions and Christian interfaith practices within the broader framework of the theological conversation regarding the association between Christian beliefs and practices.

The third strand is the pneumatological framework that I believe both holds together the other two strands and links the arguments in this volume to those I have developed elsewhere. In two previous books, *Discerning the Spirit(s): A Pentecostal-Charismatic Contribution to Christian Theology of Religions*, and *Beyond the Impasse: Toward a Pneumatological Theology of Religions*,[3] I have suggested that approaching the topic of

---

[1] My thanks to Hans Ucko, Jacques Matthey, and the WCC and Ecumenical Institute, Bossey, staffs for their hospitality to me and other consultation members over three visits to Geneva, Switzerland, from October 2003 to October 2004.

[2] See the resulting document, "Religious Plurality and Christian Self-Understanding," *Current Dialogue* 45 (July 2005): 4-12.

[3] Amos Yong, *Discerning the Spirit(s): A Pentecostal-Charismatic Contribution to Christian Theology of Religions*, Journal of Pentecostal Theology Supplement Series 20 (Sheffield, U.K.: Sheffield Academic Press, 2000), and *Beyond the Impasse: Toward a Pneumatological Theology of Religions* (Grand Rapids: Baker Academic, 2003).

theology of religions by starting with the doctrine of the Holy Spirit may open up heretofore-unforeseen possibilities for rethinking the relationship between Christianity and other faiths in our time. One of the complaints—on target, in my estimation—was that my project remained there at a high level of abstraction. In this book, I hope to remedy that fault at least in two ways: by providing concrete case studies that can ground our more theoretical considerations, and by explicating how Christian theology of religions is, or should be, bound up with interreligious practices of hospitality.

Among other concerns about my pneumatological approach to theology of religions has been the relationship between pneumatology and christology and the implications for Christian mission.[4] In this book, I seek to respond decisively to these matters by developing the trinitarian framework of my pneumatological approach and by showing how Christian beliefs about other religions are both deeply shaped by Christian practices and have normative implications for Christian missions. But I also will show that such mission in a postmodern and pluralistic world is much more complicated than some might be willing to grant so far. Let me be clear that I see the arguments in this volume as being extensions and elaborations of my pneumatological theology rather than discontinuous from my previous work in this area. Put straightforwardly, the theses being argued here are consistent with the pneumatological project I have been developing over the last ten years,[5] with the major advance in this volume consisting of making clear the connections between Christian beliefs about other faiths and Christian interreligious practices.

The three strands of this volume will be woven together in five chapters. The first will provide three case studies of interreligious interactions—in Sri Lanka, Nigeria, and the United States—in order to ground our theological reflections on an adequate empirical base. My chief aim here will be to show that in a postmodern and pluralistic world of interreligious war and violence, there are glimmers of hope manifest in various acts of interreligious hospitality. It is the latter that we need to cultivate in all its breadth and depth, and that is one of the primary reasons I have written this book.

Chapter 2 attends to the Christian theological discussion about the interrelationship between beliefs and practices. Rather than theology preceding practices or vice versa, there is increasing recognition that they are dialectically related. My distinctive contribution to this broader discussion will be to suggest a pneumatological account regarding this interrelationship. To be more precise, I will argue that the gift of the Holy Spirit results

---

    [4] E.g., Jay A. Womack and J. Scott Horrell, in *Bibliotheca Sacra* (Oct-Dec 2005): 489-91; and William T. Chandler in *Journal of the Evangelical Theological Society* 48, no. 1 (2005): 191-95.

    [5] Besides the two books already cited, see also Amos Yong, *The Spirit Poured Out on All Flesh: Pentecostalism and the Possibility of Global Theology* (Grand Rapids: Baker Academic, 2005).

not only in the many tongues manifest on the Day of Pentecost, but also in the many practices seen in the multitude of charisms in the body of Christ. Put alternatively, I suggest that the diversity of gifts of the Spirit is connected with the multiplicity of tongues to which the same Spirit gives utterance.

In chapter 3, I apply the idea of many tongues and many practices to the ongoing discussion of Christian theology of religions. Here I provide a sympathetic reading of the main theological approaches—exclusivism, inclusivism, and pluralism—and make explicit both their underlying practices and the shape of their normative commitments. While the discourse deployed in this chapter remains primarily at the level of description, its implicit argument is that many tongues and many practices are also the norm rather than the exception when thinking about both the relationship between Christianity and other faiths and the Christian mission in a world of many faiths. Just as the many tongues are not homogenized but bear witness to the glory of God in and through their particularities, so also the many practices accomplished the redemptive and sanctifying work of the Spirit as signs of the coming kingdom.

Chapters 4 and 5 argue the thesis that a pneumatological theology of hospitality provides a coherent framework for thinking about many tongues and many practices in an interfaith context. We focus first on the emerging Christian exploration of the theology of hospitality and, again, suggest pneumatological perspectives through which to push the discussion forward. More specifically, I argue that the many tongues witness to many types of hospitable practices already seen and still needed in the interfaith encounter. In our final chapter, we bring the argument full circle by elucidating how a pneumatological theology of hospitality applies to contemporary interreligious practices and to Christian mission in a multireligious, world which includes situations such as those in Sri Lanka, Nigeria, and the United States.

Rather than being merely a prolegomenon to the interfaith encounter, however, I submit that the pneumato-theological vision sketched in this volume is itself derivative from and deeply shaped by our present experiences of the many kinds of interreligious hospitality. To go further, I am convinced that such a "pneumatological imagination"—to use a term I have developed elsewhere[6]—would not have been possible apart from the practices of intra-Christian and interreligious ecumenism that emerged during the twentieth century. In that sense, while I do not conduct sustained interreligious dialogues in this book,[7] they are in fact the bedrock of the thesis argued here.

---

[6] See Amos Yong, *Spirit-Word-Community: Theological Hermeneutics in Trinitarian Perspective* (Burlington, Vt., and Aldershot, U.K.: Ashgate, 2002), part 2.

[7] My work in this area has been focused on comparative theology and comparative religion, especially with Buddhist traditions; see, e.g., Amos Yong, "Technologies of Liberation:

So who then am I addressing? I hope that those working in the areas of the interrelationship between religious beliefs and practices and of theology of hospitality will be drawn to this book. I think I have some creative and insightful theological—specifically, pneumatological—perspectives to add to these discussions. My discussion of the many tongues and many practices, for example, derives from a sustained dialogue with the Luke-Acts narrative regarding the work of the Spirit. Similarly, I hope to develop a pneumatological theology of hospitality in dialogue with the broad scope of the biblical narrative and with recent developments in the tradition of phenomenological philosophy.

But clearly, the primary readers of this volume will be those interested in interfaith relations today. At one level, I am addressing primarily other Christians, both in order to persuade those yet unconvinced about the importance of interreligious hospitality and to encourage those who are already involved in interfaith activities that their practices are intimately connected with the depth grammar of Christian convictions regarding the redemptive hospitality of God manifest in Jesus Christ by the power of the Holy Spirit. Yet at the same time, I also trust that people of other religious persuasions will find material of value in this book. Perhaps it can encourage them to return to their own traditions to identify how the virtue of hospitality has been and could be further deployed for the purposes of advancing the interfaith encounter in our time. Alternatively, perhaps they can also make clear how their beliefs and practices are intertwined, and by so doing, reveal how their deepest religious commitments open up to the kinds of interreligious practices desperately needed in an oftentimes hostile postmodern and pluralistic world.

I do, however, presume that those interested in reading this book are either already committed to such goals or are seeking to understand further the present situation and our roles in it. My goal is not to titillate the eyes and ears of those concerned only about being politically correct or interested in tolerance for tolerance sake. Here I find helpful Derek Tidball's distinction between pilgrims and tourists: the latter are those chasing about every faddish wind and tending in the process to leave litter behind, whereas the former are teleologically directed and leave their rest stops

---

A Comparative Soteriology of Eastern Orthodoxy and Theravada Buddhism," *Dharma Deepika: A South Asian Journal of Missiological Research* 7, no. 1 (2003): 17-60; idem, "The Holy Spirit and the World Religions: On the Christian Discernment of Spirit(s) 'after' Buddhism," *Buddhist-Christian Studies* 24 (2004): 191-207; idem, "The Demonic in Pentecostal-Charismatic Christianity and in the Religious Consciousness of Asia," in *Asian and Pentecostal: The Charismatic Face of Christianity in Asia*, ed. Allan Anderson and Edmond Tang (London: Regnum International; and Baguio City, Philippines: Asia Pacific Theological Seminary Press, 2005), 93-127; and idem, "Christian and Buddhist Perspectives on Neuropsychology and the Human Person: *Pneuma* and *Pratityasamutpada*," *Zygon: Journal of Religion and Science* 40, no. 1 (2005): 143-65.

transformed for the better.[8] I am not against tourism, but I see this as a work of pilgrimage rather than a sightseeing venture. My commitments are directed toward the formation of Christian character in a world of many faiths, and the outworking of Christian practices and the Christian mission in the postmodern and pluralistic times that we find ourselves. Toward that end, on with the weaving our threefold cord.

---

[8] Derek Tidball, "The Pilgrim and the Tourist: Zygmunt Bauman and Postmodern Identity," in *Explorations in a Christian Theology of Pilgrimage,* ed. Craig G. Bartholomew and Fred Hughes (Aldershot, U.K., and Burlington, Vt.: Ashgate, 2004), 183-200, esp. 196.

1

Between Terrorism and Hospitality

The Encounter of Religions in the Twenty-first Century

Many of us recall watching the circumstances unfold on our television sets on that fateful day of 11 September 2001, when two jetliners hijacked by terrorists were flown into the World Trade Center twin towers. I was teaching then at Bethel University in St. Paul, and we were watching a screen set up in one of our public lounges. In reflecting back over the years on that sequence of events, three themes have emerged that describe for me central aspects of the encounter between religions in the twenty-first century, and that frame the discussion of this book.

First and foremost are concerns with the complexity of the interreligious encounter in our time. We have since come to realize that the war on terror is not just a war fought abroad, but it involves all human beings who care for peace, justice, and freedom. More to the point, the religious, ideological, political, social, and economic struggles in various places around the world have reverberating effects for every one of us. We are past the point where wars are merely "local" or geographically circumscribed. Our globalized and globalizing world has forced the many nations, cultures, peoples, and religious traditions together. The result is what some theorists have called "glocalization,"[1] so that what happens (locally) to or through "the least of these" may have (global) consequences for any and all others, and vice versa. Truly one of the first questions in the biblical narrative— "Am I my brother's keeper?"—is no longer rhetorical but has serious impli-

---

[1] See Roland Robertson, "Glocalization: Time-Space and Homogeneity-Heterogeneity," in *Global Modernities,* ed. Mike Featherstone, Scott Lash, and Roland Robertson (London and Thousand Oaks, Calif.: Sage, 1995), 25-44.

cations not only for those threatened but for all who may or may not wish to be responsible for others.

And the truth is, second, that the human family may be more deeply divided than we would care to admit. Not long ago Harvard University professor Samuel Huntington proposed that the present world order may be divided into at least three civilizations—the Western, Islamic, and Chinese—with the latter two now retrieving and re-affirming the value of their own cultural (and even religious, in the case of Islam) achievements in response to Western colonialism and imperialism.[2] The results might be catastrophic since these developments may lead to full-scale civilizational clashes such that what happened on 9/11 is only a portent of things to come. Even if the overall scope of Huntington's thesis is unsustainable,[3] 9/11 has alerted us to the fact that none of us are immune to the threat of wars waged in the name of religion. And our growing recognition of human interdependence not only across space but also across time—generations, even centuries past—means that the victims and perpetrators are bound up in an extensive web of cause and effect such that only repentance on all sides can bring about reconciliation and peace.

But third, and here I am sounding the hopeful note of this volume, 9/11 has showed us that religious terrorism ultimately takes a back seat to the kind of hospitality advocated by the world's religions. Here I am referring to the massive mobilization of disaster relief, the charitable efforts and commitments of people, and the many acts of unrelenting kindness, all of which brought together people across traditionally divided religious lines.[4] One of America's darkest hours also brought forth the heroism, kindness, and hospitality of people of many faiths.

In this chapter, I want to explicate the first two themes—that of the complexity of the interreligious encounter in a post-9/11 world and that of the actual and potential clash of religions (if not civilizations)—and do so by attending to case studies of interreligious relations in three distinct contexts: Sri Lanka, Nigeria, and the United States. In a sense, the three cho-

---

[2] Samuel P. Huntington, *The Clash of Civilizations and the Remaking of World Order* (New York: Simon & Schuster, 1996).

[3] Jonathan Fox, *Religion, Civilization, and Civil War: 1945 through the Millennium* (Lanham, Md.: Lexington Books, 2004), ch. 6, argues that Huntington's thesis is too broad because many conflicts are ethnic and regional, not civilizational; that religion is not often the primary cause of conflict, even if religion does influence the dynamics of conflicts in various ways; and finally, that religion impacts conflicts in deeper ways than it does civilizations. There have been many other responses in the debate that Huntington's book has opened up.

[4] For an American Muslim account of some of the "acts of compassion, tolerance and friendship" in the wake of 9/11, see Riad Z. Abdelkarim, "The Muslim American Community a Year after the Attacks," in *Muslims in America*, ed. Allen Verbrugge (Detroit: Greenhaven Press, 2005), 97-103, esp. 99-100. For Christian perspectives that resisted the demonization of Islam and Muslims, see Alan F. H. Wisdom and Darrell Cole, *Straight Answers to Moral Confusion in National Crisis* (Washington, D.C.: Institute on Religion and Democracy, 2002), ch. 11 and appendix.

sen cases are arbitrary: there are many others that could have served our purposes. But Nigeria was on my radar because it involves pentecostal Christians, of whom I have a special interest having grown up in that tradition, and I live in and am therefore most familiar with the American situation. Further, I desired a diversity of empirical studies reflecting the global character of the contemporary interreligious interchange. Finally, I wanted at least one of the case studies to be focused on non-Christian interactions (Sri Lanka).

Especially in the first two cases of Sri Lanka and Nigeria, we will be discussing some very controversial issues about which there is no agreement not only between but also within the religious communities involved. My comments should be read not as being prejudicial toward one or other side of the divide (I claim no "bird's-eye view" on these matters), nor as advocating one or other political agenda (I am a theologian, not a political scientist). Rather, my goal in these case studies is to provide some empirical perspective to situate our theological reflections in the rest of this book amidst concrete developments in the complex encounter between religions "on the ground." Hence, I should caution that these case studies are neither exhaustive of what is happening in these three regions nor representative of interreligious relations worldwide. At the same time, I believe they will open up possibilities for thinking about interreligious interactions through the lens of a theology of hospitality that this book proposes.

WORLD CHRISTIANITY: MINORITY STATUS AMIDST RELIGIO-ETHNIC CONFLICT IN SRI LANKA

Our first case study focuses on Christianity in Sri Lanka. This case is of particular interest for at least three reasons: first, Christianity is a minority religion in Sri Lanka; second, Sri Lankan Christians have been implicitly drawn into the civil war in Sri Lanka that has been waged since 1983 between the Sinhalese Buddhist majority and the Tamil Hindu minority; and third, all "parties" to the conflict are negotiating local identities within the global context. In this section, we will offer an overview of the Sri Lankan conflict, present shifting Sinhalese Buddhist self-understandings over the last two generations, and describe the wide range of Christian responses from their minority locations. It will be especially important to note what practices are prominent when Christians find themselves as a minority group in the midst of an ethnically and (partly) religiously motivated conflicted situation.

THE CIVIL WAR IN SRI LANKA

Sri Lanka is an island of approximately 25,000 square miles lying about forty miles (at its shortest point) off the coast of southeast India across the

Palk Strait. A partial census in 2001 estimated a population of almost nine-teen million, with about 74 percent of these being of Sinhala or Aryan descent and mostly Buddhist, and 18 percent Tamil of Dravidian descent and mostly Hindu.[5] Christians constitute 7-8 percent of the population, almost 90 percent of these being Roman Catholic, with a larger proportion of Tamils than Sinhala (about 33 percent and 60 percent respectively) when compared to the general population.[6]

With the exception of three ceasefires in 1989-90, 1994-95, and 2002-2005, the current civil war dates back to the Colombo-centered riots in July 1983.[7] Tensions between Sinhalese and Tamils had been building up since independence (1948) in disputes over land ownership, educational and employment rights, and the national language. The Tamil demand for autonomy if not independence came to a head when—according to the most conventionally accepted account—the extremist Liberation Tigers of Tamil Eleem (LTTE) forces ambushed, killed, and mutilated an army truck of thirteen government soldiers, and the army agreed to bring the mangled corpses back to the capital city for public viewing prior to military burial. The resulting Sinhala riots against Tamils by unemployed and under-employed youth from shantytowns resulted in up to 3,000 dead, 100,000 homeless Tamils in Colombo itself, and up to another 150,000 to 175,000 displaced Tamils around the island.[8] Governmental agents were complicit in the massacre either by looking the other way during the riots or, worse, even orchestrating some of the attacks.[9] This series of events precipitated an even further radicalization of the LTTE, whose agenda since its forma-tion in 1976 has involved achieving a separate Tamil state.[10]

Over the last twenty plus years, the LTTE has consolidated its resistance and developed a global network of support that begins with sympathizers

---

[5] All census figures are taken from the Sri Lanka Department of Census and Statistics, *Census of Housing and Population 2001*, available at http://www.statistics.gov.lk/census2001/index.html (accessed 5 December 2006).

[6] On the breakdown of percentages of Christians, see S. Ratnajeevan H. Hoole, "The Eth-nic Conflict in Sri Lanka: The Christian Responses and the Nationalist Threat," *Dharma Deepika* 2, no. 2 (1996): 39-66, esp. 40-41.

[7] For details of the Colombo riots, see Stanley J. Tambiah, *Leveling Crowds: Ethnona-tionalist Conflicts and Collective Violence in South Asia* (Berkeley: University of California Press, 1996), ch. 4.

[8] The numbers of displaced Tamils are disputed. My figures come from Robert Bobilin, *Revolution from Below: Buddhist and Christian Movements for Justice in Asia* (Lanham, Md.: University Press of America, 1988), 145; and Robert I. Rotberg, "Sri Lanka's Civil War: From Mayhem toward Diplomatic Resolution," in *Creating Peace in Sri Lanka: Civil War and Reconciliation,* ed. Robert I. Rotberg (Washington, D.C.: Brookings Institution Press; and Cambridge, Mass.: World Peace Foundation, 1999), 1-16, esp. 7. This is not to overlook the many Sinhalese and Muslims also displaced by the conflict.

[9] On this point, see Stanley Jeyaraja Tambiah, *Buddhism Betrayed? Religion, Politics, and Violence in Sri Lanka* (Chicago and London: University of Chicago Press, 1992), 71-75.

[10] For an introduction to the origins of the LTTE, see Ranga Kalansooriya, *LTTE and IRA: Combating Terrorism and Discussing Peace* (Sri Lanka: Sanghinda Publishers, 2002), 12-29.

from Tamilnadu in south India, involves an international narcotics distribution network, and extends to the growing Tamil diaspora, especially in North America, Europe, and Australia.[11] Its various sources of funding have allowed the organization to procure weapons, raise funds, and conduct propaganda.[12] Along the way, the guerilla-warfare approach adopted by the LTTE has intensified to the point of involving human rights abuses (including kidnapping of children) and suicide bombings of high-ranking national (e.g., Sri Lankan president Ranasingle Premadasa in 1993) and even international officials (such as Rajiv Gandhi in 1991, who was then serving as prime minister of India). As a result, the United States Department of State has included the organization on its black list of terrorist groups since October 1997.[13]

To be sure, an increasing number of Tamils agree neither with the extremist and violent tactics nor with the secessionist political agenda of the LTTE. In fact, Tamils have long contributed to the government and civilian work force. Many own property in traditional Sinhala towns and villages, and many more in recent years have sought refuge from the LTTE in the southern part of the country. Hence, to discuss the Sri Lankan civil war between Sinhalese and Tamils is misleading insofar as neither of these ethnic groups is homogenous in terms of religious identity, socioeconomic standing, or political commitments. Therefore, we can talk about a Sinhala-Tamil conflict only in very general terms, and it is at this level of abstraction that many of the following comments need to be understood.

This said, it should still be noted that some innocent Tamils continue to be on the receiving end of the human rights abuses perpetrated by the government (often justified in its "war against terror" through the Prevention of Terrorism Act),[14] and it has been the LTTE that has taken up the Tamil

---

[11] Estimates are that there are now up to 800,000 Tamils worldwide; see Rohan Gunaratna, "Impact of the Mobilised Tamil Diaspora on the Protracted Conflict in Sri Lanka," in *Negotiating Peace in Sri Lanka: Efforts, Failures and Lessons,* ed. Kumar Rupesinghe (London: International Alert, 1998), 301-28.

[12] Note, however, that the line between authentic fundraising and intimidationist extortion is blurred with regard to LTTE tactics; see Jo Becker, "Funding the 'Final War': LTTE Intimidation and Extortion in the Tamil Diaspora," *Human Rights Watch* 18, no. 1C (2006).

[13] The LTTE remains on this list; see the U.S. Department of State's Foreign Terrorist Organizations, at http://www.state.gov/s/ct/rls/fs/37191.htm (accessed 5 December 2006); cf. M. de Silva, *Reaping the Whirlwind: Ethnic Conflict, Ethnic Politics in Sri Lanka* (Delhi: Penguin, 1998), esp. 324-30; Edward V. Linden, ed., *Foreign Terrorist Organizations: History, Tactics and Connections* (New York: Nova Science, 2004), 55-58; and Jonathan R. White, *Terrorism and Homeland Security*, 5th ed. (Belmont, Calif.: Thomson Wadsworth, 2006), 189-93.

[14] On the complicity of governmental agents in human rights abuses, see "The Fatal Conjunction: Women, Continuing Violations and Accountability," *University Teacher's for Human Rights Information Bulletin*, 25 (11 July 2001) [http://www.uthr.org/bulletins/bul25. html], accessed November 2006. While the government has acted against unjust abuses—e.g., in the sentencing to death by the Colombo high court in July 1996 of five security forces members for murder; see Paul Marshall, gen. ed., *Religious Freedom in the World: A Global*

cause against the Sinhala-dominated government. Hence, the LTTE has staked its claim—rightly or wrongly—to represent the Tamil people and demands to be reckoned with in any attempt to bring about peace on the island. But the Sri Lankan government has not been able to negotiate successfully with the LTTE, even as the Sri Lankan military has been unable to decisively defeat the rebel forces. Part of the problem is that the government has not taken effective steps to cut off the international support-and-supplies network that props up and arms the LTTE,[15] even though such support has waned considerably after 9/11. Further, there is the varied nature of the Tamil demands for rights, ranging from that of full Tamil citizenship to that of self-determination in their own Tamil Eleem ("Eleem" meaning "homeland") state.[16] The third set of complicating factors has to do with Sri Lanka's relationship with India in general and with the state of Tamilnadu in particular. When one considers that up to one-third of the Tamil population in Sri Lanka are recent descendents of or current plantation immigrant workers from south India, mostly from Tamilnadu,[17] it is understandable that favorable Tamil sentiments run high north of the Palk Strait. Tamilnadu's chief ministers have even extended material support to the LTTE and provided a safe haven for LTTE retreat and respite.

The complexities involved became most apparent during 1987 when the Sri Lankan government mounted Operation Liberation to capture Vadama-rachchi (a major crossing point between India and the Jaffna peninsula at the northernmost tip of the island) with the intention to cut off LTTE retreat lines to Tamilnadu.[18] At that point, Delhi gave clear signals that it would not allow Jaffna to be captured by the government forces and even dispatched flotillas of relief supplies to Jaffna Tamils as well as emergency airdrops, in clear violation of Sri Lankan airspace. This led finally to negotiations for a joint Indian-Sri Lankan military campaign to root out the Tamil Tigers that brought initially 10,000 Indian troops to the island, a number that increased in just a few months to 125,000. With increasing Sinhalese fears of an Indian invasion (a perpetual worry given the long history of at least sixteen major invasions of the island by Indian armies over

---

Report on Freedom and Persecution (Nashville: Broadman & Holman, 2000), 279—yet there is a fine line between official government sanctioning of human rights abuses and abuses at the hands of governmental forces acting on their own accord.

[15] On this point, see Roham Gunaratna, *Sri Lanka's Ethnic Crisis and National Security* (Colombo: South Asian Network on Conflict Research, 1998), ch. 4.

[16] See Shri D. R. Kaarthikeyan, "Root Causes of Terrorism? A Case Study of the Tamil Insurgency and the LTTE," in *Root Causes of Terrorism: Myths, Reality and Ways Forward,* ed. Tore Bjørgo (London and New York: Routledge, 2005), 131-40.

[17] See S. W. R. de A. Samarasinghe, "The Indian Tamil Plantation Workers in Sri Lanka: Welfare and Integration," in *Ethnic Conflict in Buddhist Societies: Sri Lanka, Thailand and Burma,* ed. K. M. de Silva et al. (Boulder, Colo.: Westview, and London: Pinter, 1988), 156-71.

[18] For details of Tamilnadu's role in the conflict and of the Indian intervention, see Chris Smith, "South Asia's Enduring War," in *Creating Peace in Sri Lanka*, 17-40 (see n. 8).

2,500 years) the government itself supplied arms to the LTTE to thwart the Indian intervention, thereby sabotaging the agreement. By late 1989, Delhi admitted the failure of its mission and began to withdraw.[19]

It is clear that the Sri Lankan civil war has had international ramifications. Besides deforming the entirety of the south Asian region, the economic costs of the war have also materially impacted global industry.[20] Whereas Sri Lanka experienced an economic boom from 1977 to 1982 when growth rates exceeded 6 percent per annum, after the 1983 riots these rates decelerated to about 3.7 percent over the next six years. Increase in defense expenditures correlated with decrease in foreign investment, while economic production in the north and east and the fishing industry in the northeastern provinces dissipated. Tourism all but ceased—Sri Lanka is one of few countries with beaches, mountains, ancient cities, and wildlife all within driving distances—and with it an important source of income. Irreplaceable, of course, are the loss of lives: over tens of thousands of military personnel and LTTE casualties besides civilian casualties of 20,000 to 30,000. For those who remain, there are other challenges: disabilities because of war injuries (over 20,000 wounded), the issue of displaced people, loss of wages due to work disruptions, and brain drain of skilled laborers (over 50,000 by the mid-1990s) to emigration. Besides all this is the trauma of an entire generation growing up in war, not only without education but also with the ongoing psychological problems that will persist long after any peace is negotiated.

"MAJORITY RULES": THE REVIVAL OF SINHALESE BUDDHISM

Although our objectives here are not to resolve the issues involved in the Sri Lankan civil war—for which I have neither the expertise nor the political standing—still we can and need to understand better the specifically religious dynamics present in this context. This will help us see that while there are a host of nonreligious factors driving the war, there are also undeniable religious elements at work. More importantly, such an understanding will help clarify how Sri Lankan Christian interreligious practices (to be discussed in the next section) are operative in the conflicted context of a predominantly Buddhist society.

Leading up to and since independence (1948), there have been focused and concentrated efforts to reclaim the Buddhist heritage and identity of the nation against its colonizers. Some of the most significant early efforts

---

[19] For analysis of the failed Indian intervention, see Kumar Rupesinghe, ed., *Negotiating Peace in Sri Lanka*, chs. 2-8 (see n. 11); see also Rajat Ganguly and Ray Taras, *Understanding Ethnic Conflict: The International Dimension* (New York: Addison Wesley Longman, 1998), ch. 7.

[20] Here I rely on Saman Kelegama, "Economic Costs of Conflict in Sri Lanka," in *Creating Peace in Sri Lanka*, 71-87 (see n. 8).

were led by Anagarika Dharmapala (1864-1933), a social reformer who became a monk toward the end of his life.[21] Born David Hewavitarana, he changed his name to Dharmapala, which means guardian of the dharma, to signify his untiring commitment to showing how Buddhism was just as if not more noble than Christianity for a modern Sri Lanka. Along the way, Dharmapala also worked to revitalize the Buddhist Sangha (order of monks and nuns).

By the mid-1940s and especially into the 1950s, the Sangha had emerged as a palpable force in Sri Lankan politics.[22] The year 1956 witnessed three events that signaled the arrival of the Sangha at the center of the nation's political scene. First, the Sangha-organized celebration of Buddha Jayanthi (2,500 years since the death of the Buddha and the landing of Vijaya, the first Sinhala, on the island, a midway point of the 5,000-year period the *dhamma* would last) was a turning point marking the rejuvenation of the Buddha's teachings. Second, the publication of the All Ceylon Buddhist Congress Committee of Inquiry's *The Betrayal of Buddhism* called for the establishment of a Buddhist Sasana Council to counteract the organized Protestant and the Roman Catholic churches and for a state-controlled (Sinhalese) and Buddhist-based educational system to oppose the dominant Christian educational institutions/structures.[23] Third, the election of S. W. R. D. Bandaranaike (1899-1959) as prime minister succeeded in part because of the support of the Sangha and resulted in Sinhala being established as the official language of the nation. Following this, the riots in 1958-1959, which saw hundreds of Tamils killed and over 10,000 displaced, were provoked in part by the resistance of Buddhist clergy to governmental and legislative "compromises" with the Tamils.

In many ways, the emergence of the Sangha in the Sri Lankan public square paralleled the rise of the nationalistic consciousness among the Sinhalese. While distinct, these two "movements" were and remain interdependent, bound together in part by the commitment to preserve and lift up the Buddhist legacy of the island. Known also as *sihadeepa*, which means "the island of the Sinhalese," and as *dhammadeepa*, which means "the island of the *dhamma*," the Sinhalese are proud about their claim that "Sri

---

[21] Surprisingly, there is still no full-length published scholarly study of Dharmapala's life. For an overview, see Gananath Obeyesekere, "Personal Identity and Cultural Crisis: The Case of Anagrika Dharmapala of Sri Lanka," in *The Biographical Process: Studies in the History and Psychology of Religion*, ed. Frank E. Reynolds and Donald Capps (The Hague and Paris: Mouton, 1976), 221-52.

[22] An overview of the history of the revival of the Sangha in Sri Lanka is provided by Stanley J. Tambiah, "Buddhism, Politics, and Violence in Sri Lanka," in *Fundamentalisms and the State: Remaking Politics, Economies, and Militance*, ed. Martin E. Marty and R. Scott Appleby, The Fundamentalism Project 3 (Chicago and London: University of Chicago Press, 1991), 589-619.

[23] Buddhist Committee of Inquiry, *The Betrayal of Buddhism: An Abridged Version of the Report of the Buddhist Committee of Inquiry* (Balangoda, Ceylon: Dharmavijaya Press, 1956).

Lanka is the oldest Buddhist society in the world."[24] This sense is bolstered by the sixth-century CE text, the *Mahavamsa*, which functions with canonical (Buddhist) authority for most Sinhalese.[25] While the epic narrative of the *Mahavamsa* concerns King Dutthagamini's (101-77 BCE) triumph over a Tamil general from south India in the second century BCE, it serves to reveal the mindset of the Sinhalese in terms of their self-understanding as those charged by the Buddha to maintain the *dhamma* and protect the island against the hordes of south Indian invaders. So although Tamils are represented variously in the *Mahavamsa* and not just as enemies of the Buddha's teachings,[26] the architects of the modern revival of Sinhalese Buddhism have read the text ideologically in support of Sinhala aspirations for "cultural, religious, economic, and linguistic hegemony."[27] As Stanley Tambiah notes, there is "a deep ontological commitment to the Buddhist cosmology which implies that the alien must be domesticated, subordinated, and then incorporated into its hierarchical scheme; the corollary is that anything that challenges this scheme is necessarily seen as evil, demonic, outside, and threatening to the very core of Sinhalese Buddhist identity and existence."[28]

This convergence of Sinhalese Buddhism and Sinhalese nationalism and the intransigency of the LTTE has produced an intractable stand-off. Besides insisting on the restoration of the over 250 religious sites damaged or destroyed by the LTTE during the civil war, the most vocal leaders of the Sangha have also been united against accepting any peace terms that would lead to an autonomous Tamil state. These monks' primary concerns have been not only to protect the sovereignty and integrity of the country—after all, unlike the Tamils who can retreat to Tamilnadu, there is nowhere else for the Sinhala to go or call home—but also to advance the cause of Buddhism by constitutional amendments declaring it the national religion. For the more radical members of the Sangha, threats to the priority of

---

[24] Vimal Tirimanna, "Asia: Sri Lanka," in *Religion as a Source of Violence*, ed. Wim Beuken and Karl-Josef Kuschel (London: SCM; and Maryknoll, N.Y.: Orbis Books, 1997) 23-30; quotation from p. 21.

[25] See Douglas Bullis, ed., *The Mahavamsa: The Great Chronicle of Sri Lanka* (Fremont, Calif.: Asian Humanities Press, 1999).

[26] See Gananath Obeyesekere, "Buddhism, Nationhood, and Cultural Identity: A Question of Fundamentals," in *Fundamentalisms Comprehended*, ed. Martin E. Marty and F. Scott Appleby, The Fundamentalism Project 5 (Chicago and London: University of Chicago Press, 1993), 231-56, esp. 240-41.

[27] Tessa J. Bartholomeusz and Chandra R. de Silva, "Buddhist Fundamentalism and Identity in Sri Lanka," in *Buddhist Fundamentalism and Minority Identities in Sri Lanka*, ed. Tessa J. Bartholomeusz and Chandra R. de Silva (Albany: State University of New York Press, 1998), 1-35, quote from p. 3.

[28] Tambiah, *Buddhism Betrayed?* 168-69. See also Bruce D. Kapferer, "Remythologizing Discourses: State and Insurrectionary Violence in Sri Lanka," in *The Legitimation of Violence*, ed. David E. Apter (New York: New York University Press, 1997), 159-88, esp. 169-77, for a similar discussion.

Buddhism in Sri Lankan life and culture are to be taken seriously and resisted with all possible means. Even if this involves or requires killing, such would be justified as "conventional" modes of response to this-worldly, real-life problems.[29] This posture, of course, would surprise those unfamiliar with the Sri Lankan situation, especially given the wider Buddhist tradition's well-known stance on nonviolence (*ahimsa*) and emphases on cultivating generosity and compassion. But what has emerged on the Sinhalese front are what might be called Buddhist just-war arguments whereby the commitments to pacifism and nonviolence can be overridden with good cause, such as those related to defending the dharma.[30] While only a very small number of Sinhala monks have actually participated in violent activities themselves, most support the "war against terror" (opposing the LTTE) in very concrete ways. The monks consider their preaching to the troops as merit-making, both for themselves and for the soldiers. Their sermons are designed to inspire soldiers to think particular thoughts, to nurture a posture of equanimity, to have a specific mindset so that they can be courageous in carrying out their duties. On the other hand, since preaching about the negative karma of killing in war does not promote the kind of morale that soldiers need to do their *samsaric* (this-worldly) duty, it is avoided.[31] For these and other reasons, the Sangha has not been at the forefront of leading the nation to hear out Tamil concerns.[32]

Before turning our attention to Christianity in Sri Lanka, I want to briefly note that the Sinhala-Tamil conflict has another set of interreligious implications: that concerning the small Muslim minority in the country. Mostly Moors with a tangible Sufi contingent, Muslims in Sri Lanka number about the same as Christians (approximately 7 percent of the overall population), and they also have suffered from the war. In 1990, almost 300 Muslims were killed by the LTTE, including 120 at prayer time in a mosque in Kattankudy. Shortly thereafter, the LTTE expelled 75,000 Muslims at gunpoint from the Jaffna peninsula and from their longtime homeland in

---

[29] See Oliver McTernan, *Violence in God's Name: Religion in an Age of Conflict* (Maryknoll, N.Y.: Orbis Books, 2003), 99-100. Mark Juergensmeyer writes, "I was once told by a monk who had participated in violent anti-government protests that there was no way to avoid violence 'in a time of *dukkha*'—the age of suffering that Buddhists regard as characteristic of recorded human history"; see Mark Juergensmeyer, *Terror in the Mind of God: The Global Rise of Religious Violence* (Berkeley: University of California Press, 2000), 113.

[30] See Tessa J. Bartholomeusz, *In Defense of Dharma: Just-war Ideology in Buddhist Sri Lanka* (London and New York: RoutledgeCurzon, 2002).

[31] See Daniel Kent, "Onward Buddhist Soldiers: Preaching to the Sri Lankan Army" (paper presented to the American Academy of Religion, Philadelphia, Pennsylvania, 18-21 November 2006); my thanks to Professor Kent for sharing his manuscript with me.

[32] The 10 percent of the Sangha more sympathetic to Tamil issues have usually been the younger undistinguished monks without a university education who come from poorer economic backgrounds; see Nathan Katz, "Sri Lankan Monks on Ethnicity and Nationalism," in *Ethnic Conflict in Buddhist Societies*, ed. K. M. de Silva et al., 138-52, esp. 149 (see n. 17).

the district of Mannar, and many of these have remained in refugee status since.[33] These are only two of the many incidents involving attacks against Muslims. Whereas in the decades preceding the war Muslims were more politically aggressive, their posture now is more subdued, sometimes being reduced to being "used" by the Sinhala majority as a counterweight to Tamil radicalism. On the religious, social, and cultural fronts, the Muslim response has varied across the spectrum: from assimilation into the fabric of Sinhalese life to association with a more pan-Arabic Islamic identity. Hence, Sri Lankan Muslim identities are negotiated at multiple levels: regionally and locally on the island, where the disputes are between ortho-dox Islam and the Sufi tradition; nationally, where the issues revolve around the Sinhala-Tamil conflict; and internationally, where the discourse is also shaped by resistance to secularism and the West.[34] In short, the inter-religious arena in Sri Lanka is multidimensional, with the Muslim presence adding further layers of complexity to an already intricate situation.

THE CHRISTIAN MINORITY IN SRI LANKA

The history of Christianity on the island has been mediated by colonial-ism: first the Portuguese (1505-1658), then the Dutch (1658-1796), and finally the British (1796-1948).[35] During the twentieth century, the Bud-dhist revival has slowly but surely pushed Christianity to the margins of national, social, and cultural life. The Free Education Act in 1947 was the first of a number of formal legislative procedures intended to wrest control of education from the missionaries and their schooling systems. Whereas the small minority of "Westernized" Christians (about 9 percent of the population during the mid-1940s) under the control of Western denomina-tions and churches wielded a disproportionate amount of social, economic, and political control during the colonial administration, there has been a steady decline of Christian numbers, influence, and, concomitantly, morale in the last half century.[36]

Along the way the Christian churches have not been immune to the pres-sures exerted by Sinhalese nationalist forces. Political independence fol-

---

[33] See K. M. de Silva, *Reaping the Whirlwind*, ch. 7, "The Islamic Factor"; cf. K. M. de Silva, "Sri Lanka's Muslim Minority," in *Ethnic Conflict in Buddhist Societies*, ed. K. M. de Silva et al., 202-14 (see n. 17).

[34] Victor C. de Munck, "Sufi and Reformist Designs: Muslim Identity in Sri Lanka," in *Buddhist Fundamentalism and Minority Identities in Sri Lanka*, ed. Tessa J. Bartholomeusz and Chandra R. de Silva, 110-32 (see n. 27 above).

[35] An overview is G. P. V. Somaratna, *Chronology of Christianity in Sri Lanka* (Nugegoda, Sri Lanka: Margaya Fellowship of Sri Lanka, 1998).

[36] See G. P. V. Somaratna, "Christianity in Sri Lanka, 1948-1987: Struggle for Survival," *Indian Church History Review* 22 (1988): 132-49. Some of the factors leading to the decreas-ing Christian population include comparatively lower birth rates and massive emigration since the start of the civil war.

lowed by ecclesial independence from Western mission agencies left many of the Protestant churches scrambling for funds while attempting to discern what it meant to develop an indigenous Sri Lankan ecclesial identity. On the Catholic side, Vatican II made it possible for priests to lead their parishes in similar initiatives of de-Westernization and inculturation of Sinhalese or Tamil forms of life.[37] What has emerged, however, is the gradual "Sinhalization" of the Catholic Church to the point that some "have felt their Sinhalese identity overpowering their Christian identity [to the point of] attacking Tamil Roman Catholics in the 1983 violence against Tamils."[38]

On the other hand, the presence of significant numbers of Tamil Christians means churches have been unable to ignore Tamil concerns. While the major Protestant denominations have focused more on pastoral than political activities, the Church of South India with its sizable Tamil contingent has, in the hands of certain leaders, even embraced the LTTE agenda for various stretches of time.[39] And since the emergence of liberation theology in the late 1960s, these have been joined by some Roman Catholic priests in the northern and eastern Tamil-predominant districts who have aligned themselves publicly with the Tamil cause. With the Sri Lankan priesthood thus divided between Sinhala and Tamil interests, the Roman Catholic Church has been limited to making generalized, innocuous, and uncontroversial statements calling for dialogue, peace, and prayer.

Meanwhile, there have been other developments on the Protestant side. Most important for our purposes is that the Protestant churches constituting the National Council of Churches—the Church of South India, the Salvation Army, and the Anglican, Methodist, Dutch Reformed, Presbyterian, and Baptist churches—have become more theologically liberal over time. Influenced by discourses coming out of the World Council of Churches, interreligious dialogue rather than evangelism has come to be emphasized, even as there has emerged in some quarters an increasingly relativistic perspective regarding the person and work of Christ vis-à-vis other religions and those in other faiths.[40] For these Christian minorities in the Sri Lankan context, survival required diplomacy rather than traditionally understood mission-minded zealousness.

In the last few decades, however, the southward shift of world Christianity, particularly in its evangelical, pentecostal, and charismatic forms,

---

[37] Charles R. A. Hoole, "The Church Amidst Suffering in Sri Lanka," *Evangelical Review of Theology* 13 (1989): 61-65.

[38] S. R. H. Hoole, "Ethnic Conflict in Sri Lanka," 41; cf. Jan H. Pranger, "Culture, Ethnicity, and Inculturation: Critical and Constructive Comments in Relation to Sri Lankan Contextual Theology," *Mission Studies* 18-1, no. 35 (2001): 154-80, esp. 159.

[39] S. R. H. Hoole, "Ethnic Conflict in Sri Lanka," 48-49.

[40] S. R. H. Hoole, "Ethnic Conflict in Sri Lanka," 52-53. For an overview of the Buddhist-Christian dialogue in Sri Lanka, see Whalen Lai and Michael Von Brück, *Christianity and Buddhism: A Multi-Cultural History of Their Dialogue*, trans. Phyllis Jestice (Maryknoll, N.Y.: Orbis Books, 2001), ch. 2.

has also begun to impact Sri Lanka.[41] During the mid-century period of mainline Protestant decline, classical pentecostal denominations such as the Assemblies of God also struggled, sustaining their numbers primarily through proselytism from other churches.[42] But more recently, buoyed by the support and influx of parachurch missionary organizations from various parts of the world, especially North America, mainline churches have been slowly revitalized. At the same time, a growing number of independent churches have also made their presence felt in terms of mobilizing local leadership (not only Sinhala but also Tamil), empowering the laity, and adopting indigenous forms and practices.[43] They more often have remained formally a-political, preferring instead to devote themselves to prayer and evangelism as their means of contributing to the reformation of the Sri Lankan situation.[44] Yet because of their aggressive (relatively speaking, for the Sri Lankan context) evangelistic methods and successes in gaining new converts, including highly publicized conversions of Buddhist monks, they have been criticized for unethical proselytizing tactics such as using material inducements to increase their numbers.[45] Buddhist clergy have been especially concerned about the growth of these churches, and quite a few have attempted to introduce legislation prohibiting such activities.[46] Others who have felt the Sinhalese cause threatened or thought

---

[41] For a sketch of the changing face of Christianity in the global south, see Philip Jenkins, *The Next Christendom: The Coming of Global Christianity* (Oxford and New York: Oxford University Press, 2002).

[42] G. P. V. Somaratna, *Origins of the Pentecostal Mission in Sri Lanka* (Nugegoda, Sri Lanka: Margaya Fellowship of Sri Lanka, 1997), 51-53.

[43] See Ranjit DeSilva, "House Church Movement Catches on among Sri Lanka's Urban and Rural Poor," *Evangelical Missions Quarterly* 27, no. 3 (1991): 274-78; and idem, "Beleaguered Christianity in Contemporary Sri Lanka," *Asia Journal of Theology* 9, no. 1 (1995): 47-62.

[44] Neville Jayaweera, *The Role of the Churches in the Ethnic Conflict*, Marga Monograph Series on Ethnic Reconciliation 17 (Colombo: Marga Institute, 2001), 10; cf. Charles Hoole, "Ethnic Fratricide and the Church's Witness to Intercommunal Peace in Sri Lanka," *Transformation* 15 (1998): 15-18.

[45] Mahinda Deegalle, "JHU Politics for Peace and a Righteous State," in *Buddhism, Conflict and Violence in Modern Sri Lanka*, ed. Mahinda Deegalle (London and New York: Routledge, 2006), 233-54, esp. 244 and 251. My sense is that at least some of what is happening is the result of misunderstanding since what is thought to be unethical can also be understood as being the result of access to new social (ecclesial) networks and relationships brought about by religious conversion. It has also been the case that evangelicals have often taken the lead in relief efforts, whether in response to riots, such as those of July 1983, or to the more recent devastating tsunami in December 2004; see, e.g., "Evangelical Relief Efforts are Under Way in Violent Sri Lanka," *Christianity Today* (7 October 1983): 66-67; and Manpreet Singh, "Bent But Not Broken: A Pummeled Church Helps Bury the Dead and Bring Life to Those Who Remain," *Christianity Today* 49, no. 2 (February 2005): 30-33.

[46] Shirley Lal Wijesinghe, "The Places of Worship in the Bible: A Theological Reading Prompted by the Recent Attacks on Places of Christian Worship in Sri Lanka," in *Encounters with the Word: Essays to Honour Aloysius Pieris S.J. on His 70th Birthday 9th April 2004*, ed. Robert Crusz, Marshal Fernando, and Asanga Tilakaratne (Colombo: Ecumenical Institute for Study and Dialogue, 2004), 629-39, at 638.

these Christians disrespectful of the Buddha and the dharma have gone as far as intimidating Christian workers, assaulting ministers, and burning churches.[47] On the other front, in Tamil-dominated areas, evangelicals and pentecostals are also endangered if their work is thought to undermine the LTTE agenda.[48]

Arguably these anti-Christian reactions are related to postindependence developments. It was precisely because the church bodies with a longer history on the island had shifted their forms of missionary engagement from kerygmatic proclamation to social uplift that evangelical and pentecostal missionary organizations focused on and committed themselves to the evangelistic renewal of Sri Lanka. In the process, some evangelical leaders have been careful to emphasize respectful and dialogical interactions with Buddhists and those in other faiths—for example, the work of Ajith Fernando, the National Director of Youth for Christ in Sri Lanka, especially in his emphasis on the importance of interpersonal dialogue, getting to know other religious traditions and people of other faiths, and treating those in other faiths with respect and approaching them with humility.[49] Further, even in the face of persecution, it is often the case that Sinhala Christians have risked their own lives and homes in providing refuge to Tamil Hindus threatened by mobs and violence.[50] Finally, there have also been occasions when Buddhists and Christians across the ecclesial spectrum have collaborated in the face of disaster and tragedy, most recently in response to the devastating tsunami of December 2004.[51] Still, Sinhalese Buddhist nationalists have been unprepared to deal with evangelistic strategies that brought back memories of the colonial missionary effort.[52] For many of the most politically invested Buddhist elite, too much ground has

---

[47] Marshall, gen. ed., *Religious Freedom in the World*, 281-82.

[48] As seen in the report of the murder of Assemblies of God pastor Sivanesarajah on 2 May 2000 because of his preaching pacifism to Tamil youth (which undermined the LTTE's capacity to recruit), and his ignoring LTTE demands to stop holding meetings in the rural area of Panichchankerni; see "The Fatal Conjunction: Women, Continuing Violations and Accountability," *University Teacher's for Human Rights Information Bulletin* 25 (11 July 2001) [http://www.uthr.org/bulletins/bul25.htm] (accessed November 2006).

[49] See the relevant chapters in Ajith Fernando, *The Christian's Attitude toward World Religions* (Wheaton, Ill.: Tyndale, 1987); and idem, *Sharing the Truth in Love: How to Relate to People of Other Faiths* (Grand Rapids: Discovery House, 2001); see also his call for a sensitivity to the Sri Lankan context: Ajith Fernando, "Missionaries Still Needed—But of a Special Kind," *Evangelical Missions Quarterly* 24, no. 1 (1988): 18-25.

[50] Ajith Fernando, *The NIV Application Commentary: Acts* (Grand Rapids: Zondervan, 1998), 330.

[51] Post-tsunami relief efforts evidenced "countless experiences of grassroots hospitality" between Buddhists and Christians; see Paul Jeffrey, "A Great Leveler: Sri Lanka's Factions Deal with the Tsunami," *Christian Century* 122, no. 3 (8 February 2005): 8-10, quotation from p. 9.

[52] Elizabeth J. Harris, "Christian Perceptions of the Buddha in Sri Lanka," *Swedish Missiological Themes* 90, no. 1 (2002): 39-62, esp. 62.

been reclaimed from the Christian colonizers to now be lost again to aggressive evangelical and pentecostal mission churches.

Committed Christians in Sri Lanka realize that given the existing political situation, their witness to the gospel must be borne with discernment, propriety, and wisdom. Arguably, the Christian imagination in Nigeria is similarly attuned, but its vastly different social and political circumstances have produced an entirely contrasting set of interreligious attitudes and practices.

WORLD PENTECOSTALISM: ISLAM AND CHRISTIANITY IN NIGERIA

Unlike in Sri Lanka, Christians are neither a small minority nor a clear majority in Nigeria. While precise demographic statistics are unavailable, there is widespread recognition that Muslims and Christians are almost numerically equivalent in the country as a whole, albeit more or less clustered in different regions. Further, while there is no ongoing civil war in Nigeria, there is a history of Muslim-Christian violence almost as long as the Sinhalese-Tamil conflict, with the potential of religiously based riots occurring at almost any time. Finally, the expanding form of Christianity in Nigeria is clearly pentecostal and charismatic, although many of these churches and their leaders are far from being politically disengaged. These and other reasons make Nigeria an important case study for those of us seeking to understand the conflict of religions in the twenty-first century. The following discussion lays out the history of Muslim-Christian violence in Nigeria before exploring Nigerian Muslim and Christian perspectives on their common struggles. Again, we will seek to highlight the wide range of Christian responses to situations of interreligious conflict.

Muslim-Christian Conflict in Nigeria

The projected population of Nigeria as of 2005 was close to 132 million, making it the most populous state in the African continent.[53] This includes innumerable different ethnic and tribal groups, the largest being the predominantly (Sunni) Muslim Hausa-Fulani in the north (about 32 percent), the religiously mixed Yoruba in the southwest (21 percent), and the predominantly Christian (Catholic) Igbo in the southeast (about 18 percent). Because of the history of the Muslim-Christian conflict and the contested political ramifications of census data, no reliable figures are available regarding the number of religious adherents. The best current estimates

---

[53] Figures range from 125,000 to 137,000, depending on one's sources. My numbers derive from the United Nation's Children's Fund Web site: http://www.unicef.org/infoby country/nigeria_1463.html (accessed 8 December 2006).

indicate that Muslims consist of between 40 and 60 percent of the population, while Christians range from 40 to 53 percent of the population, with
the different percentages dependent on who is counting and on how practitioners of African traditional religions are counted. Regardless of the
actual numbers, Muslim-Christian relations are clearly central not only to
the religious, cultural, and social life of the country but also to its political
and economic well-being.

Before turning specifically to Muslim-Christian violence, it would be
helpful to set the broader recent Nigerian context. While the role of religion in the conflicts cannot be denied, there are other extenuating circumstances. First, the history of British colonialism in the region resulted in the
arbitrary organization of different ethnic groups under one national government. Since independence (1960), this has been a perennial source of
political disputation and even violent conflict, as seen in the civil war
(1967-1970).[54] Second, in part because of ethnic strife and distrust, there
has been an entire generation of political instability featuring coups and
countercoups (motivated variously) that have in turn opened the doors for
military dictatorships and corruption in leadership at all levels of the government.[55] By 2001, Nigeria had come to rank ninetieth out of ninety-one
nations on *The Transparency International Corruption Index*, and it was
estimated that 1 percent of the population controlled 90 percent of the
nation's wealth in banks outside the country.[56] Third, the tremendous natural resources of the country, especially its massive oil deposits, have not
been harnessed for the well-being of the people, and this has resulted in
widespread poverty.[57] Since the oil boom of the late 1970s and early 1980s,
Nigeria's per capita Gross National Product (GNP) has fallen drastically
such that more than two-thirds of its population lives below the poverty
line.[58] Against this background, it should not be surprising that there exists

---

[54] For an overview, see Remi Anifowose, *Violence and Politics in Nigeria: The Tiv and Yoruba Experience* (New York: Nok Publishers, 1982). A more focused study is Yusufu Bala Usman, *The Manipulation of Religion in Nigeria, 1977-1987* (Kaduna, Nigeria: Vanguard, 1987). For a brief synopsis, see Godfrey N. Uzoigwe, "Assessing the History of Eth-nic/religious Relations," in *Inter-Ethnic and Religious Conflict Resolution in Nigeria*, ed. Ernest E. Uwazie, Isaac O. Albert, and Godfrey N. Uzoigwe (Lanham, Md.: Lexington Books, 1999), 7-17.

[55] Leo Dare, "Political Instability and Displacement in Nigeria," in *Displacement and the Politics of Violence in Nigeria*, ed. Paul E. Lovejoy and Pat Ama Tokunbo Williams, Interna-tional Studies in Sociology and Social Anthropology 67 (Leiden and New York: Brill, 1997), 22-32.

[56] Victor E. Dike, *Nigeria and the Politics of Unreason: A Study of the Obasanjo Regime* (London: Adonis & Abbey, 2003), 71 and 116.

[57] Nigeria has been losing rather than gaining ground as a developing nation; see John McCormick, *Comparative Politics in Transition* (Belmont, Calif.: Wadsworth, 1995), ch. 7.

[58] Abdul Karim Banura, "Multifaceted Ethnic Conflicts and Conflict Resolution in Nige-ria," in *Perspectives on Contemporary Ethnic Conflict: Primal Violence or the Politics of Con-viction?* ed. Santosh C. Saha (Lanham, Md.: Lexington, 2006), 173-96, data from p. 182. Early in the new century, the United Nations Development Programme ranked Nigeria as the

a high degree of economic pressures, social unrest, and ethnic tensions. When other considerations such as the instability of the economy, the question of control over and access to the nation's key natural resources, and the ethnic pride instilled by centuries of Arabic-Islamic rule in the north are factored in, the Nigerian situation is volatile indeed.

In this context we need to understand the volatility of Muslim-Christian relations in Nigeria. Since 1982—the beginning of the nation's downward economic spiral—conservative estimates show more than a dozen serious violent conflicts involving Muslims against Christians and vice versa. I will simply list some of the most prominent here,[59] and discuss only two incidents in more detail:

- December 1980, October 1982, February 1984, and April 1985— involving the extremist Maitatsine sect that sought to cleanse Nigeria from secularism, and which involved primarily Muslims against Muslims (over 6,000 killed, and over 6,000 displaced), but that included some Christian casualties and burnt church buildings;[60]
- October 1982, Kano—involving the more radical Muslim Students Society that burnt eight churches and a Christian bookshop;
- March 1987, Kaduna-Kafanchan and Kano areas—more than 160 churches burnt, 5 mosques destroyed, and thousands dead;
- May and June 1990, Kaduna and Bauchi states—hundreds injured, Christian homes burnt;
- April 1991, Katsina and Bauchi—Muslims reacting against a predominantly Christian government because of its alleged anti-Muslim stance, resulting in an estimated 2,000 dead, 1,483 churches, mosques, and houses burnt, and about 25,000 displaced;
- October 1991, Kano—Muslims responding to the Reinhard Bonnke crusade, resulting in the deaths of over 2,000 Christians, 13 churches burnt, and 22,000 displaced (see below);
- February-May 1992, Zango-Kataf area—over 5,200 Christian and Muslim deaths and many burnt homes;

---

twenty-sixth poorest country in the world; cited in Dike, *Nigeria and the Politics of Unreason*, 87.

[59] My sources are varied, but the most comprehensive surveys include Patrick Lambert Udoma, *The Cross and the Crescent: A Christian Response to Two Decades of Islamic Affirmation in Nigeria* (London: Saint Austin Press, 2002), 143-52; Jan H. Boer, *Nigeria's Decades of Blood 1980-2002*, Studies in Christian-Muslim Relations 1 (Belleville, Ont.: Essence, 2003); Carina Tertsakian, "Revenge in the Name of Religion: The Cycle of Violence in Plateau and Kano States," *Human Rights Watch* 17, no. 8A (May 2005); and Iheanyi M. Enwerem, "An Assessment of Government's Formal Responses to Ethnic/religious Riots, 1980-1990s," in *Inter-Ethnic and Religious Conflict Resolution in Nigeria*, ed. Ernest E. Uwazie, Isaac O. Albert, and Godfrey N. Uzoigwe, 121-35 (see n. 54 above).

[60] On the Maitatsine riots, see Toyin Falola, *Violence in Nigeria: The Crisis of Religious Politics and Secular Ideologies* (Rochester, N.Y.: University of Rochester Press, 1998), ch. 5.

- January 1993, Katsina state—1,000 killed, dozens of homes burnt;
- April 1994, Jos—involving Muslim perpetrators and aggressive Christian retaliation in self-defense;
- December 1998, Maiduguri—20 deaths as a result of clashes and protests over the government's allowing the teaching of "Christian Religious Knowledge" in the public schools;
- February 2000, Kaduna—1,000 killed;
- September 2001, Jos—around 1,000 people killed in six days;
- June 2002, Yelwa—up to 190 Muslims and at least 30 Christians killed;
- February-May 2004, Kano and Plateau states—numerous incidents resulting in over 1,000 (mostly Muslims) dead, tens of thousands of both Muslim and Christian refugees either displaced from their homes or made to flee the region, and the declaration of a state of emergency in Plateau state by President Olusegun Obasanjo from May 18 to November 4 (see below).[61]

This list and numbers do little, however, to give us a sense of the interreligious hostilities in Nigeria. For this, I will briefly describe the incidents at Kano in October 1991 and in the Kano and Plateau states in the first half of 2004. The riots in October 1991 were precipitated by the return to Kano of pentecostal evangelist Reinhard Bonnke, whose crusade was part of his Christ for All Nations Africa campaign designed to evangelize the continent of Africa by the year 2000.[62] Kano is a historically Islamic city, and renowned Muslim apologist Ahmed Deedat (1918-2005) already had been denied a license to hold a similar type of meeting in Kano earlier that year.[63] Given the widely recognized successes experienced by Bonnke on his first visit to Kano a few years before, Muslims pressured the government to deny Bonnke's license for this visit. When this did not happen, Muslims were deluged by Christian advertisements in public posters and space (including radio, TV, and moving vans with public address systems). When

---

[61] There is some debate about why the Christian president declared the state of emergency only in Plateau (which was governed at that time by a Christian as well), but not in Kano (a historically Muslim-dominated state); see John Okwoeze Odey, *C.A.N. My Foot: The Reckless Utterance of a Wilful President* (Abakaliki, Nigeria: St. Patrick's Parish, 2004).

[62] Rosalind I. J. Hackett, "Radical Christian Revivalism in Nigeria and Ghana: Recent Patterns of Intolerance and Conflict," in *Proselytization and Communal Self-Determination in Africa*, ed. Abdullahi Ahmed An-Na'im (Maryknoll, N.Y.: Orbis Books, 1999), 246-67, esp. 251. This was Bonnke's nineteenth crusade in Africa after his Harare (Zimbabwe) Fire Convention in 1985 challenged over four thousand pastors with the theme "Africa Shall Be Saved"; see Ogbu U. Kalu, *Power, Poverty and Prayer: The Challenges of Poverty and Pluralism in African Christianity, 1960-1996*, Studies in the Intercultural History of Christianity 122 (Frankfurt: Peter Lang, 2000), 114.

[63] One of the few scholarly articles on Deedat is by David Westerlund, "Ahmed Deedat's Theology of Religion: Apologetics through Polemics," *Journal of Religion in Africa* 33, no. 3 (2003): 263-78.

"Bonnke entered Kano in a triumphant motorcade two days before the scheduled opening,"[64] a few scuffles and arguments provoked rioting, with tragic results.

While the majority of riot-related deaths have been Christians,[65] they have retaliated aggressively and violently on numerous occasions. It has been extremely difficult to identify the originating causes of these riots because each side blames the other. At least in the Kano-Plateau riots of 2004, however, there is evidence that Christians had tired of turning the other cheek and mobilized intentionally against those they felt were their oppressors.[66] Christian atrocities have been documented in the Yelwa area when, on 2-3 May 2004, over 700 Muslims were killed, including some who sought medical help at a clinic for injuries. Finally, an equally disturbing fact is that nearly 370 Muslim women and children were abducted by the attackers, with many of the women raped, fed pork, and required to drink locally brewed alcohol (both prohibited by *Sharia* law).

While these were dark days for interreligious relations in Nigeria, there have also been some signs of hope in Muslim neighbors protecting and saving Christians and vice versa. One Christian testified, "An old Muslim man took me into his house where I stayed until 6.30 p.m.," while two elderly Christian men said they "managed to escape and were saved by a Muslim acquaintance who hid them, along with eight women and two young men, in his house close to the church premises."[67] Other Muslims warned Christians in advance of potential attacks, or gave their Christian neighbors Muslim headscarves enabling their escape from rioting areas; some even risked their own lives in the face of threatening fellow-Muslim attackers.[68] That many on both sides have been preserved from harm and death by neighbors, friends, and total strangers from the other faith shows that interreligious relations, even in Nigeria, have not been marked solely by violence.

---

[64] Paul Gifford, "Reinhard Bonnke's Mission to Africa, and His 1991 Nairobi Crusade," in *New Dimensions in African Christianity*, ed. Paul Gifford (Nairobi: All Africa Conference of Churches, 1992), 157-82, quotation from p. 171.

[65] Marshall, gen. ed., *Religious Freedom in the World*, 240, identifies thirteen thousand Christian deaths alone. But Marshall has also written as follows elsewhere: "Nigeria is one of the few areas where Christians have engaged in communal violence themselves, though most of this seems to be in reaction to the activity of Islamic radicals"; see Paul Marshall, with Lela Gilbert, *Their Blood Cries Out: The Worldwide Tragedy of Modern Christians Who are Dying for Their Faith* (Dallas: Word, 1997), 63.

[66] Carina Tertsakian writes, "The Christian attackers were so numerous and well-armed that they quickly overpowered even those Muslims who had weapons" ("Revenge in the Name of Religion," 23); for what follows, see pp. 26, 30, and 34-37.

[67] Tertsakian, "Revenge in the Name of Religion," 17-18.

[68] David L. Windibiziri, "Neighborology, Mutuality and Friendship," in *Dialogue and Beyond: Christians and Muslims Together on the Way*, ed. Sigvard von Sicard and Ingo Wulfhorst (Geneva: Lutheran World Federation, 2003), 89-95, esp. 92-93; cf. Boer, *Nigeria's Decades of Blood*, 62 and 109 n. 49.

RESISTING SECULARIZATION: MUSLIM DISCOURSES IN NIGERIA

The question remains: What exactly identifies these violent episodes as religious rather than ethnic, economic, or political? In this section, we will examine Muslim perspectives before looking at Christian viewpoints in the next. At one level, the ethnic and religious hostilities need to be understood against the background of the colonial administration.[69] During the first half of the twentieth century, the British created a system of "indirect rule" in the northern region by allowing the existing Muslim emirates—renamed "Native Authorities"—to remain in power. By the time of independence, however, many of these emirs were either being phased out of leadership or had come to retain only a ceremonial role in the public sphere.[70] There were also increasing numbers of colonially educated southerners (mostly Igbo Christians) who migrated to the northern areas, and these in many cases succeeded in taking over land long controlled by Hausa-Fulani tribes. In the process Igbos also assumed positions of political leadership. Arguably, the conflict may have been minimized if southern Nigerian migrants who moved to the north and then established themselves there actually observed the behavioral protocols of their regions rather than antagonize their Muslim neighbors in various ways after attaining political standing.[71] Last but certainly not least, the Nigerian civil war (1967-1970) was in part a dispute over which groups (Muslim or Christian) should control what space (northern and/or southern areas) of the country. From the Muslim perspective, independence meant throwing off the yoke of the colonizers (along with their seed, including southern Christian Nigerians), reasserting Nigerian Muslim identity, and reclaiming the Islamic culture and civilization from Western, secular, modernist, and Christian forces.[72]

---

[69] See Chima J. Korieh, "Islam and Politics in Nigeria: Historical Perspectives," in *Religion, History, and Politics in Nigeria: Essays in Honor of Ogbu U. Kalu,* ed. Chima J. Korieh and G. Ugo Nwokeji (Lanham, Md.: University Press of America, 2005), 109-24; and Lamin Sanneh, *Piety and Power: Muslims and Christians in West Africa* (Maryknoll, N.Y.: Orbis Books, 1996).

[70] See Jonathan T. Reynolds, "The Politics of History: The Legacy of the Sokoto Caliphate in Nigeria," in *Displacement and the Politics of Violence in Nigeria*, ed. Paul E. Lovejoy and Pat Ama Tokunbo Williams, 50-65 (see n. 55 above).

[71] On this point, see M. H. Kukah, *Religion, Politics and Power in Northern Nigeria* (Ibadan, Nigeria: Spectrum, 1993), 256. For more on the southern displacement of northerners in that region as well as the marginalization of northern migrants to the south (which also exacerbated northern-southern relations), see Kate Meaher, "Shifting the Imbalance: The Impact of Structural Adjustment on Rural-urban Population Movements in Northern Nigeria," in *Displacement and the Politics of Violence in Nigeria*, 81-92 (see n. 55 above); and Patrick J. Ryan, "In My End Is My Beginning: Muslim and Christian Traditions at Cross-purposes in Contemporary Nigeria," in *Muslim-Christian Encounters in Africa*, ed. Benjamin F. Soares, Islam in Africa 6 (Leiden and Boston: Brill, 2006), 187-220.

[72] Muslims fear "that the aim of the unholy triad of colonialism, secularism, and Christianity 'is to keep the Muslims under perpetual domination,'" and therefore often equate this

From the Muslim point of view, one of the most illuminating issues involves their insistence on governance through *Sharia* law. It needs to be recalled that *Sharia* law has been in effect at least in some respects since the early nineteenth century through the establishment of the Sokoto Caliphate by Usman dan Fodio (1744-1817).[73] Whereas full implementation of *Sharia* provided a comprehensive national legal system—addressing, for example, sumptuary laws (involving prostitution, alcohol, and gambling), *zakat* (poor tax), land reform (which would in all likelihood retrieve land from multinational corporations), economic/banking reforms, and educational reforms to include Islamic/*Sharia* courses on politics, economics, law, banking[74]—the "indirect rule" approach of the colonizers did not eliminate *Sharia* entirely. Yet, the British relegated *Sharia* to matters related to personal status and replaced *Sharia* criminal law with a version of the English Penal Code. But at independence (1960), the Northern *Sharia* Court of Appeals was established to rule on issues disputed between Muslims. With the division of the northern region into twelve states after the civil war, the practical question that emerged was how to harmonize conflicting *Sharia* decisions given the various rulings of the multiple-state *Sharia* courts of appeals. The proposal for a federal *Sharia* court of appeals in 1977 was intended to address precisely this question.

Christians rejected this proposal because they felt it symbolized the intent of Muslim northerners to Islamicize the country.[75] After two years worth of debates, the new constitution in 1979 explicitly stated there would be no state religion in Nigeria—and this was repeated in the 1999 constitution—but did provide for state *Sharia* courts of appeals even if only for issues related to Islamic personal law such as marriage, divorce, inheritances, and so forth. Yet Muslims lost much more because *Sharia* decisions could now be appealed to federal non-*Sharia* high courts. Hence they continued to search for ways to implement *Sharia* law and found such through a constitutional loophole giving states the power of self-determination with regard to the implementation of judiciary systems in state territories. In October of 1999, in part as a response to the emer-

triad with the Satanic; see Jan H. Boer, *Muslims: Why the Violence*, Studies in Christian-Muslim Relations 2 (Belleville, Ont.: Essence, 2004), 65 and 79; the quote within the quote is from the *New Nigerian* (8 November 1999), 1. See also Boer's more extensive presentation in his *Muslims: Why We Reject Secularism*, Studies in Christian-Muslim Relations 4 (Belleville, Ont.: Essence, 2005).

[73] Ibraheem Sulaiman, *A Revolution in History: The Jihad of Usman dan Fodio* (London and New York: Mansell, 1986), 22-23.

[74] Umar M. Birai, "Islamic Tajdid and the Political Process in Nigeria," in *Fundamentalisms and the State*, ed. Martin E. Marty and R. Scott Appleby, 184-203, esp. 194 (see n. 22 above).

[75] Philip Ostien, "An Opportunity Missed by Nigeria's Christians: The 1976-78 Sharia Debate Revisited," in *Muslim-Christian Encounters in Africa*, ed. Benjamin F. Soares, 221-55 (see n. 71 above), suggests that Christian foresight in this matter in the mid-to-late-1970s would have averted the emergence of *Sharia* under state implementation since 1999.

gence of a southern (Christian) president at a very precarious time in the country's history, *Sharia* was introduced in the state of Zamfara, and this was followed soon by eleven other states in the north. As was the case previously (under colonial rule and during the First Republic period before the civil war, 1960-1966), non-Muslims, including Christians, have the option of having their cases heard in the existing (Christian created) Common Law Courts.[76]

For Muslims, *Sharia* law is not merely a political system; rather, it is divinely given and intrinsic (not accidental) to fulfilling the Islamic way of life in submission to Allah. Many Muslims believe that while people of the Religions of the Book were and are tolerated under Muslim rule with their rights protected, Muslims in a secular (Christian and Western) state have had no such rights of religious freedom insofar as denial of *Sharia* is in effect a denial of the practice of Islamic faith. To counter the Christian claim that the creation of a federal *Sharia* court of appeals is equivalent to creating a Muslim state, *Sharia* apologists point out that if such were the case, Christians would not be able to opt out of *Sharia* law. By contrast, since the colonial period, the forcible removal of *Sharia* has been part of the Christian plan to exterminate Islam.[77] Moderate Muslim voices are especially careful to affirm *Sharia* as an expression of Muslim resistance to Western decadence on the one hand, but, on the other hand, to insist on *Sharia* operating within the religiously plural framework of multifaith Nigeria.[78]

Yet Christians remain unconvinced that justice is possible for non-Muslims if *Sharia* law is implemented in Nigeria. They point out that the history of *Dhimmis* (non-Muslims) in Muslim-controlled regions have included the following restrictions based on *Sharia*: on joining the army, even while having to pay for and rely on the army for defense; on holding certain positions of leadership; on exercising the right to own and control land; on living in well-built homes; on exposing crosses and other objects of worship; on having sexual relations with or marrying Muslims; on possessing arms or dressing in certain ways; on maintaining other than a standing posture in the presence of Muslims; and on disturbing Muslims (e.g., churches must be silent).[79] In the present situation, there are other concerns such as the following: that the witness of a Muslim would have greater

---

[76] Abdur Rahman I. Doi, *Non-Muslims under Shari'ah* (Brentwood, Md.: International Graphics, 1979).

[77] Ibrahim Ado-Kurawa, *Shari'ah and the Press in Nigeria: Islam versus Western Christian Civilization* (Kano, Nigeria: Kurawa Holdings, 2000).

[78] Frieder Ludwig, "Religion and Politics in Northern Nigeria: Shari'a Controversies and Christian-Muslim Relations," unpublished manuscript. My thanks to Prof. Ludwig for sharing his paper with me before publication.

[79] See Matthew Hassan Kukah and Toyin Falola, *Religious Militancy and Self-Assertion: Islam and Politics in Nigeria* (Aldershot, U.K.: Avebury, 1996), 119-20.

value than that of a woman, a Christian, or a pagan, or that there would be prejudice against those unable to swear on the Qur'an. There is also the question that while *Sharia* may work well when both parties are Muslim, what if one is not?[80] Hence, in spite of Muslim assurances, Christians remain concerned that later expansion of *Sharia* law would severely curtail non-Muslim freedoms.

At the same time, it should also be acknowledged that Muslim fears about Christian secularization of Nigeria are no less well grounded than Christian fears about Muslim Islamization.[81] Such Muslim aspirations were most clearly signaled in Nigeria's surreptitiously changing its status from observer to full member of the Organization of Islamic Conference (OIC) in 1986, membership in which was limited only to sovereign Muslim states.[82] At one point, the OIC's charter included the objective "to propagate Islam and acquaint the rest of the world with Islam, its issues and aspirations," and cited the Declaration of the Third Islamic Summit of 1981: "Strict adherence to Islam and Islamic principles and values, as a way of life, constitutes the highest protection for Muslims against the dangers which confront them. Islam is the only path which can lead them to strength, dignity and prosperity and a better future."[83] These moves were motivated by the Muslim concern that a secular state would in effect empower Christians and result in negative implications for Muslim with regard to the national calendar, religious holidays, control of public education, and Nigeria's international relations, among other issues. Hence, the political disputes in Nigeria have retained an undeniably religious character. In the end, many Muslim theopoliticians continue to insist it is insufficient to win the game of electoral politics because that would be to capitulate to a foreign system of social organization rather than to abide under religiously sanctioned dictates.[84] After all, to accept the separation of religion and politics (of church/mosque and state) is to accommodate to a secular framework of understanding.[85]

Yet, there is also a growing contingent of Muslims who recognize that as a religiously plural state, Nigerians of all faiths must learn to get along with one another. A few Muslims have begun to call for an end to the "silent majority syndrome" so that extremist Muslims do not represent the

---

[80] John Okwoeze Odey, *The Sharia and the Rest of Us* (Abakaliki, Nigeria: St. Patrick's Parish, 2000), esp. ch. 4; and Udoma, *The Cross and the Crescent*, 101-26.

[81] On the issue of Islamization, see Falola, *Violence in Nigeria*, ch. 3.

[82] For discussion of this issue, see Udoma, *The Cross and the Crescent*, 126-33.

[83] Lamin Sanneh, *The Crown and the Turban: Muslims and West African Pluralism* (Boulder, Colo.: Westview, 1997), 220. For the current OIC charter, see the "About OIC" link at http://www.oic-oci.org/.

[84] William Miles, "Muslim Ethnopolitics and Presidential Elections in Nigeria," *Journal of Muslim Minority Affairs* 20, no. 2 (2000): 229-41.

[85] Simeon O. Ilesanmi, *Religious Pluralism and the Nigerian State* (Athens, Ohio: Ohio University Center for International Studies, 1997), ch. 4.

public face of Islam to the world, whether in Nigeria or elsewhere.[86] Within Nigeria, moderate and progressive Muslim voices are urging acceptance of a secular state for the sake of peace.[87] Isn't this what Nigerian Christians are seeking?

RESISTING ISLAMIZATION AND "CASTING OUT THE EVIL ONE": NIGERIAN CHRISTIANITIES

The answer to the previous question depends on which Christian one asks. In what follows, we survey the responses of the Christian Association of Nigeria (CAN), the Roman Catholic Church, and the growing pentecostal-charismatic churches.

Although officially founded in 1976, CAN has its roots in the earlier Northern Christian Association (NCA), an ecumenical initiative formed out of concerns related to the centralization of power in the federal military government, the consolidation of power in the northern region states under Hausa-Fulani Muslims, and the agenda of the military class to unify the nation under Islam.[88] Over the years, CAN led initiatives to address Christian concerns such as Christian school autonomy; censorship of Christian media; the provocative use of loudspeakers in mosques and near church buildings; the denial of expatriate quotas to Christian institutions; the use of government subsidies for Muslim pilgrimages to Mecca without making such funds available for Christians; the imposition of Muslim authorities over Christians; the disproportionate number of Muslim appointees to governmental positions; and rights related to church buildings, female fashions, and the media.[89] But while CAN began with a "pol-

---

[86] Liyakat Takim, "Peace and Conflict Resolution in the Islamic Tradition," in *Religion, Terrorism and Globalization: Nonviolence—A New Agenda,* ed. K. K. Kuriakose (New York: Nova Science, 2006), 109-20, esp. 109.

[87] Most often these are scholars in conversation with Christian and African-tradition religionist academics; see, e.g., Sam Babs Mala and Z. I. Oseni, eds., *Religion, Peace and Unity in Nigeria* (Ibadan, Nigeria: Nigerian Association for the Study of Religions, 1984); C. S. Momoh, et al., eds., *Nigerian Studies in Religious Tolerance,* 4 vols. (Ibadan: Shaneson C. I., and Lagos: CBAAC/NARETO, 1988-1989); Jacob K. Olupona, ed., *Religion and Peace in Multi-Faith Nigeria* (Ile-Ife, Nigeria: Obafemi Awolowo University, 1992); R. D. Abubakre, ed., *Studies in Religious Understanding in Nigeria* (Ilorin, Nigeria: Nigerian Association for the Study of Religion, 1993).

[88] In addition, CAN sought to bring about collaboration between a wide range of Christian churches so as to foster church unity, develop the Christian Health Association of Nigeria, issue joint statements related to government policies and activities, write syllabi for schools, support the Bible Society of Nigeria, and fund and develop media training for the purposes of evangelization; see Bauna Peter Tanko, *The Christian Association of Nigeria and the Challenge of the Ecumenical Imperative* (1991; reprint, Jos, Nigeria: Fab Anieh, 1993), 128-31.

[89] Jan H. Boer, *Christians: Why This Muslim Violence,* Studies in Christian-Muslim Relations 3 (Belleville, Ont.: Essence, 2004), 93-101. Of course, it should be noted that Muslim perspectives on almost all of these issues are exactly reversed from that of Christians.

itics of quiet diplomacy" for its first ten plus years, by the mid-1980s, in response to the riots and Nigeria's full membership in the OIC, it had developed a "militant politics," led in part by the fiery archbishop A. O. Okogie. CAN's projects involved the massive use of media, engagement with members of the military council, and use of the court system.[90] While it is impossible to link CAN directly with any of the violence perpetrated by Christians in Nigeria, it is arguable that its operations as a network not only informed Christian public opinion but also mobilized Christian responses to the riots. CAN's unspoken motto was voiced by Christians fed up with Muslim violence: that the Bible is silent about what should happen after one's cheek has been slapped the second time.[91]

With regard to the Roman Catholic Church (RCC) in Nigeria, a number of trends can be identified.[92] At the political level, responses have usually been registered through CAN—often to voice criticisms of what is perceived as unfair governance. Going beyond political statements, RCC leadership also sought to implement Vatican II initiatives emphasizing engagement in dialogue with people of other faiths.[93] While the goal of increasing understanding of other religions is essential, these dialogues are for the most part limited to academics. From the point of view of the RCC's spiritual vitality, however, Nigerian clerics seem to be concerned less with Islam than with pentecostalism. After all, Catholic Christians who leave the Catholic Church are not converting to Islam but are joining pentecostal churches.[94]

The emergence of pentecostal and charismatic churches and Christians (PCCs) in Nigeria during the last thirty years further complicates an

---

[90] Iheanyi M. Enwerem, *A Dangerous Awakening: The Politicization of Religion in Nigeria* (Ibadan, Nigeria: IFRA, 1995), 119. Reflecting this alarmist posture of Nigerian Christians over the 1980s and into the 1990s, Tanko Yusuf, CAN's first president and later Nigerian ambassador, wrote a book in 1995 to show that "Islam's fundamentalist Muslims seek to control not only Nigeria but also the world"; see Tanko Yusuf and Lillian V. Grissen, *That We May Be One: The Autobiography of Nigerian Ambassador Jolly Tanko Yusuf* (Grand Rapids, and Cambridge, U.K.: Eerdmans, 1995), xvi.

[91] Kalu, *Power, Poverty and Prayer*, 156.

[92] I regret that the analysis of Roman Catholic priest Casimir Chinedu O. Nzeh, *From Clash to Dialogue of Religions: A Socio-Ethical Analysis of the Christian-Islamic Tension in a Pluralistic Nigeria*, European University Studies 23, Theology 745 (Frankfurt: Peter Lang, 2002), came to my attention too late to incorporate into this book.

[93] Victor Chukwulozie, *Muslim-Christian Dialogue in Nigeria* (Ibadan: Daystar, 1986), ch. 8.

[94] See, e.g., Evaristus Bassey, *Pentecostalism and the Catholic Church in Nigeria* (Calabar, Nigeria: Mariana, 1993); John A. Farounbi, *A Brief History of Pentecostal Movement in Nigeria* (Mushin, Nigeria: Lemuel Publishers, 1997); Emmanuel Onuh, *Pentecostalism: Selling Jesus at a Discount* (Nsukka, Nigeria: Goodwill of God Apostolate, 1999); Jerome N. Okafor, ed., *The Challenge of Pentecostalism* (Awka, Nigeria: Mercury Bright Press, 2004); and Hilary C. Achunike, *The Influence of Pentecostalism on Catholic Priests and Seminarians in Nigeria* (Onitsha, Nigeria: Africana First, 2004).

already hotly contested interreligious arena.[95] Besides revitalizing Christianity by competing for the allegiance of the Christian faithful with historic Protestant and Roman Catholic churches in Nigeria, PCCs have also aggressively engaged the interreligious arena. On the one hand, PCCs have adopted earlier missionary polemics against African traditional religions. They remain concerned that even the retrieval of African culture—for example, such as which occurred at FESTAC 1977 (the second World Black and African Festival of Arts and Culture)—was and would be "an open door to the demonic" in terms of reinstilling the covenants with the indigenous religious traditions and their spiritual entities.[96] On the other hand, PCCs not only counter the Islamization of Nigeria but sought to do so by evangelizing both the nation and, as we have seen in Reinhard Bonnke's "Africa for Christ" crusades, the entire continent.[97]

For our purposes, it is important to recognize not just the PCC commitment to mission and evangelism but also the tactics and, especially, the rhetoric that is often employed. The inflammatory nature of PCC modes of evangelization can be identified at multiple levels. First, PCC "political theology" is not based on political action but on fasting, prayer, spiritual warfare, and even exorcism and ministries of deliverance against the principalities, powers, and covenants of the heavenly realms.[98] Following

---

[95] This would include also neo-pentecostal churches. For discussion of the categories, see Matthews A. Ojo, *The End-Time Army: Charismatic Movements in Modern Nigeria* (Trenton, N.J., and Asmara, Eritrea: Africa World Press, 2006), 9-12. In what follows, I use "PCC(s)" in an all-inclusive sense to refer to pentecostal and charismatic type movements, churches, and Christians in Nigeria.

[96] Joseph Thompson, "Rising from the Mediocre to the Miraculous," in *Out of Africa: How the Spiritual Explosion among Nigerians Is Impacting the World*, ed. C. Peter Wagner and Joseph Thompson (Ventura, Calif.: Regal, 2004), 19-36, esp. 26-28. For more coverage of this issue, see Rosalind I. J. Hackett, "Discourses of Demonization in Africa and Beyond," *Diogenes* 50, no. 3 (2003): 61-75; and the work of Ogbu U. Kalu, "Estranged Bedfellows? The Demonisation of the Aladura in African Pentecostal Rhetoric," *Missionalia* 28, no. 2/3 (2000): 121-42; idem, "Preserving a Worldview: Pentecostalism in the African Maps of the Universe," *PNEUMA* 24, no. 2 (2002): 110-37; idem, "Pentecostal and Charismatic Reshaping of the African Religious Landscape in the 1990s," *Mission Studies* 20, no. 1 (2003): 84-111; and idem, *The Embattled Gods: Christianization of Igboland, 1841-1991* (Trenton, N.J., and Asmara, Eritrea: Africa World Press, 2003), 334.

[97] Thus the back flap of *Battle Cry for the Nations: Rekindling the Flames of World Evangelization*, ed. Timothy O. Olonade (Jos, Nigeria: CAPRO Media, 1995), announces that this book is designed to mobilize the church to evangelize the "unreached millions" caught up in "idolatry and Islam."

[98] Kalu, *Power, Poverty and Prayer*, ch. 5. In this regard, Nigerian PCC beliefs and practices mirror developments in world PCC circles—e.g., Jean DeBernardi, "Spiritual Warfare and Territorial Spirits: The Globalization and Localisation of a 'Practical Theology,'" *Religious Studies and Theology* 18, no. 2 (1999): 66-96—although one of the effects of this spiritualization of Nigerian politics is that PCCs are less motivated to address corruption and other national problems at their social, economic, political, and structural levels; see Paul Gifford, "The Bible as Political Document in Africa," in *Scriptural Politics: The Bible and the Koran as Political Models in the Middle East and Africa*, ed. Niels Kastfelt (Trenton, N.J., and Asmara, Eritrea: Africa World Press, 2004), 16-28, esp. 21-23.

from this, second, there is consistent demonization not only of African religions but also of Islam in PCC literature. For PCCs, Ishmael is outside the covenant, born to Hagar "the bondwoman" because of Abraham's lack of faith (see Gal 4:22-31); Mohammad is not a prophet but an epileptic and womanizer; and Allah is not the supreme God but one of 360 gods in the Ka'abah of pre-Islamic Arabia; hence, Islam is idolatry. Muslims are caught up "in Satan's bondage," and PCCs reject as demonic several core Islamic symbols such as the moon, the star, and Islamic rituals.[99] Third, and perhaps most provocative in terms of its practical effects, PCCs have employed the full range of media and technology in their evangelism campaigns— loudspeaker public address systems, cassettes, videos, CDs, DVDs, radio, TV, and the Internet—all of which not only clearly publicize the PCC understanding of other religions but also generate new forms of interreligious animosity and hostility.[100] Of course, Muslims also produce such defamatory literature and media, and the result is an intensification of interreligious "hate" rhetoric that further destabilizes the region rather than provides a platform for building a harmonious multifaith Nigeria.[101]

Finally and perhaps most interestingly for our purposes, PCC engagement with the public sphere has also expanded over the last few decades so

---

[99] See Steve Brouwer, Paul Gifford, and Susan D. Rose, *Exporting the American Gospel: Global Christian Fundamentalism* (New York & London: Routledge, 1996), 173-75; Rosalind I. J. Hackett, "Radical Christian Revivalism in Nigeria and Ghana: Recent Patterns of Intolerance and Conflict," in *Proselytization and Communal Self-Determination in Africa*, ed. Abdullahi Ahmed An-Na'im (Maryknoll, N.Y.: Orbis Books, 1999), 246-67, esp. 252; idem, "Managing or Manipulating Religious Conflict in the Nigerian Media," in *Mediating Religion: Conversations in Media, Religion and Culture*, ed. Jolyon Mitchell and Sophia Marriage (London and New York: T & T Clark, 2003), 47-63, esp. 58; Ruth Marshall-Fratani, "Mediating the Global and Local in Nigerian Pentecostalism," in *Between Babel and Pentecost: Transnational Pentecostalism in Africa and Latin America*, ed. Andre Corten and Ruth Marshall-Fratani (Bloomington, Ind.: Indiana University Press, 2001), 80-105, esp. 102-3; Ogbu U. Kalu, "Sharia and Islam in Nigerian Pentecostal Rhetoric, 1970-2003," *PNEUMA* 26, no. 2 (2004): 242-61, esp. 256-58; and Matthews A. Ojo, "American Pentecostalism and the Growth of Pentecostal-Charismatic Movements in Nigeria," in *Freedom's Distant Shores: American Protestants and Post-Colonial Alliances with Africa*, ed. R. Drew Smith (Waco, Tex.: Baylor University Press, 2006), 155-67, esp. 167. The reference to "Satan's bondage" is in Paul Gifford, *The New Crusaders: Christianity and the New Right in Southern Africa*, rev. ed. (London and Concord, Mass.: Pluto Press, 1991), 111, while the PCC assertion that Allah is not the supreme God builds on the highly polemical book by a Muslim convert to Christianity, G. J. O. Moshay, *Who Is This Allah?* (Bucks, U.K.: Dorchester House, 1994).

[100] See Rosalind I. J. Hackett, "Devil Bustin' Satellites: How Media Liberalization in Africa Generates Religious Intolerance and Conflict," in *Religion in African Conflicts and Peacebuilding Initiatives: Problems and Prospects for a Globalizing Africa*, ed. Sakah Mahmud, Rosalind I. J. Hackett, and James Smith (Notre Dame, Ind.: University of Notre Dame Press, 2008), in press. Thanks to Prof. Hackett for sending me a draft copy of this paper.

[101] Toyin Falola points out that in light of the emerging Muslim literary and media propaganda, "hate crimes are rationalized in religious terms: the holy books provide psychological support for all sorts of crimes, including murder" (*Violence in Nigeria*, ch. 9, quote from p. 264).

as to involve not only voting but also campaigning for public office and the courting of other explicitly political relationships.[102] The emergence of former general Olusegun Obasanjo from prison, during which he had a "born-again" experience, and then his run for the presidency in 1999, brought out massive PCC support.[103] Before and since, PCCs have been associating themselves with public figures, sometimes through CAN but other times on their own accord, especially in the cases of the more high profile, independent PCC organizations.

All is not bleak, however, for interreligious relations in Nigeria. There are signs some PCCs are recognizing that different attitudes need to be cultivated that will allow them to listen to, understand, and work together with Muslims for peace in Nigeria. In some cases, PCC involvement with CAN has helped moderate intolerant and negative perceptions of Islam among their constituencies so that "by the mid-1990s, Pentecostals were participating in the inter-faith dialogues that were held under the auspices of CAN."[104] Leading the way has been pentecostal pastor James Movel Wuye. After losing his right arm during the February 1992 riots in the Zango region, Wuye began searching for alternatives to violent responses in the Nigerian context. He met Ustaz Muhammad Nurayn Ashafa, who lost his brothers in the same Zango conflict, and after coming to realize they had wrongly perceived each other and their religious traditions, they founded the Muslim/Christian Youth Dialogue Forum. Together they published *The Pastor and the Imam*, in which they confessed, "We, as Christian and Muslim youth leaders who have played significant roles in past conflicts and became victims through the physical and psychological injuries that we sustained, came to realise that there is a need for a better approach to our conflict situation."[105] Their book neither overlooks the many substantive disagreements between Christianity and Islam nor denies the importance of the work of evangelization or Islamization; but

---

[102] Matthews A. Ojo, "The Church in the African State: The Charismatic/Pentecostal Experience in Nigeria," *Journal of African Christian Thought* 1, no. 2 (1998): 25-32, esp. 27.

[103] See Asonzeh Franklin-Kennedy Ukah, "The Redeemed Christian Church of God (RCCG), Nigeria: Local Identities and Global Processes in African Pentecostalism" (Ph.D. diss., Universität Bayreuth, 2003), §§5.3.6 and 6.3.3, available at http://opus.ub.uni-bayreuth. de/volltexte/2004/73/pdf/Ukah.pdf (last accessed 10 December 2006). For introductions to Obasanjo, see Alan Rake, *African Leaders: Guiding the New Millennium* (Lanham, Md., and London: Scarecrow, 2001), 180-84; and Akin Sofoluwe and 'Leke Ogunleye, eds., *The Return of Obasanjo* (Lagos: Peekay, 1999). More sympathetic early accounts include Mansour Khalid, ed., *Africa through the Eyes of a Patriot: A Tribute to General Olusegun Obasanjo* (London: Kegan Paul, 2001), and A. Toriola Oyewo, *Obasanjo's Administration and Issues in Nigerian Government* (Ibadan, Nigeria: Jator, 2001). One of Obasanjo's more severe critics is John Okwoeze Odey, *This Madness Called Election 2003* (Abakaliki, Nigeria: St. Patrick's Parish, 2003).

[104] Ojo, *The End-Time Army*, 69.

[105] Ustaz Muhammad Nurayn Ashafa and James Movel Wuye, *The Pastor and the Imam* (Kaduna and Lagos: Christian/Muslim Youth Dialogue Forum, 1999), ix.

it does lay out seventy scriptural texts each from the Bible and the Qur'an that provide common ground for the beginning of dialogue. They conclude by proposing collaboration via creating a platform for dialogue, fostering mutual respect for one another and for each other's religious tradition, resisting forced/unethical conversions, engaging in joint forgiveness-and-reconciliation initiatives, committing to the fight against injustice, and working together toward socioeconomic development. Might PCCs and Muslims live in peace as neighbors in Nigeria after all?

WHERE THE WEST MEETS THE REST: MULTICULTURALISM AND INTERRELIGIOUS RELATIONS IN THE UNITED STATES

In the American context, some Muslims have also recognized the possibility of PCCs cooperating rather than colliding with Muslims for the betterment of their communities.[106] Of course, the situation in the United States is much different from either that of Sri Lanka or Nigeria. In this section, I want to highlight these differences by describing America as a multicultural and multireligious country, and then observe the responses to this pluralistic situation on both the "left" and "right" side of the religious spectrum. Throughout we will note the wide range of interreligious practices at work in the contemporary American scene.

Multiculturalism and Multireligiosity in a Democratic and Secular Society

In 2001, Diana Eck, a leading Harvard University professor, published a book with the subtitle *How a "Christian Country" Has Now Become the World's Most Religiously Diverse Nation.*[107] Coming out of the "Pluralism Project" research initiative—which continues to the present—Eck's book provides a snapshot of multicultural and multireligious America at the turn of the twenty-first century.[108] The following recent estimates (2004) suggest that besides about 160 million Christians, there are millions of Americans who belong to non-Christian faith traditions.

---

[106] See Khalid Abdullah Tariq Al Mansour, *The Pentecostals: The Good, the Bad, the Ugly* (n.p.: First African Arabian Press, 1991), ch. 18, who sees real potential for African American PCCs and African American Muslims to work together to address the social and economic challenges confronting the black American community.

[107] Diana L. Eck, *A New Religious America: How a "Christian Country" Has Now Become the World's Most Religiously Diverse Nation* (New York: HarperSanFrancisco, 2001).

[108] The following statistics come from the Pluralism Project Web site, which is continuously updated; see http://www.pluralism.org/index.php.

- Baha'i—up to 767,000
- Buddhism—up to 4 million
- Hinduism—about 1,200,000
- Islam—up to 4,390,000
- Jainism—up to 75,000
- Judaism—up to 6,150,000
- Paganism (including witches and neopagans)—up to 1,000,000
- Sikhism—approximately 250,000
- Zoroastrianism—about 18,000

Although the actual percentage of non-Christians remains small, with almost 18 million Americans belonging to or affiliated with the world's major religious traditions, the United States is the most religiously diverse nation on earth. There is simply no denying the demographic diversification of American religiosity over the last generation owing to immigration, globalization trends, and transnational movements.[109]

However, there are definitely also ideological agendas that multicultural and multireligious America has produced. To simplify an otherwise enormously complex discussion, it could be argued that there are two trends at work: a progressive trajectory wishing to preserve the constitutionally guaranteed rights of religion and conscience that emerged out of America's founding by refugees and immigrants seeking such freedoms, and a conservative mentality seeking to focus on retrieving and emphasizing the Judeo-Christian legacy of the founding fathers of the nation. For those in the former camp, American multiculturalism and multireligiosity are potential resources that will strengthen the nation in an increasingly shrinking global village while an overemphasis on the Judeo-Christian tradition would necessarily exclude the flourishing of diversity and pluralism needed for American leadership in the twenty-first century.[110] On the other side, conservatives counter that American greatness was made possible precisely because of its Judeo-Christian heritage and that uncritical embrace of multiculturalism and multireligiosity will undermine the cohesiveness needed to sustain the American democratic vision.[111] Where progressives recognize multicultural and multiracial families and seek to approve transracial adoptions, conservatives anticipate the destabilizing of the family; if pro-

---

[109] See Peter W. Williams, *America's Religions: From Their Origins to the Twenty-First Century* (Urbana, Ill., and Chicago: University of Illinois Press, 2002), 6-11.

[110] See William Scott Green, "Diversity and Tolerance: Religion and American Pluralism," in *The Religion Factor: An Introduction to How Religion Matters*, ed. William Scott Green and Jacob Neusner (Louisville, Ky.: Westminster John Knox Press, 1996), 257-68; and Barbara A. McGraw and Jo Renee Formicola, eds., *Taking Religious Pluralism Seriously: Spiritual Politics on America's Sacred Ground* (Waco, Tex.: Baylor University Press, 2005).

[111] See Alvin J. Schmidt, *The Menace of Multiculturalism: Trojan Horse in America* (Westport, Conn., and London: Praeger, 1997); and Russell Kirk, *The Roots of American Order*, 4th ed. (Wilmington, Del.: ISI Books, 2003).

gressives want to emphasize a multicultural, multireligious, and bilingual education, conservatives see political correctness and an ideology of relativism. Where progressives want to open up immigration and defend affirmative action, conservatives are concerned about the unraveling of the American way of life; and so on.[112] Where in some quarters of the country this distinction between "progressives" and "conservatives" does not accurately reflect the emergence of a *via media*, in many other parts the culture wars continue to rage.

Part of the challenge is that whereas there is a constitutional separation of church and state in America—which means that there is no state-sponsored religion—there is an inseparable connection between religion and politics. This connection is no less present in the United States than it is in either Nigeria or Sri Lanka. Further, religious practices have political implications and vice versa, and it is impossible to divide our lives into an allegedly objective public political sphere and a purportedly subjective private religious domain.[113] This means at least two things. First, at the political level, many Americans realize they need to find a middle way between left and right, between progressive and conservatives, between pluralism and homogeneity, and so forth. How this is done is the million dollar political question, but there can be no doubt this is a conversation all concerned Americans need to engage for the future not only of this country but also of its place in the world affairs of the twenty-first century.[114]

Second and concurrently with the first, at the religious level Americans recognize the importance of nurturing both religious particularity and interreligious understanding and relationships. This involves working together to protect and preserve the religious freedoms they have in ways that allow for the flourishing of all religious traditions, including presently marginalized religious communities. At the same time, there is the acknowledgment that in a post-9/11 world, no religious tradition exists in isolation from all others. Therefore, there is an urgent need for collaboration across religious lines in developing safe public spaces wherein all citizens can learn more about other religious ways of life. From this, perhaps it will be possible for Americans to cultivate relationships of solidarity that respect religious differences but yet are committed to working amidst such differences for the common good. What is required is not a bland tolerance but a vision for a respectful mutuality that is able to engage in dialogue about ultimately meaningful (religious) convictions and yet at the same time is strong enough to sustain commitments relevant to the public good.

---

[112] An introduction to these debated issues can be found in Eleanor Stanford, ed., *Interracial America: Opposing Viewpoints* (Detroit: Thomson Gale, 2006).

[113] See Robert Booth Fowler et al., *Religion and Politics in America: Faith, Culture, and Strategic Choices*, 3rd ed. (Boulder, Colo.: Westview, 2004).

[114] One suggestion from David A. Hollinger, *Postethnic America: Beyond Multiculturalism* (New York: Basic Books, 1995), builds on America's diversification while resisting the anarchic threats of an uncritical ideology of pluralism.

All this sounds nice and good. But pluralism means Americans probably have different ideas about what should be done and how to go about doing such. In the next two sections, we look respectively at responses to religious pluralism in America as seen in the development of interreligious dialogue and in the circles of evangelical Christianity.

FROM THE PARLIAMENT OF RELIGIONS TO THE AMERICAN
ACADEMY OF RELIGION

Given the centrality of religious freedom to the history of the United States, it should not be surprising that the World's First Parliament of Religions was held in Chicago in September 1893 in conjunction with the Columbian Exposition.[115] Thousands of Americans and people from all over the world heard speeches and papers by representatives of the various Christian churches (Orthodox, Roman Catholic, and the different Protestant denominations) as well as Judaism, Islam, Hinduism, Buddhism, Jainism, Confucianism, Taoism, Shintoism, Zoroastrianism, and other less-well-known religious traditions. Christian voices dominated the conversation, but for the first time the world's religious traditions were gathered in one place with each given a platform to present its ideas. By the time of the second Parliament one hundred years later, globalization had commenced in earnest and the Christian dominance in 1893 had been replaced by a genuine ecumenical and interfaith process and multireligious framework.[116]

In retrospect, the First Parliament gave impetus to the modern ecumenical and interfaith movements and contributed to the emergence of the academic study of religion in North America.[117] With regard to the latter, the Parliament revealed the value of learning about other religious traditions on their own terms. From this the discipline of *Religionswissenschaft* (the scientific study of religion, comparative religion, or the history of religions) developed.[118] Yet the research carried out by these scholars was better classified within the arts and humanities—for example, involving literature,

---

[115] The documents of the Parliament were published immediately in John Henry Barrows, ed., *The World Parliament of Religions*, 2 vols. (Chicago: Parliament Publishing Company, 1893).

[116] See Wayne Teasdale and George F. Cairns, eds., *The Community of Religions: Voices and Images of the Parliament of the World's Religions* (New York: Continuum, 1996).

[117] Diana L. Eck, "Foreword," in *The Dawn of Religious Pluralism: Voices from the World's Parliament of Religions, 1893*, ed. Richard Hughes Seager (La Salle, Ill.: Open Court, 1993), xiii-xvii. For further assessment of the First Parliament, see also the essays in Eric J. Ziolkowski, ed., *A Museum of Faiths: Histories and Legacies of the 1893 World's Parliament of Religions* (Atlanta: Scholars Press, 1993), part 3.

[118] See Joseph M. Kitagawa and Joachim Wach, eds., *The History of Religions: Essays on the Problem of Understanding* (Chicago: University of Chicago Press, 1967); and Eric J. Sharpe, *Comparative Religion: A History*, 2nd ed. (La Salle, Ill.: Open Court, 1986).

art, ethics, Catholic studies, Jewish studies, and so on[119]—than the "harder" sciences. Those attempting the latter were trained more often in psychology, anthropology, and sociology, and there was little collaboration across these disciplinary boundaries during the first half of the twentieth century.

At the same time, scholars of religion came to progressively see there could be no tight disciplinary boundaries separating the various approaches to the study of religion. Rather, our cumulative understanding of religion could actually be enhanced by a multidisciplinary approach. The beginnings of an institutional rearrangement reflecting such an emerging consensus occurred in 1963 when the scholarly organization National Association of Biblical Instructors changed its name to the American Academy of Religion (AAR) precisely in order to facilitate a wider conversation among the many specialized approaches to the study of religion.[120] The result was the opening up of the AAR to include multidisciplinary approaches to the study of religion. Members of the AAR now bring to bear on the study of religion the disciplinary tools of the cognitive and biological sciences, sociology, political science, economics, psychology, ethnicity, gender, anthropology, cultural studies, and others, but also a hermeneutics of suspicion informed by Marxist, Freudian, Nietzschean, and postcolonial theories.[121] Along with this proliferation of methodologies and theoretical tools in the study of religion has been also the appearance of multiple religious perspectives in the AAR: more and more of its membership include people from diverse faith backgrounds or even no faith at all.

Amidst this "zoo" that is the AAR there are at least three identifiable trajectories that parallel the wider debates in American society about religious pluralism. On the one side are those who are cynical about the direction of the AAR and concerned that the study of religion is disintegrating under a myriad of ideological interests.[122] On the other side are those convinced that for all its intentions and changes the AAR continues to be dominated (wrongly, for them) by theological (especially Christian religious) interests and that what is needed is a more scientifically and empirically shaped framework for the study of religion.[123] In the middle, I would

---

[119] Paul Ramsey, John Frederick Wilson, and George F. Thomas, eds., *The Study of Religion in Colleges and Universities* (Princeton: Princeton University Press, 1970).

[120] See the "Editorial Preface" to *The Journal of Bible and Religion* 33, no. 1 (1965): 3-4.

[121] Willi Braun and Russell T. McCutcheon, eds., *Guide to the Study of Religion* (London and New York: Cassell, 2000).

[122] Paul V. Mankowski, "What I Saw at the American Academy of Religion," *First Things* 21, no. 1 (March 1992); 36-41.

[123] Representative of those in this camp is Donald Wiebe—e.g., "A Religious Agenda Continued: A Review of the Presidential Addresses of the American Academy of Religion," *Method & Theory in the Study of Religion* 9, no. 4 (1997): 353-75; idem, "Against Science in the Academic Study of Religion: On the Emergence and Development of the American Academy of Religion," in *The Comity and Grace of Method: Essays in Honor of Edmund F. Perry*, ed. Thomas Ryba, George D. Bond, and Herman Tull (Evanston, Ill.: Northwestern

argue, are those who are concerned that the study of religion is inclusive of all religions, that it deploys whatever tools might be amenable to fostering a better understanding of what is being studied, and that it does not reduce religion to other non-religious categories of explanation. Those working broadly within this framework wrestle with difficult methodological (What difference does the perspectives of insider or outsider make in the study of religion or are the lines between the two unambiguous?), pedagogical (What is the difference between being a *confessor* of a religion and being a *professor* of a religion in the college or university classroom?), and political-ethical (What are the political implications of categorizations made by scholars of religion on those whom they study?) questions.[124] We will return to some of these issues later.

AMERICAN CHRISTIANS AND INTERRELIGIOUS RELATIONS

While these debates have been occurring in the AAR, American churches have also been wrestling with how to respond to the increasing sense of religious pluralism after the First Parliament. Although by no means occurring overnight, between 1893 and 1993 intra-Christian ecumenism slowly expanded to include interreligious relations. The First Parliament focused discussion on a conversation that was later picked up, successively, by the International Missionary Council and then the World Council of Churches (WCC). Throughout the histories of both organizations the question of interreligious relations was hotly debated, but over time interreligious dialogue came to be embraced as part of the mission of the WCC.[125]

David Bosch has called attention to how the evolution of themes in WCC conferences devoted to the relationship of Christianity and other faiths has reflected the progression of Christian consciousness (my emphases in what follows):

- Commission for World Mission and Evangelism meeting in Mexico City (1963): "The Witness of Christians *to* Men of Other Faiths" (one-way monologue directed *at* religious others, although they are recognized as being of faith rather than not);
- East Asia Christian Conference in Bangkok (1964): "The *Christian Encounter* with Men of Other Beliefs" (Christian initiative emphasized, although such interactions involve the responses of people of other faiths);

University Press, 2004), 58-83; and idem, *The Politics of Religious Studies: The Continuing Conflict with Theology in the Academy* (New York: St. Martin's Press, 1999).

   [124] These issues are discussed in Russell T. McCutcheon, ed., *The Insider/Outsider Problem in the Study of Religion: A Reader* (London and New York: Cassell, 1999).

   [125] See Franklin H. Littell, ed., *The Growth of Interreligious Dialogue 1939-1989: Enlarging the Circle*, Toronto Studies in Theology 46 (Lewiston, Queenston, and Lampeter: Edwin Mellen Press, 1989).

- Ajaltoun (Lebanon) (1970): "Dialogue *between* Men of *Living* Faiths" (people of other faiths affirmed positively and as equal dialogue partners);
- Chiang Mai (Thailand) (1977): "Dialogue *in Community*" (fully mutual emphasis, including a gender inclusive approach).[126]

On the Roman Catholic side, Vatican II opened the church to engaging not only in the intra-Christian ecumenical discussion but also in interreligious dialogue.[127] These developments in the WCC and the Catholic Church have raised the question of the relationship between dialogue and proclamation. While there are a few who polarize the issue in terms of advocating only one or the other kind of activity as legitimate Christian witness in a pluralistic world, most wrestle with the recognition that authentic evangelism includes dialogue and vice versa.[128] On the practical level, most mainline Protestant and Catholic churches in the United States have adopted a posture emphasizing working with organizations representing other faith traditions to achieve common social and political goals, and building relationships with people of other faiths.[129]

These questions are also debated among American evangelicals. While it is surely unfair to divide evangelical approaches into two camps,[130] I suggest there are also conservative and progressive trajectories that frame the discussion of evangelical theology of religions and their concomitant practices. On the conservative side, the most vocal have not denied the importance of dialogue but insisted dialogue must always serve the purposes of witness and evangelism understood in traditional terms.[131] There are also

---

[126] David J. Bosch, *Transforming Mission: Paradigm Shifts in Theology of Mission* (Maryknoll, N.Y.: Orbis Books, 1991), 484.

[127] Robert B. Sheard, *Interreligious Dialogue in the Catholic Church since Vatican II: An Historical and Theological Study*, Toronto Studies in Theology 31 (Lewiston, Queenston, and Lampeter: Edwin Mellen Press, 1987); and Francesco Gioia, ed., *Interreligious Dialogue: The Official Teaching of the Catholic Church (1963-1995)* (Boston: Pauline Books & Media, 1997).

[128] See Don Pittman, Ruben L. F. Habito, and Terry C. Muck, eds., *Ministry and Theology in Global Perspective: Contemporary Challenges for the Church* (Grand Rapids: Eerdmans, 1996); for a brief synopsis of how Roman Catholics are wrestling with this issue, see John Borelli, "Interreligious Dialogue and Mission: Continuing Questions," in *Evangelizing America*, ed. Thomas P. Rausch (New York and Mahwah, N.J.: Paulist Press, 2004), 172-98.

[129] E.g., Harold Coward and Gordon S. Smith, eds., *Religion and Peacebuilding* (Albany: State University of New York Press, 2004).

[130] I discuss the complexity of North American evangelicalism and cite the pertinent literature in my "The Word and the Spirit, or the Spirit and the Word? Exploring the Boundaries of Evangelicalism in Relationship to Modern Pentecostalism," *Trinity Journal* n.s. 23, no. 2 (2002): 235-52.

[131] See Ronald H. Nash, *Is Jesus the Only Savior?* (Grand Rapids: Zondervan, 1994), 165-69; and Millard J. Erickson, *How Shall They Be Saved? The Destiny of Those Who Do Not Hear of Jesus* (Grand Rapids: Baker, 1996), ch. 14.

some in this camp who have bemoaned the trends toward multiculturalism and multireligiosity in America, believing these have nurtured relativism, decentered Christian faith in the marketplace of competing religions and philosophies, and popularized "spirituality" rather than authentic religious commitment.[132] For many traditional American evangelicals, the important practices include preaching or bearing witness in such a way as to lead non-Christians to conversion to Christ.

No self-identifying evangelical would deny the importance of public and interpersonal evangelism. At the same time, other evangelicals, such as those associated with the Emerging Church movement, have opted for a less traditional set of approaches to Christian mission. In contrast to attempts to more clearly mark the boundaries between the church and the world, Emerging churches have a much more fluid, organic, and relational self-understanding.[133] In this framework, strangers are welcomed and engaged following the inclusive practices of Jesus. Such "practices of inclusion" include creating safe places in the welcome space, getting to know and embracing others who are different, nurturing attitudes that are transparent and humble rather than arrogant, replacing verbal apologetics with relational approaches, and resisting "having an agenda" and allowing instead the agenda to emerge from the relationship. Therefore when applied to relating with people of other faiths, Emergent churches emphasize genuine dialogue, encourage visiting other sacred sites and even participating in their liturgies, and insist on learning about the lives and religious commitments of others. All of these activities are informed by the conviction that there is much to be learned from other cultures, even to the point of being evangelized by those of other faiths in ways that transform Christian self-understandings.[134] For these progressive evangelicals, evangelizing those in other faiths involves not merely rational apologetics but an embodied and holistic approach that engages people by beginning with where they are, while adapting to those situations in risky ways for the sake of the gospel.[135]

---

[132] E.g., David F. Wells, *Above All Earthly Powr's: Christ in a Postmodern World* (Grand Rapids, and Cambridge, U.K.: Eerdmans, and Leicester, U.K.: InterVarsity Press, 2005).

[133] See Eddie Gibbs and Ryan K. Bolger, *Emerging Churches: Creating Christian Community in Postmodern Cultures* (Grand Rapids: Baker Academic, 2005); cf. Ray Sherman Anderson, *An Emergent Theology for Emerging Churches* (Downers Grove, Ill.: InterVarsity, 2006).

[134] See Gibbs and Bolger, *Emerging Churches*, ch. 6, including the following report from Spencer Burke's community in Newport Beach, California: "We have a community hermeneutic. We read other sacred writings, then get back to Scripture and decide together how to interpret what we have read from the literature that other religions hold to be sacred" (p. 132).

[135] Missiologists advocating the adaptation of old rites or even the creation of new symbols and rituals shaped by the interreligious encounter include Michael Frost and Alan Hirsch, *The Shaping of Things to Come: Innovation and Mission for the 21st-Century Church* (Peabody, Mass.: Hendrickson, and Erina, Australia: Strand, 2003), 189-94. See also Terry Muck, *Alien Gods on American Turf* (Wheaton, Ill.: Victor/Christianity Today, 1990), esp. ch.

At one level, my choice of focusing our case studies in these three contexts has been fairly arbitrary: why not any other three countries or interreligious situations? And even in the three cases under consideration, I have in no wise provided an exhaustive assessment of interreligious relations, much less offered a comprehensive typology of different kinds of interreligious interactions worldwide. Yet I believe our discussion so far has been productive of a more limited set of goals. First, I wanted us to observe the many different social and political contexts within which interreligious encounters are taking place, and to note that even in these various locales, multiple forms of interreligious engagements are occurring. Second, I began this chapter with reference to Huntington's thesis of the "clash of civilizations" and noted its limitations. I think it is clear in our case studies, however, that interreligious violence is an undeniable factor of our global situation. While this does not require complete acceptance of Huntington's thesis, Christian theological reflection on interreligious relations cannot ignore the association of religion and violence in a post-9/11 world. Last but not least, our case studies have also noted positive interreligious relations featuring hospitality, dialogue, and mutuality among people of different faith traditions. Together, these observations lead me to believe that Christians need to articulate a multifaceted theology of religions and theology of interreligious engagement that more adequately underwrites the broad range of practices required for a complex post-9/11 world of many faiths. The next three chapters of this book will be preoccupied with precisely such a task before we return in our concluding chapter to revisit the question of Christian practices in Sri Lanka, Nigeria, and the United States as well as in interfaith zones around the world.

6, "Loving Neighbors"; and Irving Hexham, Stephen Rost, and John W. Morehead II, eds., *Encountering New Religious Movements: A Holistic Evangelical Approach* (Grand Rapids: Kregel, 2004).

2

Performing Theology

The Interrelationship between Christian Beliefs and Practices

Our constructive theological proposal depends on my making the case for seeing an intimate relationship between Christian beliefs—including doctrines and theologies—and Christian practices. If the previous chapter provided some of the empirical data informing our theology of Christian practices, this chapter focuses on the theoretical interconnections between theology and practices. While this relationship may be taken for granted in certain quarters, we would do well to pause and reflect on this issue for at least two reasons. First, all too often the relationship between Christian theologies of religion and Christian practices vis-à-vis the religions has not been spelled out. Since this linkage is central to the case being made in the remainder of this book (chapters 3 to 5), I want to be sure the constructive part of our argument is established on an adequate theoretical and theological foundation. Hence, it is important to see the general connection between beliefs and practices—the focus on this chapter—before proceeding to discuss the relationship between Christian theologies of religion and Christian interreligious practices.

Second, as we have now seen from the preceding chapter, the question of Christian practices in a post-9/11 world of many faiths is not an inconsequential one for Christian theology of religions. Christians need to give much more sustained reflection to the implications of their theologies of religion for Christian attitudes and actions regarding other faiths. But while these are valid practical concerns, Christian theological reflection cannot be normed merely by pragmatic constraints. Of course, Christian theology must be politically relevant, not merely (even if at times necessarily) "politically correct." But Christian theology must also provide explicit theological warrants not only for its practices but also for how those practices are informed by beliefs and vice versa. Hence, we need to clearly articulate the theological rationale for holding tightly the relationship between Christian beliefs and practices that undergirds the performative theology of interreligious praxis to be developed later in this book. Failing this, we might either simply provide instrumental rationales for dealing with the complexities of life in a multireligious world or articulate Christian beliefs about the religions without interrogating their concomitant policies and practices.

Our argument here will proceed in three steps, correlating with the three sections of this chapter. First, I want to demonstrate the interconnectedness between beliefs (doctrine and then theology) and practices by attending to the experiences of the early church. I will show that the early Christians did not bifurcate these two domains but that each flowed forth from the other. Second, I will present an overview of recent theoretical explications of how Christian beliefs and practices are interrelated. In this section, I will draw from philosophers such as J. L. Austin and Nicholas Wolterstorff, and theologians such as George Lindbeck and Kevin Vanhoozer, in developing my own theologically thick account of the interaction between Christian beliefs and practices. Finally, I will attempt to advance the contemporary discussion by sketching a pneumatological theology of Christian beliefs and practices that is relevant to the pluralistic world of our post-9/11 era. In further dialogue with pneumatological theologians such as D. Lyle Dabney and Reinhard Hütter, I seek to articulate what I am calling a pneumatological and performative theology according to the maxim, "many tongues equals many practices." Our goal in the big scheme of things is to provide a pneumato-theological framework for understanding the relationship between beliefs and practices that can in turn inform our view of how Christian theologies of religions are connected to the variety of Christian interreligious practices.

BELIEFS AND PRACTICES IN THE EARLY CHURCH

The earliest Christians did not reflect theoretically on the interrelationship between their beliefs and their practices. I hope to show, however, that this is because they presumed their interconnection rather than their disparateness. This can be seen in the apostolic witness preserved in the Christian Testament, in the later christological controversies, and in the fourth-century debates about the divinity of the Holy Spirit. In each case, we will see that Christian beliefs emerged out of and were intrinsically tied in with their practices.

BELIEFS AND PRACTICES IN THE FIRST-CENTURY CHURCH

I suggest we view the interrelationship between early Christian beliefs and practices along four lines. First, let me recapitulate what we should not need to be reminded of: that the accounts of Christian beliefs accessible to us now are available only because of the preservation of occasional docu-ments composed by the earliest Christians in response to specific situations, needs, and experiences. What we now call the Christian Testament emerged out of the earliest Christian communities' having to find encour-agement and consolation in living out their faith, having to answer funda-mental questions, and having to settle disputes about divergent practices. Many of these earliest Christian communities were under real or potential threat of persecution, not unlike the churches in Sri Lanka today. In these minority situations, some Christians were urged to live quiet and peaceful lives in relation to their surrounding neighbors (1 Thess 4:11; 2 Thess 3:12; 1 Tim 2:2), while others found themselves in conflict with other religious groups.[1] At a fundamental level, the earliest Christians did not live by "the book"; rather, what we now call "the book" arose out of their attempts to live faithfully as followers of Jesus Christ empowered by the Holy Spirit.

But, second, the earliest Jewish Christians did live according to the Law, the Prophets, and the Writings. Yet the author of the second letter to Tim-othy writes,

> But as for you, continue in what you have learned and firmly believed, knowing from whom you learned it, and how from child-hood you have known the sacred writings that are able to instruct you for salvation through faith in Christ Jesus. All scripture is inspired by God and is useful for teaching, for reproof, for correc-tion, and for training in righteousness, so that everyone who belongs to God may be proficient, equipped for every good work. (2 Tim 3:14-17)

Observe two points: (a) the scriptures (sacred writings) make people wise for salvation,[2] and (b) the teachings of scripture (doctrines) may inform, but do so for the larger purpose of correcting, shaping, and equipping the believer for good works. In other words, the scriptures are not merely cat-alogues of beliefs, although they certainly include such lists, propositions, and assertions. Rather, the scriptures are inspired by God—with inspiration usually connected to the Holy Spirit—for specific purposes related to Christian practices, life, and, ultimately, salvation.

Third, we can see this interconnection between beliefs and practices in the earliest Christian understanding of "faith." Against attempts to reduce or define faith solely in terms of either doctrines to be understood, affirmed, and confessed on the one side, or in terms of inexpressible feelings to be

---

[1] I deal with the case of Christians and Jews in the Johannine community in my "'The Light Shines in the Darkness': Johannine Dualism and Christian Theology of Religions Today," *Journal of Religion* (under review).

[2] On this point, see the extended argument by Telford Work, *Living and Active: Scripture in the Economy of Salvation* (Grand Rapids: Eerdmans, 2002).

embraced on the other, the earliest Christians recognized that their belief "in" God involved trusting God affectively, surrendering one's life to God unconditionally, and being obedient to God even to the point of death.[3] Christian faith involved and brought together the cognitive, affective, and practical dimensions of human life. Hence, the fourth evangelist saw the interconnectedness between belief and Christian life—for example, "But these are written so that you may come to believe that Jesus is the Messiah, the Son of God, and that through believing you may have life in his name" (John 20:31)—even as the author of the letter to the Hebrews noted in a mantra-like account that it was "by faith" that the ancient Israelite heroes went out and accomplished great feats (Hebrews 11). Similarly, this assumed connection between beliefs and practices makes sense of the claims that "For by grace you have been saved through faith, and this is not your own doing; it is the gift of God—not the result of works, so that no one may boast" (Eph 2:8-9), on the one hand, and that faith without works is dead (Jam 2:14-26), on the other. The disagreements between *sola fideists* and those who affirm the importance of works break down once we realize there are no truly-held beliefs unexpressed through works or authentic christo-form and Spirit-empowered practices unshaped by beliefs.[4]

Finally, because our focus in chapter 4 will be on Luke-Acts, let me briefly discuss this two-volume work when viewed through the lens that see early Christian beliefs and practices as connected. Luke tells his readers that his explicit intention is to clarify and confirm for them "the truth concerning the things about [Jesus Christ] which you have been instructed" (Luke 1:4; cf. Acts 1:1). At the same time, there is widespread scholarly consensus that the Spirit-empowered life of Jesus told in the Gospel provides the paradigm for the Spirit-empowered life of Christian discipleship told in Acts.[5] At least three levels of interconnections between beliefs and practices can be discerned here: (1) the interconnections that existed in the life of Jesus and the early Christian community as described in the Luke-Acts narrative;[6] (2) the intentions of Luke as the author of Luke-Acts not

---

[3] In the Christian Testament, faith is "unreserved trust that the love of God will reach out to those who turn to it without reservation"; see Terence Penelhum, ed., *Faith* (New York: Macmillan, 1989), 5.

[4] An extended argument on this point is provided by Frank D. Macchia, *Justification in the Spirit: Towards a Trinitarian Soteriology*, Pentecostal Manifestos 2 (Grand Rapids: Eerdmans, forthcoming).

[5] E.g., Robert P. Menzies, *Empowered for Witness: The Spirit in Luke-Acts*, Journal of Pentecostal Theology Supplement Series 6 (Sheffield: Sheffield Academic Press, 1994); and Max Turner, *Power from on High: The Spirit in Israel's Restoration and Witness in Luke-Acts*, Journal of Pentecostal Theology Supplement Series 9 (Sheffield: Sheffield Academic Press, 1996).

[6] The interrelationship between who Jesus was and what Jesus did is clarified through an assessment of what Jesus did through what he said; on this point, see Anthony C. Thiselton, "Christology in Luke, Speech-Act Theory, and the Problem of Dualism in Christology after Kant," in *Jesus of Nazareth: Lord and Christ—Essays on the Historical Jesus and New Tes-*

only to inform but also to encourage and inspire his readers to live out their Christian discipleship by the power of the Holy Spirit; and (3) the effects that the work accomplishes in transforming the lives of its readers and shaping their practices. The latter two levels of interconnections between beliefs and practices are also known as the illocutionary and perlocutionary aspects of speech-acts, and we will return to discuss these notions in more detail later (see pp. 47-50).

CHRISTOLOGY AND SOTERIOLOGY: ORTHODOXY AND ORTHOPRAXIS

If the earliest Christians lived out of the assumption that their beliefs and practices were interrelated, so also can we detect this same supposition at work in the fourth-century church fathers who were materially responsible for the formulation and reception of Christian doctrine. In this section, I want to focus our discussion on St. Athanasius (c. 296-373) in order to observe this pattern at work.

Well known as the champion of Christian orthodoxy because of his stand against Arianism after the Council of Nicea (325), Athanasius worked tirelessly to defend the divinity of Christ during the fourth-century debates.[7] His opponents were the strict Arians, who rejected all nonbiblical terms for describing the relationship between the Father and the Son, and the semi-Arians, who were willing to entertain the notion of the Son as being of "like substance" (*homoiousios*) as the Father because the Son was begotten of the Father—that is, "He is the image of the invisible God, firstborn of all creation" (Col 1:15). Athanasius countered that the Son was of "the same substance" (*homoousios*) as the Father, alike in all respects except in his begottenness.[8] Sometimes Athanasius's high christology is abstracted from the rest of his theological system with the result that its performative aspects are either obscured or neglected altogether. But when the links between Athanasius's understanding of the person of Christ and the saving works of Christ are made explicit, we can observe how the orthodox doctrine of Christ is interrelated with what we might call orthopraxis—the right practices that (ought to) mark Christian faith and discipleship.

Synthesizing but also building on the teachings of earlier church fathers such as Irenaeus of Lyons, Origen, and Clement of Alexandria, Athanasius understood salvation as the redemption of humankind and its completion

---

tament Christology, ed. Joel B. Green and Max Turner (Grand Rapids: Eerdmans; and Carlisle, U.K.: Paternoster, 1994), 453-72.

[7] For a general introduction to Athanasius, see Alvyn Pettersen, *Athanasius* (Harrisburg, Pa.: Morehouse, 1995). Details about Athanasius's apologetic engagements with Arianism are provided by Khaled Anatolios, *Athanasius* (London and New York: Routledge, 2004), 1-38.

[8] For details about the debate over "consubstantiality," see Bernard Lonergan, *The Way to Nicea: The Dialectical Development of Trinitarian Theology*, trans. Conn O'Donovan (Philadelphia: Westminster, 1976), ch. 9.

by God according to the image of the Second Adam. More specifically, the Second Adam (Christ) came so human beings "may escape from the corruption that is in the world because of lust, and may become participants in the divine nature" (2 Pet 1:4b). What the fall had taken away in terms of humans losing the likeness of the divine nature, redemption in Christ has restored in terms of union with God. Thus did Athanasius understand salvation in terms of divinization or deification (*theosis*).[9]

Now we can see why Athanasius insisted on defending the *homoousios*. If salvation involves the restoration of human union with God, then only God could have accomplished redemption. For this reason, Christ, the divinely appointed means of redemption, had to be fully divine or he would not have been able to reverse the curse of the fall and unite humanity (and human nature) with God. Hence Athanasius wrote, "The Word of God came in His own person, that, as He was the Image of the Father, He might be able to create afresh the man after the image"; more tersely, "For He was made man that we might be made God."[10] And it was this idea that was crucial in the argument against the Arians: "Therefore He was not man, and then became God, but He was God, and then became man, and that to deify us"; and again: "For therefore did He assume the body originate and human, that having renewed it as its Framer, he might deify it in Himself, and thus might introduce us all into the kingdom of heaven after His likeness. For man had not been deified if joined to a creature, or unless the Son were very God."[11]

I am thus suggesting that Athanasius's defense of the *homoousios* is not just a speculative idea but that it was intimately bound up with his doctrine of salvation. Once this connection is understood, the implications for Christian practices are more clearly seen. At this level, the life of Christ becomes paradigmatic for the lives of his followers, and Athanasius makes this explicit in his *Vita Antony*.[12] Written after the death of Antony in 356, the *Vita Antony* became almost immediately a classic of Christian hagiography. Yet, I see that the central features of Antony's life are simply a divinely empowered repetition of the life of Christ. If the goal of the incarnation was redemption and union with God, then the life of Antony reflects the practices through which such deification is realized. Hence, like Jesus, Antony maintains a life of prayer, especially early in the mornings, and of

[9] For further discussion of Athanasius's theology of deification, see Jules Gross, *The Divinization of the Christian according to the Greek Fathers*, trans. Paul A. Onica (Anaheim, Calif.: A & C Press, 2002), 163-75.

[10] Athanasius, *On the Incarnation of the Word*, §§13.7 and 54.3, in *Nicene and Post-Nicene Fathers*, 2nd series, vol. 4, ed. Philip Schaff and Henry Wace (1892; reprint, Peabody, Mass.: Hendrickson, 1994), 43 and 65.

[11] Athanasius, *Against the Arians*, I.39 and II.70, in *Nicene and Post-Nicene Fathers*, 329 and 386.

[12] St. Athanasius, *The Life of Antony and the Letter to Marcellinus*, trans. Robert C. Gregg (New York: Paulist Press, 1980).

spiritual exercises and disciplines; Antony confronts and overcomes the devil and his demons in the wilderness; and Antony exemplifies the holiness without which no one can either see or be united with God—all through the gracious workings of the divine Son of God. Not to be overlooked is that Antony "abhorred the heresy of the Arians, and he ordered everyone neither to go near them nor to share their erroneous belief."[13] After all, the divine Word became flesh so as to restore human communion with God, and those who are being saved cannot but acknowledge their exemplar as Jesus the God-man.

The *Vita Antony*, therefore, manifests the orthopraxis that gives meaning to the *homoousios*. Whereas the Arian parties also appealed to the life of Antony in support of a moralistic and ascetical soteriology wherein human salvation is possible through the imitation of the ethical sonship of Jesus conferred by divine adoption, Athanasius's affirmation of Jesus' divinity secured human salvation on the basis of the eternal sonship of the Logos revealed in the life of Jesus: it is now the grace of the savior that empowers the life of obedience and faithful discipleship (as seen in the life of Antony) toward deification or union with God.[14] Hence there is movement in Athanasius's christology "from economy to theology,"[15] from the revelation of God in the life of Jesus to the being of God understood as Father and Son. But I would also add that in view of the wider Athanasian corpus, the movement from economy to theology continues in the ongoing life of Christian discipleship as empowered by divine grace. Christian beliefs about the divinity of Christ are shaped by and in turn inform Christian practices of being transformed into the image of Christ and being made partakers of the divine nature.

PNEUMATOLOGY, TRINITARIAN THEOLOGY, AND LITURGICAL PRACTICES

What then about the Holy Spirit? In this section, I want to extend the argument in the preceding by suggesting that Christian orthodoxy regarding the Holy Spirit was intimately tied in with Christian practices.

In a set of letters after the *Vita Antony*, Athanasius turned to address those who denied the full divinity of the Holy Spirit.[16] Extending the sote-

---

[13] *Vita Antony*, §69, in *The Life of Antony*, trans. Gregg, 82. Athanasius describes Antony's energetic resistance against the Arians in §§68-70, 89, and 91.

[14] On how Antony's life is interpreted by Arianism in contrast to Athanasius's *Vita Antony*, see Robert C. Gregg and Dennis E. Groh, *Early Arianism—A View of Salvation* (Philadelphia: Fortress, 1981), esp. ch. 4.

[15] On this point, see Catherine Mowry LaCugna, *God for Us: The Trinity and Christian Life* (New York: HarperSanFrancisco, 1991), esp. 24-30.

[16] See the introduction to C. R. B. Shapland, trans., *The Letters of Saint Athanasius concerning the Holy Spirit* (London: Epworth Press and Methodist Publishing House, 1951); references to this text will be made parenthetically by book, paragraph, and page numbers.

riological-divinization logic of his christology, Athanasius argued that "it is through the Spirit that we are all said to be partakers of God," and that "by participation in the Spirit, we are made 'sharers in the divine nature'" (I.24: 125-26). Indeed, it is asked, "Who will unite you to God, if you have not the Spirit of God, but the spirit which belongs to creation?" (I.29: 138). But more to the point, Athanasius observes that the Christian rite of initiation accomplishes human salvation and union with God when invoked in the fully trinitarian formula of baptism in the name of the Father, Son, and Holy Spirit. Hence, reducing the status of the Holy Spirit to that of a creature undermines baptismal faith so that the catechumen "has neither the Son nor the Father, but is without God, worse than an unbeliever, and anything rather than a Christian" (I.30: 140).[17]

This connection between orthodoxy and orthopraxis is even more clearly articulated in St. Basil of Caesarea (c. 330-379). Reaffirming the Christian conviction that salvation comes by the regenerating grace of baptism, Basil agrees with Athanasius both that if Christians are divinized or made to become like God through the Holy Spirit then the Spirit must be divine and that the salvific efficacy of Christian baptism invoking the trinitarian formula of Father, Son, and Holy Spirit cannot but mean that the Spirit is equal in divinity to the Father and the Son.[18] But Basil goes beyond Athanasius to argue for the divinity of the Spirit in connection with the Christian practice of singing doxologies not only to the Father and the Son but also to the Holy Spirit. To be more precise, whereas Basil's critics had charged him with liturgical novelty by worshiping the Father and Son *with* the Holy Spirit, the bishop of Caesarea countered that their customary practice of worshiping the Father and the Son *in* the Spirit did not mean the Spirit was subordinated in deity. Rather, "Both doxologies are used by the faithful, and so we use both; we believe that either one ascribes perfect glory to the Spirit."[19] In this case, we have a clear example of Christian practices informing theological reflection, on the one hand, even as we notice how doctrinal formulation and clarification returns to legitimate Christian practices, on the other.

Now I need to be clear about my argument at this point. I am less concerned with defending the details of the early church fathers' views regarding deification, baptismal regeneration, liturgical practices, or even doxological or ritual formulations, although I do believe that sufficiently

---

[17] For an extended discussion of the patristic understanding of the work of the Holy Spirit in relationship to Christian initiation in general and to Christian baptism in particular, see Killian McDonnell and George T. Montague, *Christian Initiation and Baptism in the Holy Spirit: Evidence from the First Eight Centuries*, 2nd rev. ed. (Collegeville, Minn.: Liturgical Press, 1994).

[18] St. Basil the Great, *On the Holy Spirit*, trans. David Anderson (Crestwood, N.Y.: St. Vladimir's Seminary Press, 1980), §§9.23, 10.26, 12.28, and 15.35-36.

[19] Basil, *On the Holy Spirit*, §25.59.

clarified and qualified, they remain informative for the contemporary church.[20] My point here and in this chapter is to make explicit the connections between Christian beliefs and practices. I have argued so far that Christian orthodoxy is intimately connected with Christian practices. In particular, the arguments for the divinity of the Son and the Spirit emerged out of and were intended to shape Christian practices.[21]

This interweaving of beliefs and practices can be seen in the aphorism attributed to a fifth-century theologian, Prosper of Aquitaine (c. 390-465): *lex orandi lex credendi*—or the "rule of prayer equals the rule of doctrine."[22] The early church fathers would not have understood Christian doctrine as separate from Christian practices. Rather, the full range of Christian practices—liturgical, spiritual, exercitive, and so forth—was understood to be soteriological in some respect, mediating the saving works of God in the lives of believers and the believing community. Doctrinal affirmations, hence, were second-order reflections emerging out of Christian practices, even as once received, they became first-order, oftentimes unspoken, rules that in turn shaped and normed the dynamics of Christian orthopraxis.

Theologians are now beginning to retrieve this linkage of beliefs and practices long after they had been sundered in many ways by early modern rationalism, individualism, and positivism.[23] But we need a bit more help to understand the challenges involved once we shift from the early church to the contemporary world.

---

[20] Elsewhere, I have suggested how the patristic notions of *theosis* and baptismal regeneration may be retrieved and reinterpreted for our time; see Amos Yong, *The Spirit Poured Out on All Flesh: Pentecostalism and the Possibility of Global Theology* (Grand Rapids: Baker Academic, 2005), chs. 2-3.

[21] For a more extended argument of this point, see Boris Bobrinskoy, *The Mystery of the Trinity: Trinitarian Experience and Vision in the Biblical and Patristic Literature*, trans. Anthony P. Gythiel (Crestwood, N.Y.: St. Vladimir's Seminary Press, 1999), 145-96.

[22] On Prosper, see Geoffrey Wainwright, *Doxology: The Praise of God in Worship, Doctrine and Life* (New York: Oxford University Press, 1980), 225-27. For more recent reflections, see W. Taylor Stevenson, "Lex Orandi—Lex Credendi," in *The Study of Anglicanism*, ed. Stephen Sykes, John Booty, and Jonathan Knight (London: SPCK; and Minneapolis: Fortress, 1988), 187-202; and Michael Downey, "*Lex Orandi, Lex Credendi*: Taking It Seriously in Systematic Theology," in *A Promise of Presence: Studies in Honor of David N. Power, O.M.I.*, ed. Michael Downey and Richard N. Fragomeni (Washington, D.C.: Pastoral Press, 1992), 3-26.

[23] I am thinking specifically of works such as David S. Cunningham, *These Three Are One: The Practice of Trinitarian Theology* (Malden, Mass.: Blackwell, 1997); and Catherine Pickstock, *After Writing: On the Liturgical Consummation of Philosophy* (Oxford, U.K., and Malden, Mass.: Blackwell, 1998)—both of which capture the heart of the Athanasian-Basillian position I have presented here. Cunningham's argument is that trinitarian beliefs are intricately tied in with ecclesial practices, even as Pickstock's thesis is an attempt to retrieve and restore the patristic vision of the interrelatedness of Christian identity and the liturgical shape of the ecclesial community.

THEOLOGY AND/AS PERFORMANCE

In this section, I want to explore more recent attempts to rethink what the early Christians took for granted, namely, the mutuality of beliefs and practices.[24] To do so, I will discuss the emergence of speech-act theory before turning to its application with regard to Christian doctrine and to Christian theology. My goal is not to present an exhaustive discussion of these matters. Rather, I intend to tease out from speech-act theory a basic understanding of theology as performance, noting the distinction between beliefs and practices but resisting their bifurcation. Our success here will set us up for further discussion of the relationship between beliefs and practices via contributing a pneumatological perspective in the third section of this chapter.

SPEECH ACTS: THEORY AND APPLICATION

Speech-act theory is a relatively recent phenomenon in the philosophy of language that emerged out of the analytic tradition of philosophy.[25] A reconsideration of the connection between language and action was launched in the English-speaking world by Oxford philosopher J. L. Austin (1911-1960). Initially, performative utterances were distinguished from constantive utterances. The latter are more descriptive and could be said to be either true or false, while the former are statements through which the speakers are *doing* something rather than merely just *saying* something.[26] Examples of performative speech acts include the following statements: "I do" (in a marriage ceremony); "I apologize" (after my treading on your toe); or "I baptize you in the name of the Father, the Son, and the Holy Spirit" (in a Christian ritual context). In these cases, each saying is also a doing, a performance that brings about a new state of affairs. Further, none of these sayings could be said to be true or false in the conventional senses of those terms. But performatives could be either happy or unhappy (felic-

---

[24] Recent articulations of this mutuality include Miroslav Volf and Dorothy C. Bass, eds., *Practicing Theology: Beliefs and Practices in Christian Life* (Grand Rapids: Eerdmans, 2002); Stanley Hauerwas, *Performing the Faith: Bonhoeffer and the Practice of Nonviolence* (Grand Rapids: Brazos Press, 2004); and Lawrence S. Cunningham, *Francis of Assisi: Performing the Gospel Life* (Grand Rapids: Eerdmans, 2004).

[25] See Barry Smith, "Towards a History of Speech Act Theory," in *Speech Acts, Meaning and Intentions: Critical Approaches to the Philosophy of John R. Searle*, ed. Armin Burkhardt (Berlin and New York: Walter de Gruyter, 1990), 29-61.

[26] See J. L. Austin, "Performative-Constantive," in *The Philosophy of Language*, ed. J. R. Searle (London: Oxford University Press, 1971), 1-12; and idem, "Performative Utterances," in *The Philosophy of Language*, ed. A. P. Martinich, 2nd ed. (New York and Oxford: Oxford University Press, 1990), 105-25.

itous or infelicitous). Austin suggested they could be criticized as happy or adequate if (a) there are conventional procedures governing the saying of certain utterances; (b) they are articulated in the right situation (there is a proper "fit" between the utterance and the situation); (c) the speaker is sincere about what is said (a much more subjective criterion); or (d) there is no "breach of commitment" between the utterance and what the speaker does next (e.g., in keeping his or her wedding vows, there is "rightness" between the utterance and later events). However, Austin observed that, on closer examination, constantives are also performatives to the extent that the speaker is also doing something with words, even if merely attempting to communicate (true) information to others.

In his posthumously transcribed and published William James lectures at Harvard University, "How to Do Things with Words,"[27] Austin discussed three kinds of performative speech acts: locutionary, illocutionary, and perlocutionary. The locutionary speech act is more or less a descriptive sentence whose chief function is to inform—for example, "She said to me, 'You can't do that.'" In this case, the audience is being informed by the speaker of what a third party said to the speaker. Locutionary statements are then, generally speaking, true or false—true in this case if in fact someone had said to the speaker, "You can't do that"; false if not. The illocutionary act has a certain conventional force whereby we are intending to do something with our sentences or statements such as warn, persuade, promise, and so forth—for example, "You can't do that." In this case, the words "You can't do that" function prohibitively. The speaker means to bring about a change of circumstances by saying these words to his or her audience. The perlocutionary act is more appropriately understood as a perlocutionary effect as it points to what is affected or achieved through our saying something—for example, "She stopped me."[28] Perlocutionary statements thus describe the effects on the hearer or reader, usually recording the exchange from their points of view. But note also that successful illocutionary acts may produce perlocutionary effects that are intended by the speaker (such as captured by the saying, "You scared me!").

Building on Austin's work, J. R. Searle introduced a further distinction relevant for our purposes, that between the *logic of assertion* and the *logic of promise*.[29] In the former, the intent of the utterance is to get the words to match the way the world is, and as such these utterances are assertions. The latter sayings, however, have the inverse function of getting the world to match the words, such as when we make promises or give commands.

---

[27] J. L. Austin, *How to Do Things with Words*, 2nd ed. (Cambridge, Mass.: Harvard University Press, 1975).

[28] These examples are from Austin, *How to Do Things with Words*, 102.

[29] See John R. Searle, *Expression and Meaning: Studies in the Theory of Speech Acts* (Cambridge: Cambridge University Press, 1979), esp. 12-15.

Various aspects of the work of Austin and Searle have begun to be applied to biblical interpretation. Anthony Thiselton, among others, has argued that carefully used, speech-act theory can illuminate aspects of the scriptural texts heretofore unnoticed.[30] For example, various biblical genres—such as blessings and curses, promises, and warnings—take on new meaning as illocutionary acts. Further, there is now the question about the "direction of fit" that speech-act theory calls attention to: Do we apply the logic of assertion or the logic of promise to the scriptural texts? Is it not the case that the biblical claims were intended in some respects to describe the world (e.g., as fallen) and in other respects to effect changes in the world (e.g., the promise of redemption)? At the same time, Thiselton recognized that the "felicitousness" of the scriptural texts depended on their having been authoritatively said. So, for example, the force of the prophets declaring, "Thus saith the Lord," depends on their not lying; or the validity of the announcement of Jesus that "You are forgiven" assumes he has the authority to forgive sins. In each of these cases and more, speech-act theory has shed light on the performative aspect of the biblical texts.

Yet speech-act theory illuminates not only how various scriptures function performatively but also how they can be understood in illocutionary terms. Philosopher Nicholas Wolterstorff has argued for the plausibility of understanding scripture as "double agency discourse" in a similar sense to how secretaries write and then sign executive documents or how ambassadors represent their governments and nations to others.[31] In this way, scripture is "divine discourse" in its being deputized or appropriated by God, but this does not undermine the integrity of the human authors of scripture. Hence, we can speak of various levels of illocutionary discourse in scripture, whether of that intended by the individual authors or of that intended by God. At the same time, Wolterstorff also notes that illocutionary analysis can be applied not only to the individual sayings of scripture but also to the scriptures' various units or genres, to its many books or letters as integral wholes (this is how Wolterstorff explains the divergences of the four Gospels), and even to the whole of the Bible as the "*one* book of God."[32]

At this last level, we could understand the entire Bible as an illocutionary speech act of God.[33] For example, the scriptures not only describe the

---

[30] Anthony C. Thiselton, *New Horizons in Hermeneutics* (Grand Rapids: Zondervan, 1992), ch. 8; and idem, *Thiselton on Hermeneutics: Collected Works with New Essays* (Grand Rapids, and Cambridge, U.K.: Eerdmans, 2006), essays in part 2.

[31] Nicholas Wolterstorff, *Divine Discourse: Philosophical Reflections on the Claim That God Speaks* (Cambridge: Cambridge University Press, 1995).

[32] Wolterstorff, *Divine Discourse*, 53, italics in original.

[33] See Timothy Ward, *Word and Supplement: Speech Acts, Biblical Texts, and the Sufficiency of Scripture* (Oxford: Oxford University Press, 2002), esp. 197-207.

covenant between God and Israel and the church but also can be understood to be the covenant itself; and insofar as covenanting is an illocutionary speech act, to that same extent scripture as a whole can be understood covenantally in terms of the logic of promise.[34] By extension, individual statements in a sermon can function as illocutions, even as the entire sermon can be an illocutionary act (e.g., that invites, or warns, or encourages, according to the various homiletic genres). Similarly, such a line of analysis can be applied to doctrinal and theological systems as a whole.

CHRISTIAN DOCTRINE AS ECCLESIAL GRAMMAR

It was the Lutheran ecumenical theologian George Lindbeck who called attention to the similarity between how doctrines function with regard to religious traditions and how grammars serve languages.[35] Whereas a cognitivist approach to religion understood doctrines in propositional terms focused on the question of truth (the classical tradition), and whereas (what Lindbeck calls) an "experiential-expressivist" approach understood doctrines in symbolic terms focused on inner feelings, existential attitudes, and overall orientations (the tradition of modern liberalism), Lindbeck proposes instead a cultural-linguistic alternative that understands doctrines as illocutionary rules informed by and in turn formative for the religious community's practices. This postliberal option emphasizes religious traditions as entire ways of life embodied in texts (myths and narratives), rites, and other practices, which in turn combine to serve as comprehensive interpretive schemes (doctrines) that claim to be able to account for all of reality. Just as grammars dictate the use of language and language shapes the nature of experience, to that same degree, narratives and doctrines dictate the practice of religion and shape the nature of religious experience.

While Lindbeck's proposal was designed to deal with intra-Christian ecumenical concerns, he based his theory primarily on breakthroughs in the philosophy of language (drawing from Austin and, especially, the linguistic philosopher Ludwig Wittgenstein) and cultural anthropology (Clifford Geertz).[36] Lindbeck argued that his proposed cultural-linguistic theory of

---

[34] E.g., Kevin Vanhoozer, "From Speech Acts to Scripture Acts: The Covenant of Discourse and the Discourse of Covenant," in *After Pentecost: Language and Biblical Interpretation*, ed. Craig Bartholomew, Colin Greene, and Karl Möller (Grand Rapids: Zondervan, 2001), 1-49. I will return to Vanhoozer's work momentarily.

[35] See George A. Lindbeck, *The Nature of Doctrine: Religion and Theology in a Postliberal Age* (Philadelphia: Westminster, 1984). Before Lindbeck, others had made similar points—e.g., Mary-John Mananzan, O.S.B., *The "Language Game" of Confessing One's Belief: A Wittgensteinian-Austinian Approach to the Linguistic Analysis of Creedal Statements*, Linguistische Arbeiten 16 (Tübingen: Max Niemeyer Verlag, 1974)—but it was the *Nature of Doctrine* that effectively launched the "postliberal" movement.

[36] Wittgenstein and Geertz both helped Lindbeck view religion as a cultural and linguistic system; see Geertz's "Religion as a Cultural System," in his *The Interpretation of Cultures: Selected Essays* (New York: Basic Books, 1973), ch. 4.

doctrine had to be, at least in principle, also applicable to issues related to extra-Christian or interreligious ecumenism. At this level, Lindbeck made five points:[37] (1) that a cultural linguistic approach did not presume a common framework between religious traditions either for adjudicating conflicting truth claims or for assuming a common-core religious experience lying behind the diverse doctrinal assertions; (2) that because of this possibility regarding the incommensurability of religious traditions,[38] we should proceed cautiously in comparing religious traditions and not rush to make claims regarding the superiority of any one religious tradition over others; (3) but insofar as religious traditions make such claims, these have to be understood eschatologically (to use theological language) or performatively according to the logic of promise as awaiting actualization or realization rather than as accomplished matters of fact; (4) that rather than religious doctrines expressing the experiences of salvation, salvation is instead the process of being shaped, formed, and transformed by religious doctrines (by their illocutionary acts and their perlocutionary effects, to use Austinian language);[39] and (5) that there are hence many different modes of interreligious engagement, and the processes of interreligious dialogue arise ad hoc out of the encounter between representatives of the various traditions as they discover similarities and differences in beliefs and practices. In the postliberal scheme of things, the logic of any religion, as spelled out by its rules and doctrines, is shaped by its communal practices—its interpretive, ritual, institutional, and interpersonal performances—so that its adherents both interpret the world according to how they see the world fitting into their ways of thinking, on the one hand, even as they engage the world according to their rules of thought in order to change it, on the other hand.[40]

---

[37] See Lindbeck, *Nature of Doctrine*, ch. 3.

[38] Elsewhere, Lindbeck discusses this incommensurability in terms of "untranslatability," by which he means that religions as comprehensive ways of life and thought are (a) not fully translatable into the language of another tradition, and (b) would resist such translation, preferring instead to itself translate every other conceivable reality, including the realities of other religions, into its own terms; see Lindbeck, "The Gospel's Uniqueness: Election and Untranslatability," in his *The Church in a Postliberal Age*, ed. James J. Buckley (Grand Rapids, and Cambridge: Eerdmans, 2002), ch. 14.

[39] So Lindbeck said, citing Austin, that "a religious utterance … acquires the propositional truth of ontological correspondence only insofar as it is a performance, an act or deed, which helps create that correspondence" (*Nature of Doctrine*, 65).

[40] Here, Lindbeck's work intersects with those of a number of other theorists, both philosophers and theologians, such as C. S. Peirce's notion of the meaning of beliefs as unfolded in practices; Alisdair MacIntyre's notion of tradition as arguments that meanings are based on social practices; Stanley Hauerwas's claim that truthfulness lies in the practices of the community; Hans Frei's insistence that narratives shape both (non-discursive) practices and (discursively articulated) beliefs; Ronald Thiemann's proposal regarding the gospel as narrative promise; James W. McClendon Jr.'s suggestion that biography is intimately linked to theology and vice versa; Johann Baptist Metz's argument for the interrelatedness of fundamental theology and political theology; Helmut Peukert's theology of communicative action;

Lindbeck's work has generated a good deal of discussion, even an entire "postliberal" theological school or movement.[41] Because we cannot afford to get sidetracked with all of the controversy, I want to focus briefly on the implications of the cultural-linguistic theory for interreligious relations. Two points are especially noteworthy. First, if religious traditions as comprehensive ways of life and thought are in fact distinct as whole systems, then it would be inadequate for us to compare them as being equally (or not) salvific. Insofar as Islam, Buddhism, and Hinduism, for example, each provides a range of practices commensurate with their ideals and goals, to the same degree none of them can be said either to aspire to Christian salvation or to provide the requisite practices pertinent to obtaining or receiving such salvation.[42] In this case, Christian theologies of exclusivism, inclusivism, and pluralism all miss the mark because they do not engage other religious traditions on their own terms.[43] On the other hand, if Christianity is itself a comprehensive system of life and thought, these theologies of religions are various ways that Christians attempt to account for and engage other faith traditions. We will return to discuss this issue in more detail in the next chapter.

But second, if the main lines of the cultural-linguistic theory of religion are correct—and for the record, I think that they are—then fully understanding the logic of any doctrinal or theological system requires partici-

Nicholas Lash's idea that theological languages shape the practices that provide access to God, etc. For discussion of many of these ideas in relationship to the postliberal school of thought, see Adonis Vidu, *Postliberal Theological Method: A Critical Study* (Milton Keynes, U.K., and Waynesboro, Ga.: Paternoster, 2005). I assess McClendon's project in my essay "The 'Baptist Vision' of James William McClendon, Jr.: A Wesleyan-Pentecostal Response," *Wesleyan Theological Journal* 37, no. 2 (Fall 2002): 32-57.

[41] See, e.g., Bruce D. Marshall, ed., *Theology and Dialogue: Essays in Conversation with George Lindbeck* (Notre Dame, Ind.: University of Notre Dame Press, 1990); Timothy R. Phillips and Dennis L. Ockholm, eds., *The Nature of Confession: Evangelicals and Postliberals in Conversation* (Downers Grove, Ill.: InterVarsity Press, 1996); and Jeffrey C. K. Goh, *Christian Tradition Today: A Postliberal Vision of Church and World*, Louvain Theological and Pastoral Monographs 28 (Louvain: Peeters Press, 2000).

[42] From the Christian point of view, the one exception may be the Jewish tradition. But even here, we have to be careful to walk a fine line between continuity and discontinuity, between understanding the church as a new Israel in some sense and yet avoiding a supersessionistic interpretation of such relationship. Lindbeck himself attempts such a *via media* in his "The Church as Israel: Ecclesiology and Ecumenism," in *Jews and Christians: People of God*, ed. Carl E. Braaten and Robert W. Jenson (Grand Rapids, and Cambridge, U.K.: Eerdmans, 2003), 78-94, and does so by insisting on, among other points, the importance of the church being ready to share in the sufferings of Israel.

[43] This is the point of J. A. DiNoia, O.P., "Varieties of Religious Aims: Beyond Exclusivism, Inclusivism, and Pluralism," in *Theology and Dialogue: Essays in Conversation with George Lindbeck*, ed. Bruce D. Marshall (Notre Dame, Ind.: University of Notre Dame Press, 1990), 249-74. In a later book, DiNoia provides a book-length argument defending this hypothesis—*The Diversity of Religions: A Christian Perspective* (Washington, D.C.: Catholic University Press of America, 1992).

pating in or embracing its practices.[44] This does not mean understanding cannot be achieved apart from such an endeavor, but it does mean the insider-outsider distinction is not an unimportant one when it comes to the meaning and truth of religious, doctrinal, and theological claims. Further, this does not mean interreligious engagement is impossible, but it does mean such can proceed only ad hoc, and that its shape, scope, degree of depth, and so forth, will depend on various factors such as who is involved, the context or background of the encounter, and the practices deployed. Finally, Lindbeck himself grants that the cultural-linguistic theory of religion does not eliminate a propositional understanding of doctrinal references, but it does mean that the significance of such assertions cannot be abstracted from ways of life as a whole. In this case, the adjudication of divergent doctrinal claims is as much a matter of the disputants engaging in religious (and interreligious) practices as it is a matter of them apologizing for or clarifying religious beliefs.

Having said this, there remains a nagging concern that any Christian community's "performance" of the scriptures "makes it so" in a way that shields it from criticism. Is Lindbeck's cultural-linguistic theory of doctrine susceptible of being used to legitimize the dismissal of other points of view because they are neither congruent with one's beliefs nor informed by one's practices? While there are valid arguments for forms of Christian sectarianism that can serve as correctives to Christian expressions that are overly accommodating to cultural dynamics and fads, there are also unhealthy fundamentalisms shaped by religious (even "biblical") convictions and forms of life that are immune to external criticism. In the big picture, I will argue that the space for self-reflexivity and criticism is opened up precisely in the hospitable encounter with the stranger, the alien, and even the religious other. But if so, then the concern arises from the other side of the skeptical response to Lindbeck: that cultural-linguistic systems are never as homogeneous as one might think, and, in that case, insiders and outsiders are not so clearly demarcated and boundaries are blurred, especially in a global and postcolonial situation where migration and hybridity are so prevalent. In these cases, what keeps Christian communities from fragmentation? Is what is needed not a dynamic internal to the cultural-linguistic theory of doctrine that can move, invite, and even sustain such engagement, but do so in ways that maintain continuity with the historic Christian tradition? I suggest that a "pneumatological assist" to Lindbeck's proposal is precisely what is required,[45] and for this, we turn to the work of evangelical-ecumenical theologian Kevin Vanhoozer.

---

[44] I have argued this point in my "The Spirit Bears Witness: Pneumatology, Truth and the Religions," *Scottish Journal of Theology* 57, no. 1 (2004): 14-38.

[45] Jane Barter Moulaison, *"Lord, Giver of Life": Toward a Pneumatological Complement to George Lindbeck's Theory of Doctrine*, Editions SR 32 (Waterloo, Ont.: Wilfrid Laurier University Press, 2007), is suggestive along these lines, although not as helpful with regard to the question of Christianity's relationship to the world's religions.

THEOLOGY AS DRAMATIC PERFORMANCE

Building on Lindbeck's work, Vanhoozer has been concerned to recenter scripture at the heart of the theological task. Hence, he calls his project "a canonical-linguistic approach to Christian theology."[46] Drawing also from continental philosophy, speech-act theory,[47] and dramatic theory, Vanhoozer provides not only a theory of doctrine but also an overarching vision of the theological enterprise understood according to the model of dramatic performance.

Vanhoozer's project is subtle and his argument sophisticated. For our purposes, however, it can be summarized thus: the gospel is itself a drama whose director is God, whose script is the canonical scriptures, whose players or actors (dramaturges) are theologians in particular and the church in general, and whose stage is the church and whose theater is the world.[48] For Vanhoozer, as for Wolterstorff, scripture is understood as a canon of God's illocutionary speech acts. Hence, scripture is to be privileged so that the interpretive community—including the dramaturges—always attempts to perform the drama in accordance with the illocutions of the canonical authors, including God. Put alternatively, the players and actors as members of the church seek to be appropriately effected (the perlocutionary sense) by the canonical illocutions.

As with any dramatic play, the performance of the gospel must be enacted not woodenly but creatively, and not irresponsibly but faithfully. Hence, theologians as dramaturges have as their task "that of knowing how to transpose the drama of redemption into the present in a different cultural key."[49] Faithfulness to the canonical script involves, then, what Vanhoozer calls "dramatic fittingness" (recall Austin's notion of the felicitousness or happiness of performatives) so that it "will require different performances in different situations. This is a kind of relativism, to be sure, but one that *establishes* rather than undermines biblical authority."[50] This

---

[46] Kevin J. Vanhoozer, *The Drama of Doctrine: A Canonical-Linguistic Approach to Christian Theology* (Louisville: Westminster John Knox, 2005).

[47] See Vanhoozer's earlier books: *Biblical Narrative in the Philosophy of Paul Ricoeur: A Study in Hermeneutics and Theology* (Cambridge: Cambridge University Press, 1990); *Is There a Meaning in This Text? The Bible, the Reader, and the Morality of Literary Knowledge* (Grand Rapids: Zondervan, 1998); and *First Theology: God, Scripture, and Hermeneutics* (Downers Grove, Ill.: InterVarsity; and Leicester, U.K.: Apollos, 2002).

[48] This is the argument of *The Drama of Doctrine*; a shorter version anticipating the book is Kevin J. Vanhoozer, "The Voice and the Actor: A Dramatic Proposal about the Ministry and Minstrelsy of Theology," in *Evangelical Futures: A Conversation on Theological Method*, ed. John G. Stackhouse (Grand Rapids: Baker, 2000), 61-106. Other recent efforts to discuss theology in dramatic terms are Michael S. Horton, *Covenant and Eschatology: The Divine Drama* (Louisville, Ky.: Westminster John Knox, 2002); and Richard Heyduck, *The Recovery of Doctrine in the Contemporary Church: An Essay in Philosophical Ecclesiology* (Waco, Tex.: Baylor University Press, 2002).

[49] Vanhoozer, *Drama of Doctrine*, 254.

[50] Vanhoozer, *Drama of Doctrine*, 261, italics in original.

is because dramatic fittingness ensures that the canonical illocutions are norms that guide Christian performances in different ways in different times and places.

Yet, it is important to note that dramatic and performative fittingness requires not only fidelity but also improvisation.[51] Nicholas Lash, Vanhoozer's *Doktorvater* (and to whom *The Drama of Doctrine* is dedicated), had already compared the task of performing the scriptures to that of playing a score of one of Beethoven's quartets or enacting *King Lear*. In each case, "as the history of the meaning of the text [or score, or play] continues, we can and must tell the story differently. But we do so under constraint: what we may *not* do, if it is *this* text which we are to continue to perform, is to tell a different story."[52] Going one step beyond Lash, N. T. Wright proposed that biblical interpretation should be understood in terms of the church's performance of the scriptural narrative and how this might be parallel to a group of actors' performance of an unwritten fifth act of a Shakespearean play based on the script of the first four acts.[53] In line with Wright's hypothetical scenario, a Lukan perspective would ask how the church faithfully improvises the performance of the twenty-ninth chapter of Acts in times and places far removed from Theophilus's original situation. With Lash and Wright, this Lukan-inspired query raises the important issue for Vanhoozer: To what degree is performative creativity or novelty constrained by the canonical script when the stage has been shifted to and set up in a very different context?

It is here that Vanhoozer's understanding of the Holy Spirit comes into view.[54] He affirms that the church can be understood as a performance of the Holy Spirit insofar as the play is faithful to the canonical script. Hence, he agrees with Reinhard Hütter, who argues that the work of the Spirit is to be found in the practices of the church (see below, pp. 59-62). More precisely, for Vanhoozer the Holy Spirit is the "executor" of the Word in at least three senses: as prompting the canonical authors; as enlivening the canonical script; and as bringing about faithful improvisations through the dramaturgical performances. As such, the Spirit brings about the perlocutionary effects of the canonical illocutions.[55] Hence, Vanhoozer affirms

---

[51] See the concluding ch. 8, "Improvisation and Inspiration," in Frances Young, *The Art of Performance: Towards a Theology of Holy Scripture* (London: Darton, Longman & Todd, 1990), which suggests that the improvisation that goes with biblical interpretation always falls short of the originally inspired version, but at the same time anticipates "the great eschatological performance to come" (p. 182). I am not as pessimistic as Young, as the following discussion shows.

[52] See Nicholas Lash's essay, "Performing the Scriptures," in his *Theology on the Road to Emmaus* (London: SCM, 1986), ch. 3, quotation from p. 44, italics in original.

[53] N. T. Wright, *The New Testament and the People of God* (Minneapolis: Fortress, 1992), 140-43.

[54] See *Drama of Doctrine*, chs. 6-7.

[55] Vanhoozer, *Is There a Meaning in This Text?*, 428-29.

both a unified understanding of the canonical text and a plurality of per-locutionary results: "*I affirm a 'Pentecostal plurality,' which maintains that the one true interpretation is best approximated by a diversity of particu-lar methods and contexts of reading.* The Word remains the interpretive norm, but no one culture or interpretive scheme is sufficient to exhaust its meaning, much less its significance."[56] In this way, Vanhoozer insists on understanding how the "spirited practices" of the church are normed by the scriptural canon.[57]

Now as we have already noted, Vanhoozer's dramatic theory is not just a canonical supplementation to Lindbeck's cultural-linguistic theory; rather, Vanhoozer's is an expansion from a doctrinal theory toward a the-ory of theology. In other words, Vanhoozer is concerned not only with the nature of doctrine but also the nature of theology in general. At this level, Vanhoozer is led to ask the more general hermeneutical and epistemolog-ical questions. Whereas the hermeneutical tradition from Friedrich Schleiermacher to Hans-Georg Gadamer suggested that human under-standing happens somewhat miraculously, Vanhoozer boldly suggests a Christian theological framework for explicating human understanding. More precisely, insofar as certain virtues such as openness, humility, and attention are needed in order for understanding to "happen," and to "the extent that these virtues are fruits of the Spirit, or at the very least evi-dences of common grace, a hermeneutics will be able to get beyond 'thin' descriptions of the event of understanding only by employing distinctly theological categories ... [To] the extent that the interpretative virtues ... are spiritual virtues, it may be that the Spirit performs a ministry of 'word' and [the matter of the text] as well."[58] In short, Vanhoozer's canonical-lin-guistic theory requires a robust pneumatological-theological framework.

PERFORMING PNEUMATOLOGY
IN A PLURALISTIC WORLD

So far in this chapter we have, first, suggested that the earliest Christians assumed the interconnectedness of beliefs and practices, and, second, drawn from speech-act theory, Lindbeck's rule theory of religion and doc-trine, and Vanhoozer's canonical-linguistic approach of doctrine and theol-ogy to explicate this interrelationship. I agree with Lindbeck that Christian beliefs cannot be abstracted from Christian practices, even as I concur with

---

[56] Vanhoozer, *Is There a Meaning in This Text?*, 419, italics in original.

[57] Vanhoozer, *Drama of Doctrine*, esp. 226-31.

[58] Kevin J. Vanhoozer, "Discourse on Matter: Hermeneutics and the 'Miracle' of Under-standing," in *Hermeneutics at the Crossroads*, ed. Kevin J. Vanhoozer, James K. A. Smith, and Bruce Ellis Benson (Bloomington and Indianapolis: Indiana University Press, 2006), 3-34, quotations from pp. 25-26.

Vanhoozer that the theological task of connecting the script of beliefs with dramatic performances is pneumatologically sustained through and through. In what follows, I build on Lindbeck's and Vanhoozer's proposals toward what I call a performative pneumatological theology of religions.[59] We proceed first with some introductory remarks on the renaissance of pneumatological theology in our contemporary pluralistic world in dialogue with D. Lyle Dabney, then observe, using the work of Reinhard Hütter, the many works of the Spirit in the practices of the church, before ending with some suggestions for understanding the plurality of the Spirit's works at the interface where the church meets and interacts with the world of the many religions. I propose that the many works and tongues of the Spirit of Pentecost open up to many practices vis-à-vis the religions.

"STARTING WITH THE SPIRIT": THEOLOGY FOR A POST-CHRISTENDOM ERA

Among the many theological developments during the last generation, I suggest two that seem to complement each other and that may somehow be related. I am referring to the renaissance in pneumatology (the doctrine of the Holy Spirit) and the emergence of postmodern theology. Let me begin with the former.

In 1958 Henry Pitt Van Dusen's *Spirit, Son and Father: Christian Faith in the Light of the Holy Spirit* signaled the reemergence of the Spirit in theological discourse after a long history of subordination during which she had come to be known as the "silent" or "shy" member of the Trinity.[60] In the past half century, there has been a heightened sensitivity to pneumatology and to pneumatological perspectives in theology.

---

[59] Hence, I am attempting to do for theology of religions what others have attempted to do for other theological *loci:* reinterpret them as performatives rather than merely as assertions; e.g., with regard to the doctrine of creation, Donald D. Evans, *The Logic of Self-Involvement: A Philosophical Study of Everyday Language with Special Reference to the Christian Use of Language about God as Creator* (London: SCM, 1963), and with regard to the doctrine of the final consummation, Robert John Schreiter, *Eschatology as a Grammar of Transformation: A Study in Speech Act Theory and Structural Semantics and Their Application to Some Problems in Eschatology* (Oxford: Parchment, 1974).

[60] Henry Pitt Van Dusen, *Spirit, Son and Father: Christian Faith in the Light of the Holy Spirit* (New York: Charles Scribner's Sons, 1958). See also William Hordern and Frederick Dale Bruner, *The Holy Spirit—Shy Member of the Trinity* (Minneapolis: Augsburg Fortress, 1984). I discuss aspects of the renaissance in pneumatology in my "A Theology of the Third Article? Hegel and the Contemporary Enterprise in First Philosophy and First Theology," in *Semper Reformandum: Studies in Honour of Clark H. Pinnock,* ed. Stanley E. Porter and Anthony R. Cross (Carlisle, U.K.: Paternoster Press, 2003), 208-31. For an argument defending the use of the feminine pronoun for the Holy Spirit, see Donald L. Gelpi, *The Divine Mother: A Trinitarian Theology of the Holy Spirit* (Lanham, Md.: University Press of America, 1984).

One of the most important books on the Holy Spirit since Van Dusen's is Michael Welker's "realistic" biblical pneumatology.[61] In a careful reading of the biblical narratives, Welker discovers the Holy Spirit's redemptive works in diverse modes and places: in the midst of suffering and affliction (e.g., the exodus and the exile); in the political power structures of ancient Israel; in the prophetic voices from the margins; in the ambiguous cultic technology of the Levitical priesthood, the tabernacle, and the temple; in the countercultural and counterimperial experiences of women, the young, and slaves; in the rejected and crucified man from Galilee, etc. He argues that a realistic portrait of the Spirit emergent from the biblical canon reveals a diversity of expressions, manifestations, and activities.

This is nowhere clearer than in the outpouring of the Spirit on the Day of Pentecost and in the book of Acts. In his reading of the Pentecost narrative,[62] Welker makes two observations: (1) the miracle of understanding occurs not through a unified voice or language but through the cacophony of many tongues and languages; and (2) the Spirit brings about a new community out of radical diversity even while ensuring that diversity is preserved (e.g., through the speaking in many tongues). To be sure, there is a unified testimony given by the many tongues to the wondrous works of God (Acts 2:11), but make no mistake about it: the particularities of the many tongues are not obliterated in the Pentecost account; rather, they are redeemed in all of their particularity for the purposes of God. Hence, Welker concludes that the many tongues of Pentecost signify nothing less than that "God affects a world-encompassing, multilingual, polyindividual testimony to Godself."[63]

D. Lyle Dabney suggests that Welker's pneumatology is pertinent precisely because it is able to account for and engage the pluralistic consciousness characteristic of our postmodern situation.[64] If the classical theological tradition of the church fathers and the medieval schoolmen were focused on God the creator, and if the protesting theologies of the Reformers were centered on God the Son, Dabney suggests that contemporary theology should now "act its age," and do so by starting with God the Spirit. This is because the Spirit is capable of "keeping up with" (so to

[61] Michael Welker, *God the Spirit*, trans. John F. Hoffmeyer (Minneapolis: Fortress, 1994).
[62] Welker, *God the Spirit*, 230-39.
[63] Welker, *God the Spirit*, 235.
[64] D. Lyle Dabney, "Starting with the Spirit: Why the Last Should Now Be First," in *Starting with the Spirit: Task of Theology Today II*, ed. Gordon Preece and Stephen Pickard (Adelaide, Australia: Australia Theological Forum, and Openbook Publishers, 2001), 3-27; see also Dabney, "Otherwise Engaged in the Spirit: A First Theology for the Twenty-First Century," in *The Future of Theology: Essays in Honor of Jürgen Moltmann*, ed. Miroslav Volf, Carmen Krieg, and Thomas Kucharz (Grand Rapids: Eerdmans, 1996), 154-63; and idem, "Why Should the Last Be First? The Priority of Pneumatology in Recent Theological Discussion," in *Advents of the Spirit: An Introduction to the Current Study of Pneumatology*, ed. Bradford E. Hinze and D. Lyle Dabney (Milwaukee, Wis.: Marquette University Press, 2001), 238-61.

speak) and speaking into our sense of awareness of reality as dynamic, processive, relational, and "irreducibly pluralistic." Now that the hegemony of the West has given way to the rest and now that the universal reason of the Enlightenment has given way to the fluidic multiplicity of postcolonial discourses, the center no longer holds. More theologically pertinent is the disintegration of Christendom. By this, Dabney is referring not only to the emergence of the pluralism of denominations out of the one, holy, catholic church, but also to the gradual but irreversible disestablishment of the church from the center of society. It is this postmodern and post-Christendom situation that needs the power of God as represented in and manifested through the many tongues of the Spirit.

The many tongues of Pentecost hence call forth in our time a "thoroughly ecumenical theology." This means neither a new uniformity to replace the diversity of churches—in fact, the many churches may better speak the many tongues needed to bear witness to God in a pluralistic world—nor simply "the task of resolving our 'internal' disputes concerning faith and practice," as important as this is; rather, a pneumatologically generated ecumenical theology includes both a reclamation and reappropriation of the various traditions of the churches in order to engage "the common task of living and thinking as disciples of Christ in the new 'external' situation in which we now find ourselves, of participating in God's ongoing mission of reconciliation."[65] This new ecumenism therefore celebrates the *diversity* of the churches even as it seeks to overcome the *divisions* between the churches.

But now the question arises: What kinds of practices have nurtured this pneumatological renaissance and what kinds of practices are congruent with and embody Welker's realistic biblical pneumatology and Dabney's ecumenical vision that starts with the Spirit?

"SUFFERING DIVINE THINGS": THE SPIRIT AND THE PRACTICES OF THE CHURCH

We have already seen that the connection between pneumatology and theology includes the connection between orthodoxy and liturgical practices (see above, pp. 44-47). Here, I suggest that the many tongues of Pentecost are performed by the power of the Spirit through the various core practices of the church. My primary dialogue partner in what follows is the former Lutheran and now Roman Catholic theologian Reinhard Hütter.[66]

---

[65] Dabney, "Starting with the Spirit," 26-27.

[66] See Reinhard Hütter, *Suffering Divine Things: Theology as Church Practice*, trans. Doug Scott (Grand Rapids, and Cambridge, U.K.: Eerdmans, 2000); further references to this book will be made parenthetically in the text as *SDT* followed by page number(s). Note also James J. Buckley and David S. Yeago, eds., *Knowing the Triune God: The Work of the Spirit in the Practices of the Church* (Grand Rapids: Eerdmans, 2001).

Building on but going beyond Lindbeck, among others, Hütter suggests that theology and doctrine should be understood or seen as the practices of the Spirit in and through the church. His key terms are *pathos*, by which he means the sense of "suffering" that comes as a result of being shaped by (an) other(s); *poiesis*, which is the sometimes artistic (Aristotle) making or doing of "something," with the focus on the product or the "thing" produced; and *praxis*, which is the activity of doing in and for itself with the focus on virtue, rather than on a resulting product. Hütter thus argues, "The poiesis of the Holy Spirit constitutes the pathos of theology insofar as theology is shaped by the *poiemata* of the Holy Spirit, namely, by the core practices of the church and by church doctrine ... Theology is undertaken, engaged, performed 'in' the work of the Holy Spirit, in the temporal and thus ecclesial development of God's *oikonomia*" (*SDT* 114). If for Welker (and Dabney) the many tongues of Pentecost are God the Spirit's multilingual and polyphonic testimony of Godself to the world, for Hütter the core practices of the church are palpable means of the Spirit's gracious presence and activity in the world.

As with others who have attempted to articulate a pneumatologically robust ecclesiology—most notably the Eastern Orthodox theologian John Zizioulas[67]—Hütter's view of the church is intimately linked to a perichoretic vision of the Trinity. Inasmuch as each of the trinitarian persons is constituted by relations with the other two, in that sense, identity is received through the other two—"that is, it is *pathically* constituted ... The pathos of life in faith then means participation in the Spirit in God's triune life, that is, in the pathos constituting the love between Father, Son, and Holy Spirit" (*SDT* 117). Further, as Jesus Christ is himself pathically constituted by the Holy Spirit, so also is the church. Hence, the church is neither merely being nor act, neither merely institution nor event, neither merely office nor charism of the Spirit. Rather, being a Christian and being the church "involves pathos, namely a state of being eschatologically qualified that is *not* however an *active* anticipation of something still to come, but rather the condition of *being* seized by the eschaton that *even now* is commencing" (*SDT* 120, italics in original). Hütter writes,

> The human being is entirely the receiving party here, whereas the Spirit's own actions are genuine poiesis; for the Spirit creates a *nova creatura*, in a hidden way now, but later openly. "Pathos" is on the human side the only possible mode of redemption ... In this pathos people become "persons," that is, they receive their essence—that which qualifies them—from communion with the triune God ... As

---

[67] See also my own attempt to sketch a robustly pneumatological ecclesiology, partly in dialogue with Zizioulas, in *The Spirit Poured Out on All Flesh: Pentecostalism and the Possibility of Global Theology* (Grand Rapids: Baker Academic, 2005), ch. 3.

works of the Holy Spirit they [Christians in particular and the church in general] are the pathos of the trinitarian economy of salvation that actually determines or shapes us. At the same time we are ourselves also "there as agents," that is *actively* present in [the virtuous praxis of] praise, confession, prayer, obedience, and discipleship. (*SDT* 125)

Hence, the orthopraxis of the church (and her members) manifest in its core practices constitutes the salvific-economic mission of the Holy Spirit. And just what are these core practices? As a Lutheran theologian (at the time of his writing this book), Hütter begins with the seven principal means of Christian sanctification identified in the historic Lutheran tradition: the preaching of the word of God; baptism; Eucharist, or the Lord's Supper; the office of the keys as church discipline; ordination and ministerial offices; public prayer, praise, thanksgiving, and instruction; and discipleship in suffering (*SDT* 129-32). While these are real human activities, human hearts and lives are transformed (perlocutionarily effected) by the actions of the Holy Spirit through these practices.

But from this, Hütter proceeds to argue that *doctrina*—which includes, for Hütter, the biblical canon, articles or confessions of faith, and the task of theological reflections—is part of the core practices of the church through which the sanctifying work of the Spirit occurs. *Doctrina* is the work—*poiesis*—of the Holy Spirit that is soteriologically directed in the sense of making God present and transforming believers into the image of Christ. More precisely, the practices of the church, including *doctrina*, are "enhypostatically" constituted in the Holy Spirit's person and works (*SDT* 132-33, 137). In this sense, human beings are the pathic recipients—perlocutionary effects of (to use the language of speech-act theory)—the Spirit's *poiesis*: "The human being remains the one who *through* these works of the Holy Spirit is qualified and receives a new 'form,' the one who thus is modeled through the Spirit of Christ, the *forma fidei*" (*SDT* 132). The result is a robust pneumatological and trinitarian ecclesiology—a vision of the church as the body of Christ constituted by core practices empowered by the Holy Spirit.

Yet a question similar to the one raised at the end of our discussion of Lindbeck (see above, pp. 50-54) arises again precisely at this juncture: Are the core practices identified by Hütter normative for the rest of the Christian churches? At an ecumenical level, are they in a sense "too Lutheran" so that other Christian communities would need a "Lutheran conversion" in order to encounter the full scope of the Spirit's *poiemata*? At a global and interfaith level, do they presume that the works of the Spirit are limited not only to the Christian churches but to Lutheran forms of Christian practice in particular? Now if the presence and activity of the Spirit are not limited to Lutheran expressions and practices (and I do not believe they are), then might Christians in general also find the winds of the Spirit blowing outside of whatever Lutherans consider their core practices to be? My argument in the big picture of this volume is that the Christian practice of hospitality is the means through which Christians encounter the *poiesis* of the Spirit not only in and through other Christian movements (the ecumenical context) but also through those "outside" the church.

PNEUMATOLOGICAL PERFORMANCE: MANY TONGUES, MANY PRACTICES

I now wish to extend Dabney's first theology of the Spirit for a post-Christendom world in concert with Hütter's pneumatological theology of ecclesial practices toward a pneumatological theology of interreligious praxis. To do so, I need to identify how the church bears witness to the world through the Holy Spirit. There are three movements to my argument.

First, I suggest that the many tongues of Pentecost anticipate, herald, and even paradigmatically manifest the many gifts—*poiemata* (works)—of the Spirit in, to, and through the churches. In the congregational context, St. Paul identifies nine gifts "for the common good" (1 Cor 12:7). Yet the many gifts correlate with, are dispersed throughout, and are expressed through the many members of the body of Christ (1 Cor 12:12ff.). In fact, the distinctiveness of many members of the body is constituted by their having been given many different gifts. In asking the following questions— "Are all apostles? Are all prophets? Are all teachers? Do all work miracles? Do all possess gifts of healing? Do all speak in tongues? Do all interpret? (1 Cor 12:29-30)—the answer is clearly "No!" Hence, the many gifts through many members are the *poiemata* of the Spirit for the edification of the body.

Yet, the gifts of the Spirit are designed not only for the believing congregation but also for those who may be on the margins, or even those without. In fact, St. Paul explicitly says that the gifts of tongues and prophecy function differently in the congregational setting when unbelievers are present (1 Cor 14:22-24). Further, in another epistle, after identifying a number of "gifts that differ according to the grace given to us" (Rom 12:6-8), the apostle goes on to urge,

Contribute to the needs of the saints; extend hospitality to strangers. Bless those who persecute you; bless and do not curse them. Rejoice with those who rejoice, weep with those who weep. Live in harmony with one another; do not be haughty, but associate with the lowly; do not claim to be wiser than you are. Do not repay anyone evil for evil, but take thought for what is noble in the sight of all. If it is possible, so far as it depends on you, live peaceably with all. Beloved, never avenge yourselves, but leave room for the wrath of God; for it is written, "Vengeance is mine, I will repay, says the Lord." No, "if your enemies are hungry, feed them; if they are thirsty, give them something to drink; for by doing this you will heap burning coals on their heads." Do not be overcome by evil, but overcome evil with good. (Rom 12:13-21)

While most of these exhortations could apply also to those in the household of faith, they are clear expressions of the Christian virtues and of the grace of the Holy Spirit when manifest to unbelievers—for example, strangers, one's persecutors, the lowly, perpetrators of injustice, one's enemies—who are not only outside the body of Christ but also opposed to the saints.[68]

Second, I suggest that the many gifts of the Spirit at work through the church for the sake of the world are part of the divinely appointed means of grace through which the world is drawn into the saving work of God in Christ. But how is the salvation of God to be understood? Elsewhere I have argued that salvation is a multidimensional and dynamic work of God's Spirit.[69] The multidimensionality of salvation refers, in no necessary order, to the recognition and confession of sin, and to repentance from it; to the moral and spiritual transformation of human hearts by the Spirit; to the interpersonal healing and reconciling community that is the body of Christ; to the transformation of communities, societies, and even nations into realms of justice, peace, and righteousness; to the mending and redemption of the world, the cosmos, as a whole; to eschatological union with God— or *theosis*, as the Eastern Orthodox churches would say, etc. Relatedly, the dynamic process of salvation includes human conversion by the power of the Spirit throughout their lives. Thus, conversion through the Holy Spirit's means of grace involves, variously, taking responsibility for the different domains of life: the intellectual, the affective, the moral, and the sociopolitical.[70] Specifically, Christian conversion occurs when the encounter and union with Christ by the Spirit occurs, which in turn transforms all other conversions. At the same time, this does not diminish the importance of conversion in these various domains either before or after specifically Christian conversion. Rather, Christian conversion is itself facilitated by other forms of conversion—these are the constitutive works of the Spirit apart from which Christian conversion is impossible—even as it in turn provides a christomorphic shape to the converted and converting life.

---

[68] These exhortations complement others given to the diaspora Christians of Asia Minor: "Conduct yourselves honourably among the Gentiles, so that, though they malign you as evildoers, they may see your honourable deeds and glorify God when he comes to judge … For it is God's will that by doing right you should silence the ignorance of the foolish. As servants of God, live as free people, yet do not use your freedom as a pretext for evil. Honour everyone. Love the family of believers. Fear God. Honour the emperor" (1 Pet 2:12, 15-17).

[69] In what follows, I summarize a pneumatological soteriology defended at length in *The Spirit Poured Out on All Flesh*, ch. 2.

[70] Here I draw specifically on Donald L. Gelpi, *The Conversion Experience: A Reflective Process for RCIA Participants and Others* (New York and Mahwah, N.J.: Paulist Press, 1998), esp. chs. 2-3.

Within this soteriological framework, then, I present the third step of my argument in the form of a hypothesis: insofar as Christian conversion is a complex and multifaceted process, and Christian salvation is a holistic and multidimensional work (*poiesis*) of the Holy Spirit, Christian praxis intended to bear witness to the God of Jesus Christ to a post-Christendom and postmodern world needs to take many forms, and this multiplicity of forms is manifest in the diversity of tongues and gifts of the Spirit. The many gifts of the Holy Spirit, which include many languages, discourses, and tongues, are the means through which Christian witness is borne and the salvation of the world is effected. So, on the one hand, insofar as Christians intend to bear witness to the gospel in a pluralistic world, they will adopt a variety of practices and speak a diversity of languages commensurate with their audiences in different times and places. On the other hand, inasmuch as people have received the gift of the Holy Spirit in their own times and places, they will testify to what God has done in their own tongues and in their own ways. Put succinctly, I suggest that the many tongues of Pentecost open up to many Christian practices in a pluralistic world, and vice versa. The remainder of this book consists of an extended explication and defense of this theological hypothesis specifically with regard to the world of many faiths.

In this chapter, we have explored the emergence of Christian doctrine from Christian practices, analyzed theological accounts of the interrelationship between beliefs and practices, and provided a pneumatological perspective on the performative aspects of Christian theology in a pluralistic world. I do insist we take seriously the interrelatedness of beliefs and experiences, doctrines and practices, theologies and performances. Neither one nor the other side is to be privileged or subordinated. The hermeneutical spiral requires that we move from beliefs informing practices, even as such are proceeded by practices shaping beliefs. I suggest that a pneumatological approach is better capable of sustaining this dialectical relationship without collapsing onto one or the other side.[71] We are now ready to see how a pneumatological theology of religions and interreligious praxis—in which "many tongues equals many practices"—plays out in a post-9/11 world of many faiths.

---

[71] This point is highlighted in my *Spirit-Word-Community: Theological Hermeneutics in Trinitarian Perspective* (Burlington, Vt., and Aldershot, U.K.: Ashgate, 2002), esp. 10-11, as central to the argument of that book.

3

Performing Theology of Religions

Christian Practices and the Religions

In the remainder of this book, I want to test the hypothesis of "many tongues equal many practices" by exploring the relationship between Christian theologies of religion and Christian practices vis-à-vis the interreligious encounter. The constructive aspect of my theological proposal is that the Christian doctrine of hospitality provides a rich framework to think about how the many tongues, gifts, and works of the Spirit enable and empower a wide range of Christian practices with regard to other religious traditions in general and people of other faiths in particular. In a world of interreligious violence, war, and terrorism (as seen in chapter 1 above), Christians can and should respond with acts of interreligious hospitality. But before proceeding to that part of the argument in chapters 4 and 5, we need to attend in a more descriptive fashion to how contemporary options in Christian theology of religions are shaped by and inform different Christian practices in the encounter between religions.

In what follows, I provide accounts of the interconnectedness of beliefs and practices in exclusivistic, inclusivistic, and pluralistic theologies of religions, and discuss them successively in the three sections of this chapter. I will argue that each position involves doctrinal and theological convictions that are more commensurate with certain practices and less amenable to others. So far as I am aware, what follows is the first sustained explication of how Christian theologies of religions assume and inform Christian interreligious practices. At this point in the book, however, this thesis should not be surprising. If, as we have shown in the previous chapter, Christian beliefs are intertwined with Christian practices, so also, as we shall demonstrate next, the theologies of exclusivism, inclusivism, and pluralism are interwoven with practices enacted amidst the interfaith encounter.

Three disclaimers need to be registered at this point. First, I will not be insisting that each of these theological positions correlate in a one-to-one fashion with the postures and practices I discuss under that category. Any theology of religions could certainly make allowances for all of the practices discussed in this chapter, even as any type of interreligious practice could find justification in more than one theological perspective. I am simply suggesting that exclusivist, inclusivist, and pluralist theologies of religion are more consistent with and tend to certain kinds of postures and practices and vice versa.

Second, no more or less should be assumed of or imputed to the authors who I will be discussing and citing; most theologians are far too complex to fit neatly into exclusivist, inclusivist, or pluralist camps, and so my presentation will be necessarily selective, guided by how I assess the commensurability of their beliefs and practices. But since my goals in this chapter are more descriptive than prescriptive, I will be exercising a hermeneutics of charity with the works of the theologians of religions discussed. My goal is primarily to understand how their beliefs about other religions are related to the interreligious practices they think important to cultivate (and vice versa), and only secondarily to interact critically with their work.

One final but major caveat needs to be noted before proceeding. There is emerging almost a consensus that the categories of exclusivism, inclusivism, and pluralism are no longer viable for our time.[1] I myself argued in a previous book that "the exclusivist-inclusivist-pluralist categories may have outlived their usefulness."[2] If so, why use this classification to assess the relationship between theologies of religions and interreligious practices? Let me respond briefly along two lines.

First, while I remain persuaded that the paradigm as a whole needs to be rethought at a theological level (which I hope to contribute to in the last two chapters of this book), I am close to being convinced that exclusivism, inclusivism, and pluralism exhaust the spectrum of *logical* possibilities in response to the soteriological question, "Is there only one true religion or are there many?"[3] And since these have been until now the traditional way

---

[1] E.g., Veli-Matti Kärkkäinen, *An Introduction to the Theology of Religions: Biblical, Historical and Contemporary Perspectives* (Downers Grove, Ill.: InterVarsity Press, 2003), prefers ecclesiocentric, christocentric, and theocentric categories, while Paul F. Knitter, *Introducing Theologies of Religions* (Maryknoll, N.Y.: Orbis Books, 2002), identifies four models: replacement (only one true religion), fulfillment (one fulfills many), mutuality (many true religions in dialogue), and acceptance (many true religions—so be it).

[2] Amos Yong, *Beyond the Impasse: Toward a Pneumatological Theology of Religions* (Grand Rapids: Baker Academic, 2003), 22-29, quotation from p. 28.

[3] This question was asked by Schubert M. Ogden, *Is There Only One True Religion or Are There Many?* (Dallas: Southern Methodist University Press, 1992), and answered modally to the effect that "there could be many true religions"; yet Ogden himself admitted that his response was a version of inclusivism, which he called "pluralistic inclusivism." More recently, it was Perry Schmidt-Leukel, "Exclusivism, Inclusivism, Pluralism: The Tripolar

of categorizing the types of Christian responses, it seems like a convenient way to go for this more descriptive portion of my argument.

But even if exclusivism, inclusivism, and pluralism retain their validity when understood with regard to the question of eschatological salvation, there are related matters regarding how salvation is worked out historically and about God's historical self-revelation that complicate the present application of these categories. Hence, second, my primary focus here is not to assess the truth or falsity of these theological positions in (eschatological) abstraction but to explore the concrete relationships between beliefs and practices vis-à-vis the religions in the here and now. For this purpose, the threefold typology provides a suitable framework within which we can examine the issues. In fact, a secondary hypothesis to be tested concerns the viability of many practices with regard to the interreligious encounter. If we do, in fact, determine that many practices are not only plausible but even necessary, then we may need to go beyond the categories of exclusivism, inclusivism, and pluralism in order to develop a more integrative and theologically sound perspective on the religions. Such a theological vision will be able to embrace the many practices correlative with these three positions without having to endorse all of their theological claims (which may be logically and eschatologically incompatible anyway).

TRADITIONAL EXCLUSIVISM: DOCTRINES AND PRACTICES

The main features of traditional Christian exclusivism regarding the religions are well captured in the following maxims: "no other name"; "how shall they believe if they have not heard"; and "no salvation outside the church." The three subsections that follow take up and explore each of these in order, focusing on the kinds of Christian postures and commitments such convictions nurture and the corresponding practices they inculcate. I suggest throughout that exclusivistic theologies of religions are premised on a fundamental discontinuity between Christianity and other religions, and hence reflect a more oppositional form of Christian performances in the interreligious encounter.

Typology—Clarified and Reaffirmed," in *The Myth of Religious Superiority: Multifaith Explorations of Religious Pluralism,* ed. Paul F. Knitter (Maryknoll, N.Y.: Orbis Books, 2005), 13-27, who convinced me that the threefold typology does indeed cover the logical possibilities of types of responses, and Kristin Beise Kiblinger, *Buddhist Inclusivism: Attitudes toward Religious Others* (Burlington, Vt., and Aldershot, U.K.: Ashgate, 2005), who persuaded me that this typology covers the range of logical possibilities even for nontheistic traditions such as Buddhism. My book proceeds from the conviction that the response of theology is not constrained by these logical possibilities, even if it remains influenced by them.

"No Other Name": Marking Christian Identity

The earliest Christians declared in the face of persecution by the authorities, "This Jesus is 'the stone that was rejected by you, the builders; it has become the cornerstone.' There is salvation in no one else, for there is no other name under heaven given among mortals by which we must be saved" (Acts 4:11-12). While some Christians have insisted this text is silent about the unevangelized and about other religions, others point out that the phrase "under heaven given among mortals" denotes the breadth, applicability, and reach of this assertion of the apostle Peter.[4] Hence, there can be no doubt about the absoluteness, uniqueness, and exclusiveness of Jesus' salvific power. Two sets of extended comments emerge from a consideration of this view: that pertaining to Christian identity and that pertaining to Christian mission. I will deal with the latter momentarily, and focus here on the former.

"No other name" for Peter and the early Christians denoted their absolute allegiance to Jesus Christ amidst a hostile social and political arena.[5] Opposed seemingly by the entire spectrum of the Jewish leadership—the priests, captain of the temple, Sadducees, rulers, elders, scribes, the high priest and the priestly family (Acts 4:1, 5, 6)—the apostolic leaders were nevertheless emboldened to reaffirm their commitment to Jesus of Nazareth, who was able to heal and save his people from their sins. Similarly, in the Gospel of John, the Johannine community's devotion to Jesus—who said "I am" the bread of life, the light of the world, the door of the sheep, the good shepherd, the resurrection and the life, the way, the truth, and the life, and the true vine (John 6:35; 8:12; 10:7-9, 11-14; 11:25; 14:6; 14:1-5)—incurred the wrath of the Jewish leadership so that the followers of Jesus were expelled from the synagogue.[6] In this sociopolitical context, the claim that there is "no other name under heaven given among mortals by which we must be saved" is a declaration of the commitment of the earliest Christians, even to the point of undergoing persecution and, ultimately as in the case of St. Stephen, martyrdom.

These affirmations about the uniquely saving power of Jesus were and remain nested within a wider set of beliefs and practices.[7] Chief among

---

[4] R. Douglas Geivett and W. Gary Phillips, "A Particularist View: An Evidentialist Approach," in *More Than One Way? Four Views on Salvation in a Pluralistic World,* ed. Dennis L. Ockholm and Timothy R. Phillips (Grand Rapids: Zondervan, 1995), 211-45, esp. 230-31.

[5] Allan A. Boesak, "In the Name of Jesus: Acts 4:12," *Journal of Theology for Southern Africa* 52 (1985): 49-55.

[6] See my discussion in "'The Light Shines in the Darkness': Johannine Dualism and the Challenge of Christian Theology of Religions Today," *Journal of Religion* (under review), part 2.

[7] Vinoth Ramachandra, *The Recovery of Mission: Beyond the Pluralist Paradigm* (Grand Rapids: Eerdmans, 1996), ch. 6.

them are the convictions that there is one God who is the creator of all; that through the sin and fall of humanity, the world has become estranged from God; that God has taken it upon himself not only to reveal himself to the world but to save the world through his Son, Jesus Christ; and that God has set apart a chosen people—Israel in former times, the church in the present dispensation—to bear witness to the works and words of God so that all may be saved and may worship and honor God.[8] Exclusivists admit that for reasons not clearly known to us, God has chosen to mediate salvation through the particular events of Israel, his Son Jesus Christ, and the church. All of these convictions mark the identity of the people of God as separate from other groups, nations, and peoples of the world.

In this view, then, there is a marked and even radical discontinuity between Christian faith and other religions. Christian *faith* identifies the only people who have been formed, called, and constituted by God, while other *religions* merely reflect the many ways in which human beings have attempted to search for and reach out to what they believed was beyond them.[9] Hence, "There is no room for alternative pathways or a more generic theism when the truth about Jesus is known. Christian theologians who baulk at the particularity of God's revelation in Christ and seek a more optimistic evaluation of the world's religions are striving against the grain of the gospel itself."[10] In fact, there is no point of contact between Christian faith and other religions except that of the missionary because the religions, including Christian faith, constitute comprehensive ways of life and thought emanating from wholly different experiences and intending to achieve very different ends.[11]

---

[8] This is summarized by Harold Netland, *Encountering Religious Pluralism: The Challenge to Christian Faith and Mission* (Downers Grove, Ill.: InterVarsity; and Leicester, U.K.: Apollos, 2001), 315-24.

[9] This view was first argued by Karl Barth, "The Revelation of God as the Abolition of Religion," in *The Doctrine of the Word of God*, vol. 1, pt. 2 of *Church Dogmatics*, trans. G. T. Thomson and Harold Knight (Edinburgh: T. & T. Clark, 1956), §17. Recent scholars such as J. A. DiNoia, "Religion and the Religions," in *The Cambridge Companion to Karl Barth*, ed. John Webster (Cambridge: Cambridge University Press, 2000), 243-57, have pointed out that Barth's theology of religions, when gleaned from his wider corpus, is much more nuanced than this (see chapter 5, pp. 151-53). In certain evangelical Christian circles, however, this reading of Barth lies behind emphasizing the uniqueness of Christian *faith* over and against other *religions*—e.g., David W. Baker, ed., *Biblical Faith and Other Religions: An Evangelical Assessment* (Grand Rapids: Kregel Academic, 2004).

[10] Mark D. Thompson, "The Uniqueness of Christ as the Revealer of God," in *Christ the One and Only: A Global Affirmation of the Uniqueness of Jesus Christ*, ed. Sung Wook Chung (Grand Rapids: Baker Academic, 2005), 90-110, quote from p. 109.

[11] This was argued by Hendrik Kraemer, *The Christian Message in a Non-Christian World* (New York: Harper & Brothers; and London: International Missionary Council, 1938), esp. 142; cf. Tim S. Perry, *Radical Difference: A Defence of Hendrik Kraemer's Theology of Religions*, Editions SR 27 (Waterloo, Ont.: Wilfrid Laurier University Press, 2001).

The claim "no other name!" (note the exclamation point) captures precisely this radical otherness between Christ—his uniqueness, absoluteness, decisiveness, unsurpassableness, normativeness, and finality—and other religious figures, between Christian faith and other religions. At this level, there may not even be (in principle, if not in reality) any sense of animosity, haughtiness, or triumphalism that accompanies such a claim insofar as it is first and foremost a designation regarding Christian self-understanding. Thus, it can be readily understood how Christian self-identity is countercultural, sectarian, and oppositional to the dominant social ethos, forces, and movements.[12]

What kind of attitudes, convictions, and concerns regarding other religions does the assertion "no other name!" express? Because God is not seen as equally revealed in all religions, when Christians encounter or interact with people of other religions, they do so "with the assumption that they have ... definitive truth about God and the human predicament which is absolute and nonnegotiable."[13] Two corollaries follow: put positively, Christians have access to religious truth that is not merely symbolic or metaphorical but which can be propositionally expressed; and, put negatively, Christians cannot approach interreligious dialogue as a common quest for truth. This means also that Christians should be alert to the destructive syncretism that can occur if they uncritically entertain the ideas and practices of other religions.

But why then should Christians interact or dialogue with people of other religions? While a dialogical posture demonstrates the willingness to treat other human beings respectfully and evinces humility, sensitivity, and courtesy toward those in other religions, ultimately, "dialogue is effective for effective evangelism."[14] With this, we see how "no other name!" not only informs Christian identity but also shapes Christian mission.

"HOW SHALL THEY BELIEVE IF THEY'VE NOT HEARD?" PERFORMING CHRISTIAN EVANGELISM

If there is "no other name" then how are people saved? Here exclusivists call attention to St. Paul's letter to the Romans:

---

[12] For a contemporary argument regarding this sectarian character of the church which is described as a "colony," see Stanley Hauerwas and William H. Willimon, *Resident Aliens Live* (Nashville, Tenn.: Abingdon, 1989), and idem, *Where Resident Aliens Live* (Nashville, Tenn.: Abingdon, 1996).

[13] Harold A. Netland, *Dissonant Voices: Religious Pluralism and the Question of Truth* (Grand Rapids: Eerdmans; and Leicester, U.K.: Apollos, 1991), 291. Much of what I say in this paragraph is an adaptation of what Netland identifies as disconcerting about the interreligious encounter from a conservative evangelical point of view.

[14] Netland, *Dissonant Voices*, 298.

If you confess with your lips that Jesus is Lord and believe in your heart that God raised him from the dead, you will be saved. For one believes with the heart and so is justified, and one confesses with the mouth and so is saved ... For, "Everyone who calls on the name of the Lord shall be saved." But how are they to call on one in whom they have not believed? And how are they to believe in one of whom they have never heard? And how are they to hear without someone to proclaim him? And how are they to proclaim him unless they are sent? As it is written, "How beautiful are the feet of those who bring good news!" But not all have obeyed the good news; for Isaiah says, "Lord, who has believed our message?" So faith comes from what is heard, and what is heard comes through the word of Christ. (Rom 10:9-10, 13-17)

The implications of this passage are (a) only those who believe and confess Jesus is Lord are saved; (b) the only way people can come to believe in Jesus as Lord is by hearing the gospel, since they have not been able to believe the message of the Old Testament prophets (signified by the reference to Isaiah); and (c) the only way the gospel will be taken to all people is if the church commits itself to sending evangelists and missionaries to the ends of the earth.[15]

Two convictions follow from an exclusivist reading of this text. First, general revelation is sufficient to inform people of their sin and their need for redemption, but insufficient to actually effect their salvation. For those who believe that St. Paul in Romans 2 suggests that Gentiles will be judged according to their responses to the light they have received—whether in the law or in their consciences—exclusivists counter both that the ungodly have known but suppressed the truth on the one hand (Rom 1:18-20) and that "there is no one who is righteous, not even one" (Rom 3:10), on the other hand.[16] Hence, general revelation cannot itself save, but it does provide sufficient information so that the ungodly, including those who have never heard and those in other religions, realize they have sinned against God.[17]

---

[15] John Piper, *Let the Nations Be Glad! The Supremacy of God in Missions*, 2nd rev. ed. (Grand Rapids: Baker Academic, 2003), 63, 145-47.

[16] Douglas Moo, "Romans 2: Saved Apart from the Gospel?" in *Through No Fault of Their Own? The Fate of Those Who Have Never Heard*, ed. William V. Crockett and James G. Sigountos (Grand Rapids: Baker, 1991), 137-45.

[17] Ramesh P. Richard, *The Population of Heaven: A Biblical Response to the Inclusivist Position on Who Will Be Saved* (Chicago: Moody, 1994), 86-90. The two classes of exceptions may be those who are severely intellectually disabled and those who dies as infants, neither of whom can be said to have ratified the Adamic sin and accepted the effects of that sin

Second, because general revelation is impotent for salvation but potent for condemnation, the Great Commission is an essential aspect of Christian life and discipleship. Christian evangelism and mission flow directly out of the exclusivist conviction "No other name!": "The only compulsion that sends us out is the realization that all are lost eternally unless they hear the good new [*sic*] we have heard and repent and believe in the Lord Jesus Christ."[18] There is urgency to the Christian mission that proceeds from the belief that faith and salvation are dependent on the proclamation of the gospel.[19] Nonexclusivist theologies of the unevangelized and theologies of religions all involve "cutting the nerve cord of evangelism."[20] More damaging, nonexclusivist approaches "strongly dispose people toward actions that can compromise the church's mission on earth and place obstacles in the way of evangelism."[21]

"How can they believe if they have not heard?" can thereby be understood as an illocutionary question that is designed to produce certain modes of engagement (perlocutionary effects) with people of other religions. Concerned that most forms of interreligious dialogue compromise Christian convictions about the uniqueness of Christ, exclusivists insist that dialogue must always be subservient to proclamation. In relating to people of other religions, Christians can begin with topics or issues common to both sides, but Christians must end with proclaiming the finality and uniqueness of Christ.[22] From an exclusivist point of view, dialogue must be truth-seeking encounters that emphasize finally not the commonalities or similarities between religious traditions but how Christianity differs from other religions. Hence, Christian participation in the conversation at the religious roundtable "must be missiologically focused."[23]

An important element in Christian evangelistic dialogue is apologetics. There are two types: negative apologetics provides answers (defenses) of

---

in their lives; see Millard J. Erickson, *How Shall They Be Saved? The Destiny of Those Who Do Not Hear of Jesus* (Grand Rapids: Baker, 1996), 250-52.

[18] Russell H. Dilday, Jr., "No Other Name: Acts 4:12," *Southwestern Journal of Theology* 36 (Summer 1994): 52-57, quote from p. 56.

[19] Erickson, *How Shall They Be Saved?* 260-61 and 268-69.

[20] William V. Crockett and James G. Sigountos, "Are the 'Heathen' Really Lost?" in *Through No Fault of Their Own?* ed. William V. Crockett and James G. Sigountos, 257-64, esp. 260-61 (see n. 16).

[21] Ronald H. Nash, "Restrictivism," in *What about Those Who Have Never Heard? Three Views on the Destiny of the Unevangelized*, ed. John Sanders (Downers Grove, Ill.: InterVarsity, 1995), 107-39, quote from p. 136; see also Ronald H. Nash, *Is Jesus the Only Savior?* (Grand Rapids: Zondervan, 1994), 165-69.

[22] This is the approach of Winfried Corduan, *A Tapestry of Faiths: The Common Threads between Christianity and World Religions* (Downers Grove, Ill.: InterVarsity, 2002).

[23] Timothy C. Tennent, *Christianity at the Religious Roundtable: Evangelicalism in Conversation with Hinduism, Buddhism, and Islam* (Grand Rapids: Baker Academic, 2002), 26.

Christian faith against questions and criticisms of non-Christians, while positive apologetics provides reasons for why others ought to consider abandoning their non-Christian religious beliefs and accept the Christian claims to truth.[24] Both approaches are increasingly difficult in a religiously plural world. Especially for those convinced by the Lindbeckian postliberal idea that religious beliefs and practices are intertwined, it is difficult to adjudicate conflicting truth claims across religious lines since the rationale for religious beliefs may in fact be deeply interrelated with certain types of religious practices. But exclusivists counter that if there are no context-independent criteria for adjudicating such claims then a severe form of relativism ensues.[25] There must be at least logical consistency and a moral criterion that can be applied in any critical analysis of competing religious claims to truth.

The moral criterion raises another set of issues connected to the reasons for engaging in both negative and positive apologetics. The first is the epistemic duty to consider whether other challenging claims to truth actually undermine one's own convictions and commitments. The second is the religious, even moral, obligation to convince others of the momentousness of the Christian truth claims.[26] In these ways, the exclusivist convictions about "no other name!" and "how can they believe if they have not heard?" are illocutionary speech acts designed to bolster Christian commitments to missions and evangelism, to proclamation and apologetics.

"NO SALVATION OUTSIDE THE CHURCH": FORMING CHRISTIAN COMMUNITY

If "no other name" identifies Christian self-understanding and "how can they believe if they have not heard" motivates Christian mission, then "no salvation outside the church" demarcates the boundaries of Christian community. In what follows, I want to identify three sets of Christian practices that give meaning to this Christian claim.

First, "no salvation outside the church" identifies the visible church as the locus of God's saving work in this dispensation. This involves a number of convictions related to the baptismal rite of initiation traceable to the earliest Christian communities. From the very beginning, the response

---

[24] Netland, *Encountering Religious Pluralism*, 259-60.

[25] Netland, *Encountering Religious Pluralism*, 289-90.

[26] See Paul J. Griffiths, *An Apology for Apologetics: A Study in the Logic of Interreligious Dialogue* (Maryknoll, N.Y.: Orbis Books, 1991), 14-16. Note, however, that as a Roman Catholic theologian, Griffiths is not a theological exclusivist with regard to the doctrine of salvation; also, he explicitly accepts a primary postliberal conviction—namely, that interreligious apologetics should be occasional or ad hoc, depending on the social and political context. I cite Griffiths here only because I think he articulates clearly the motivations for interreligious apologetics that animate exclusivist apologetic polemics.

to the question of how one could be saved was, "Repent, and be baptized every one of you in the name of Jesus Christ so that your sins may be forgiven; and you will receive the gift of the Holy Spirit" (Acts 2:38). This Lukan formulation was consistent with the Johannine claim (put in the words of Jesus) that "no one can enter the kingdom of God without being born of water and Spirit" (John 3:5), as well as the Pauline teaching that salvation is "not because of any works of righteousness that we had done, but according to his mercy, through the water of rebirth and renewal by the Holy Spirit" (Titus 3:5). While these latter two texts are less clear than the Lukan one about connecting baptism and salvation, there is no doubt when they are all read in light of the Petrine declaration that "God waited patiently in the days of Noah, during the building of the ark, in which a few, that is, eight people, were saved through water. And *baptism, which this prefigured, now saves you*—not as a removal of dirt from the body, but as an appeal to God for a good conscience, through the resurrection of Jesus Christ" (1 Pet 3:20-21; italics added; cf. Rom 6:1-11 and Col 2:11-12).

The Petrine image of the ark of Noah saving the remnant thus became a type of the church saving the remnant people of God. And since the keys of the kingdom were given to Peter (Matt 16:18-19; cf. John 21:15-19), the apostle and his successors became the priestly representatives of the headship of Christ and the holders of the rites of initiation into the ecclesial ark of salvation. This priestly function and role should not be underestimated. During the postapostolic period, disputes and schisms led to the emergence of the bishop as the protector of the church.

It was in the life and work of Cyprian of Carthage (200-258) that "no salvation outside the church" was most clearly articulated.[27] Note, however, that Cyprian's ideas grew out of the mid-second-century Decian persecution and the problem of the lapsed Christians posed by the Donatists. Amidst these developments that threatened the unity of the church, Cyprian urged that the locus of salvation in Christ was to be found only in the church and nowhere else. In a passage that deserves to be quoted at length, Cyprian wrote,

> Whoever is separated from the Church and is joined to an adulteress, is separated from the promises of the Church; nor can he who forsakes the Church of Christ attain to the rewards of Christ ... If any one could escape who was outside the ark of Noah, then he also may escape who shall be outside of the Church ... And does any one

---

[27] For a historical overview, see Molly Truman Marshall, *No Salvation Outside the Church? A Critical Inquiry*, NABPR Dissertation Series 9 (Lewiston, Queenston, Lampeter: Edwin Mellen, 1993), ch. 2.

believe that this unity which thus comes from the divine strength and coheres in celestial sacraments, can be divided in the Church, and can be separated by the parting asunder of opposing wills? He who does not hold this unity does not hold God's law, does not hold the faith of the Father and the Son, does not hold life and salvation.[28]

Two points should be noted from the preceeding. First, Cyprian was addressing not unbelievers outside the church or even those in other religions but schismatics and those who threatened to divide the church from within. Hence, as a speech act, "no salvation outside the church" is an illocution warning such schismatics and heretics about their divisive activities. Second, the bishop comes to represent the unity of the church, and this unity itself "coheres in [the] celestial sacraments." This means that insofar as the priesthood presided over the sacraments, to that same extent the priesthood now held the keys to the rites of initiation into the ecclesial ark of salvation.

Later developments ensured that what before was intended to separate out schismatics and heretics from the true church was now thought to refer to all nonbelievers. St. Augustine's doctrine of original sin meant all were now condemned to perish unless regenerated by Christian baptism.[29] By the time of the medieval period, the numbers of those outside the church were considerably expanded. Boniface VIII spoke in the papal bull "Unam Sanctum" about confessing "that there is only [one] holy Catholic and apostolic Church, outside of which there is neither salvation nor remission of sins."[30] The Council of Florence later said unequivocally that the church "firmly believes, professes and teaches that none of those who exist outside of the Catholic Church—neither pagans nor Jews nor heretics nor schismatics—can become sharers of eternal life; rather they will go into the eternal fire 'which was prepared for the devil and his angels' [Mt 25:41] unless, before the end of their lives, they are joined to that same church."[31]

---

[28] Cyprian, *Treatise on the Unity of the Church* §6, in Alexander Roberts and James Donaldson, eds., *Ante-Nicene Fathers: The Writings of the Fathers Down to A.D. 325*, vol. 5 (1886; reprint, Peabody, Mass.: Hendrickson, 1994), 423.

[29] Francis A. Sullivan, S.J., *Salvation Outside the Church? Tracing the History of the Catholic Response* (New York and Mahwah, N.J.: Paulist Press, 1992), ch. 3.

[30] Cited in Richard Plantinga, ed., *Christianity and Plurality: Classic and Contemporary Readings* (Malden, Mass., and Oxford: Blackwell, 1999), 124.

[31] Cited in Sullivan, *Salvation Outside the Church?* 6. Sullivan's book actually is written to explain how such ecclesial pronouncements can be squared with Vatican II's explicit statements that salvation does occur outside of the Roman Catholic Church, and he suggests that one reason resides in the fact that the medieval assumption of mass guilt had come to be replaced during the modern period by an assumption of innocence until proven guilty. Further the Roman Catholic notion of the development of doctrine enabled the bishops of Vatican II

In short, the emphases of "no salvation outside the church" began with the centrality of the Christian initiation rite (baptism), shifted to being an admonition to those who threatened the unity of the church (in the time of Cyprian), and was extended only later to exclude all non-Christians (during the later patristic and medieval periods). This teaching was therefore originally meant to encourage catechumens to seek after the rite of baptism, then to warn Christians against dividing the one, holy, catholic, and apostolic church, and later to caution the faithful against relationships with Jews, Muslims, pagan, and others thought to be enemies of the Christian faith. These were the sensibilities and practices nurtured and legitimated by the exclusivist conviction, "no salvation outside the church."

In the preceding pages, we have been discussing traditional Christian theological exclusivism. We have in a sense bracketed the soteriological and eschatological claims of exclusivism and focused instead on the ecclesial and historical practices that have been shaped by and also inform such claims. I have characterized exclusivist theologies of religion as focused on the demarcation of Christian identity and community (the point of "No other name!"), as committed to Christian mission in general and evangelism more specifically (as captured by the maxim, "How shall they believe if they have not heard?"), and as related to episcopal leadership and directed toward catechetical formation (reflected in "No salvation outside the church"). In each of these ways, exclusivism is constituted by distinct and important ecclesial practices. Regardless of where one finally lands with regard to the soteriological-eschatological implications of exclusivism, many of its practices nevertheless remain central to Christian life and faith. Witness, evangelism, and formation are ongoing tasks of Christian discipleship regardless of one's theology of religions. Might we be able to develop a theology of Christian practices that includes such elements without necessarily embracing all of the beliefs related to theological exclusivism? In the following section, we will ask a similar question with regard to theological inclusivism.

INCLUSIVISM AND THE RELIGIONS: THEOLOGIES AND PERFORMANCES

If exclusivism emphasizes the discontinuity between Christian faith and other religions, inclusivism alleviates some of the tension by thinking about the relationship more in terms of a spectrum of continuity. Other religions would still be subordinated to Christian faith, and Christian faith would

---

to understand how different social and political circumstances at different times and places are later clarified.

continue to fulfill the highest aspirations of other religions. From a missiological perspective, other religions may even prepare the way for the Christian gospel in a similar if not identical way as the religion of ancient Israel
prepared the way for the messiah. In this section, we will examine, respectively, the various missiological, dialogical, and interreligious practices fostered by inclusivistic types of theologies of religions.

INCARNATION AND PENTECOST: PERFORMING CONTEXTUAL MISSIOLOGY

If exclusivism highlights the uniqueness of Christ, the church, and the
Christian faith, inclusivism is convinced that much more can and needs to
be said about these matters vis-à-vis other religious figures, other religious
communities, and other faiths (note: not just other "religions"). Hence,
inclusivists suggest that while Christ is the absolute, normative, decisive,
and even final revelation, he is not necessarily the *only* revelation of God.[32]
Jesus might be the unique savior of humankind, but such uniqueness could
be understood not in an exclusionary sense of a boundaried individual but
in an inclusionary sense of one who was able to open up to, receive, and
even transform all others.[33] In this case, one could still affirm with the
Johannine community all of the "I am's" of Jesus Christ yet also recognize
that he was the true light who enlightens everyone (John 1:9).[34]

Similarly, the Holy Spirit is surely to be understood as being the Spirit of
Jesus as well as the one who animates and empowers the church as the living body of Christ. But the Spirit is also the Spirit of creation and of all
creatures even as it is the Spirit whose breath gives life to all people.[35] This
means that while the works of the Spirit in the church are distinct from the
works of the Spirit in the world, nevertheless, there is continuity rather
than discontinuity between the two. In this view, the church is "representative rather than constitutive of salvation because not all who ultimately
participate in God's salvific purpose are visibly attached to this community
of faith which remains in direct continuity with the earthly ministry of

---

[32] See Carl Braaten, *No Other Gospel! Christianity among the World's Religions* (Minneapolis: Fortress, 1992), ch. 4. There is a subtle but substantive difference between the claim
that Jesus is truly savior (Braaten), and the claim that he is not the only savior. This latter is
defended, for example, by Paul F. Knitter, in the opening and concluding chapters to *The
Uniqueness of Jesus: A Dialogue with Paul F. Knitter,* ed. Leonard Swidler and Paul Mojzes
(Maryknoll, N.Y.: Orbis Books, 1997), and it moves us from inclusivism to pluralism.

[33] See Gabriel Moran, *Uniqueness: Problems or Paradox in Jesus and Christian Traditions*
(Maryknoll, N.Y.: Orbis Books, 1992), esp. ch. 5.

[34] This is the most cited text in Jacques Dupuis' inclusivistic theology of religions; see
Dupuis, *Toward a Christian Theology of Religious Pluralism* (Maryknoll, N.Y.: Orbis Books,
1997).

[35] Ken Gnanakan, *Proclaiming Christ in a Pluralistic Context* (Bangalore: Theological
Book Trust, 2000), ch. 7.

Jesus Christ."[36] Hence it is also possible to think "of a religion as a people's tradition of response to the reality the Holy Spirit has set before their eyes."[37]

If exclusivism emphasizes "no salvation outside the church," inclusivism accentuates "no salvation outside of Christ and the Spirit."[38] When incarnation and Pentecost are understood in inclusivistic terms, Christian mission is thereby characterized with a number of features that, although not present only within the inclusivist framework, is most coherent within the purview of inclusivism. While not dispensing with evangelism and proclamation, these activities are only one of many modes of missionary activities. In his *magnum opus,* missiologist David Bosch suggests that an ecumenical missionary paradigm features multiple approaches, including working toward social and economic justice on behalf of the poor and marginalized.[39] Further, the church is understood not as over-and-against others or even other religions but as participating in the mission of God "with-others," possibly even sharing in mutual witness alongside those in other faiths. Last but not least, mission is understood not in terms of the gospel as being only discontinuous with cultures and religions but in terms of the gospel being inculturated, contextualized, and indigenized in a postcolonial, post-Enlightenment, and postmodern world. While there will always be some kind of discontinuity between gospel and culture (and religion)—as that is, in part, the nature of gospel to be scandalous—yet in the inclusivist framework, such discontinuities sit amidst continuities that allow for various "points of contact" as well.

Inculturation, contextualization, and indigenization assume that all cultures and perhaps even religions are redeemable by the gospel precisely because God has entered into history in Christ and by the Holy Spirit. Hence, there are points of contact between gospel and culture and between gospel and religion, and such points of contact are seen by inclusivists as "evidence that God has not been sitting idly by waiting for human missionaries to bring the gospel to these peoples."[40] In fact, such points of con-

---

[36] Marshall, *No Salvation Outside the Church?* 231.

[37] John V. Taylor, *The Go-Between God: The Holy Spirit and Christian Mission*, 2nd ed. (London: SCM, 2004), 182; note also that Taylor's ch. 9, from where this quotation is taken, is titled "Meeting: The Universal Spirit and the Meeting of Faiths."

[38] Here I am paraphrasing Hendrik Vroom, *No Other Gods: Christian Belief in Dialogue with Buddhism, Hinduism, and Islam* (Grand Rapids, and Cambridge, U.K.: Eerdmans, 1996), 142.

[39] David J. Bosch, *Transforming Mission: Paradigm Shifts in Theology of Mission* (Maryknoll, N.Y.: Orbis Books, 1991), part 3. This kind of holistic approach is also defended by Andrew Lord, *Spirit-Shaped Mission: A Holistic Charismatic Missiology* (Milton Keynes, U.K., and Waynesboro, Ga.: Paternoster, 2005).

[40] John Sanders, *No Other Name: An Investigation into the Destiny of the Unevangelized* (Grand Rapids: Eerdmans, 1992), 249.

tact are to be found not only in the cultural domain but also in the texts, rituals, spiritualities, and practices of people in other faiths.[41] In Eastern traditions, the lines between culture and religion are much fuzzier than they are in the West. Yet inclusivists are also careful to avoid syncretism: "A theology is not syncretistic if and when it uses the thought-forms of the environment in which it operates. A theology becomes syncretistic if and when in using such thought-forms it introduces into the structure ideas which change the meaning of biblical truth in its substance."[42]

For this among other reasons, missiological strategies that focus on inculturation, contextualization, and indigenization take time. Examples of such missionary approaches include the "neighborology" of Kosuke Koyama and of Sadayandy Batumalai. Koyama was a Japanese missionary to Thailand, where he wrote his widely heralded *Waterbuffalo Theology*, and then later, *Three Mile an Hour God*.[43] In the former volume, he describes "neighborology" as the process of engaging with our neighbors, including people in other faiths, not as objects (e.g., to be converted) but as neighbors who have important messages even for us Christians. Further, Jesus Christ is the neighbor to all of us. Whereas our neighbors are unconcerned with our christology, they are surely concerned about our neighborology—whether or not we are good neighbors. For the gospel to take root among the Thai, it will have to be deeply inculturated amidst a Buddhist way of life.[44]

Building on Koyama's neighborology, Sadayandy Batumalai is a Malaysian Anglican theologian who converted to Christ during his teenage years. He has written a number of books advocating a neighborly stance for Christians in the Muslim-dominated pluralistic context of Malaysia.[45] His question is how the Malaysian church can be prophetic and yet neighborly at the same time. Building bridges with Islam, Hinduism, and Buddhism in Malaysia requires patient effort. Batumalai suggests that "we visit temples and mosques, not as tourists but as pilgrims."[46] The goal is "to

---

[41] Kirsteen Kim, *Mission in the Spirit: The Holy Spirit in Indian Christian Theologies* (Delhi: ISPCK, 2003), esp. chs. 2-3.

[42] W. A. Visser 't Hooft, *No Other Name: The Choice between Syncretism and Christian Universalism* (Philadelphia: Westminster, 1963), 123.

[43] Kosuke Koyama, *Waterbuffalo Theology* (Maryknoll, N.Y.: Orbis Books, 1976), and *Three Mile an Hour God: Biblical Reflections* (Maryknoll, N.Y.: Orbis Books, 1980).

[44] For an overview of Koyama's work, see Victoria Lee Erickson, "Neighborology: A Feminist-Ethno-Missiological Celebration of Kosuke Koyama," in *The Agitated Mind of God: The Theology of Kosuke Koyama*, ed. Dale T. Irvin and Akintunde E. Akinade (Maryknoll, N.Y.: Orbis Books, 1996), 151-72.

[45] Sadayandy Batumalai, *A Prophetic Christology for Neighbourology: A Theology for a Prophetic Living* (Kuala Lumpur: Seminari Theoloji Malaysia, 1986); idem, *A Malaysian Theology of Muhibbah: A Theology for a Christian Witnessing in Malaysia* (Kuala Lumpur: Seminari Theoloji Malaysia, 1990); and idem, *An Introduction to Asian Theology: An Asian Story from a Malaysian Eye for Asian Neighbourology* (Delhi: ISPCK, 1991).

[46] Batumalai, *Introduction to Asian Theology*, 391.

interpret our knowing of Christ to our neighbours of other living faiths," and "to recast the Christian message in the religious [e.g., Islamic terminology] categories to enable others to appreciate, understand and accept our Lord Jesus Christ, as Saviour."[47] Yet alongside evangelism, the call is to respond to the cultural, social, economic, and political crises/issues of concern to all Malaysians. A theology of neighborology proposes ways forward that emphasize dialogue, learning about the "other," and working together to strengthen the nation: "The potential is considerable for making Malaysia not only an exemplary Islamic state but also an exemplary pluralistic state in the best tradition of Islam and a human society guided by God for the well being of all its members."[48]

MUTUALITY AND VULNERABILITY: ENGAGING THE INTERRELIGIOUS DIALOGUE

Clearly, the inclusivist view of the continuity (not identity) between Christianity and other faiths requires and underwrites a much more relational and dialogical mission strategy.[49] More than just dialogical, the process of interaction is genuinely exploratory.[50] Rather than adopting a polemical form of apologetics, relational and dialogical approaches emphasize that dialogue partners should be viewed as equals and that their exchanges should be characterized, as Koyama suggests, by real give-and-take.[51] In this case, interreligious dialogue becomes a Christian practice in its own right, rather than being subservient to other ends.[52]

So whereas exclusivists emphasize dialogue for the sake of proclamation or presentation of the gospel, inclusivists do not deny this kerygmatic moment when appropriate, but instead view the dialogical event as one of mutuality. Rather than there being a discontinuity between Christianity

---

[47] Batumalai, *Introduction to Asian Theology*, 420-21.

[48] Batumalai, *Islamic Resurgence and Islamization in Malaysia: A Malaysian Christian Response* (Ipoh, Malaysia: St. John's Church Anglican, 1996), 147.

[49] See, from a Roman Catholic perspective, William R. Burrows, ed., *Redemption and Dialogue: Reading Redemptoris Missio and Dialogue and Proclamation* (Maryknoll, N.Y.: Orbis Books, 1993); and, from a Protestant perspective, E. Luther Copeland, *A New Meeting of the Religions: Interreligious Relationships and Theological Questioning* (Waco, Tex.: Baylor University Press, 1999).

[50] Theron D. Price, *Revelation and Faith: Theological Reflections on the Knowing and Doing of Truth* (Macon, Ga.: Mercer University Press, 1987), 179, talks about the interreligious encounter in terms of "dialogical exploration."

[51] See David K. Clark, *Dialogical Apologetics: A Person-Centered Approach to Christian Defense* (Grand Rapids: Baker, 1999), 117. Note that Clark is an exclusivist with a fairly robust relational approach to interreligious dialogue.

[52] James L. Fredericks, *Buddhists and Christians: Through Comparative Theology to Solidarity* (Maryknoll, N.Y.: Orbis Books, 2004), 103-5, talks about "dialogue as Christian 'practice.'"

and other religions, there is rather mutual enrichment and even what might be called a "mutual asymmetrical complementarity."[53] This paradoxical description suggests that while Christianity is not identical with other faith traditions—that is, there is an asymmetrical relationship—yet there is real mutuality and reciprocity such that Christians can benefit from the dialogue process even as they hope their dialogue partners also gain something from the encounter.

But going beyond mutual personal enrichment, there is also the possibility of a mutual transformation of theological traditions out of the dialogical encounter.[54] The interreligious encounter may have implications not only for our personal self-understanding but also for our theological identity: we might actually learn something new and relevant! In this case, insiders become outsiders and vice versa, as each is the "iron" through which the other becomes sharpened and transformed (see Prov 27:17).[55] Other religious ideas and theologies are thus not just instrumental for the Christian sharing of the gospel, but are perhaps also instruments through which Christians come to a new self-awareness, even at the theological level.

This kind of mutual transformation is already taking place in the theological academy.[56] While I will leave it to representatives of other faiths to document the transformation of their own religious and theological traditions through interreligious dialogue, allow me here to very briefly identify some of the ways in which the interreligious encounter has impacted Christian theology. From out of the Christian-Jewish dialogue, for example, there has emerged a nonsupersessionist Christian self-understanding.[57] Christian-Muslim dialogue has produced expanded Christian views of prophethood and scriptural revelation.[58] Christian-Hindu dialogue has resulted in creative explorations of intertextual reading across religious tra-

---

[53] Jacques Dupuis, *Christianity and the Religions: From Confrontation to Dialogue*, trans. Phillip Berryman (Maryknoll, N.Y.: Orbis Books, 2002), 232-35 and 255-58.

[54] First clearly articulated by John B. Cobb, Jr., *Beyond Dialogue: Toward a Mutual Transformation of Christianity and Buddhism* (Philadelphia: Fortress, 1982).

[55] Thus Lamin Sanneh, *Encountering the West: Christianity and the Global Cultural Process—The African Dimension* (Maryknoll, N.Y.: Orbis Books, 1993), ch. 4, appropriately notes how religious insiders and cultural outsiders like the missionaries in Africa became religious outsiders to their own mission-sending contexts and cultural insiders to their mission contexts, and also how the religious outsider/cultural insider folk who were being missionized were at the same time also religious insider/cultural outsider folk vis-à-vis the missionaries.

[56] E.g., Gerald R. McDermott, *Can Evangelicals Learn from World Religions? Jesus, Revelation and Religious Traditions* (Downers Grove, Ill.: InterVarsity, 2000); and Mercy Amba Oduyoye and Hendrik M. Vroom, eds., *One Gospel—Many Cultures: Case Studies and Reflections on Cross-Cultural Theology* (New York and Amsterdam: Editions Rodopi, 2003).

[57] The work of Paul Van Buren, Clark M. Williamson, and Marvin Wilson are exemplary in this regard.

[58] Consult here the life work of Wilfred Cantwell Smith, Kenneth Cragg, and F. E. Peters.

ditions as well as fresh cross-religious christological categories.[59] Christian-Buddhist dialogue has called into question basic theistic assumptions across the board, given the non-theistic Buddhist worldview.[60] Christian dialogue with Chinese religious traditions has opened up new possibilities for understanding Jesus Christ as the *Dao*, the truth, and the life.[61] And this process of mutual transformation has occurred also in the Christian encounter with indigenous religious traditions in the Americas, in Africa, and in Australasia.[62] Now in all of these cases, the goal has never been to compromise Christian commitments but to engage in a dialogical quest for understanding from the standpoint of Christian faith. In the process, of course, the Christians have been enriched and transformed.

At still a third level beyond mutual enrichment and mutual transformation is what might be called authentic vulnerability.[63] The Christian quest for understanding, while never consciously intended to undermine Christian faith, may sometimes lead sojourners to embrace other faiths as their own. In a few of these cases, Christians experience transformation so radical that it might be recognized as conversion in some substantive sense to another faith. When this happens, we have gone beyond merely learning something new, but we have also been changed into completely different persons. Is this possible in and through interreligious dialogue? There are at least three levels of response.

First, it needs to be recognized that, sometimes, real conversion from one faith to another happens. This occurs, however, not only through the process of interreligious dialogue, but for many reasons. It would be inappropriate to reject interreligious dialogue simply because of the possibility of religious conversion. This means that veterans of the interreligious dialogue need to mentor others so that those who engage in interreligious dialogue can do so discerningly.

Second, rather than just exchanging one religious identity for another, there could also be conversion in some respect to another religious tradition without leaving one's home faith. This might result in what some have

---

[59] Francis X. Clooney has published a number of books that cross over into Vedantic and other Hindu religious texts, and then return to illuminate Christian theology and Bible reading. Another example of how Indian categories are reshaping the Christian view of Christ is M. Thomas Thangaraj, *The Crucified Guru: An Experiment in Cross-Cultural Christology* (Nashville, Tenn.: Abingdon, 1994).

[60] At the forefront here are people such as Lynn de Silva, Michael Von Brück, Perry Schmidt-Leukel, John P. Keenan, and others.

[61] Pertinent here is the work of Julia Ching, Robert C. Neville, and John Berthrong. See also Heup Young Kim, *Christ and the Tao* (Hong Kong: Christian Conference of Asia, 2003).

[62] As in the work of George E. Tinker, Envi Ben Udoh, A. Okechukwu Ogbonnaya, and John D'Arcy May.

[63] See David J. Bosch, "The Vulnerability of Mission," in *New Directions in Mission & Evangelization*, vol. 2: *Theological Foundations*, ed. James A. Scherer and Stephen B. Bevans (Maryknoll, N.Y.: Orbis Books, 1994), 73-86.

called dual or multiple religious identities.[64] This may or may not be syncretism understood in the sociological sense, but it assumes a syncretistic existential identity insofar as such a person grows increasingly comfortable in multiple religious domains and adept in multiple religious symbols, rites, and practices. Most often, however, people with dual or multiple religious identities retain a primary religious affiliation or commitment, and in the Christian case, this may still fit under the inclusivist banner. Much rarer are people who are *equally* at home in two or more religious traditions, in which case they may have shifted from an inclusivist to a pluralist position. We will return to further explore this point later.

But, third, it is also the case that any authentic interreligious encounter requires that we view the religious other as an equal rather than ourselves as superior. Hence, the confession that "it is almost impossible for me to enter into simple, honest, open, and friendly communication with another person as long as I have at the back of my mind the feeling that I am one of the saved and he is one of the lost."[65] If in fact we approach the religious other genuinely as an equal—that is, without an agenda that seeks only to "use" the other religion for Christian evangelistic purposes, without minimizing the significance of the religious differences, and without claiming to know in advance how the dialogue will turn out[66]—then we cannot dismiss the real possibility that we might indeed change our minds. Many have actually converted in the process, even those who began with a certain degree of religious maturity.

It is important to remember, however, that for an authentic meeting of different views, dialogue partners need to bring their own religious convictions. Precisely for this reason, most meaningful interreligious dialogues involve people who are sincerely committed to their own faith. For such persons, while it may be theoretically possible to change one's mind to the point of converting to another faith, in reality committed dialogue partners find their own views stretched but deepened even further precisely through the interreligious encounter.[67] When set within a Christian theological

---

[64] E.g., Catherine Cornille, ed., *Many Mansions? Multiple Religious Belonging and Christian Identity* (Maryknoll, N.Y.: Orbis Books, 2002); see also John H. Berthrong, *The Divine Deli: Religious Identity in the North American Cultural Mosaic* (Maryknoll, N.Y.: Orbis Books, 1999); and Jeannine Hill Fletcher, *Monopoly on Salvation? A Feminist Approach to Religious Pluralism* (New York and London: Continuum, 2005), esp. ch. 4, "We Are All Hybrids."

[65] Lesslie Newbigin, *The Open Secret: Sketches for a Missionary Theology* (Grand Rapids: Eerdmans, 1978), 196. Newbigin also goes on to say that to assume the other to be saved is also improper. Hence there has to be a real mutual openness to discovering the truth, whether of salvation or otherwise.

[66] For discussion, see Fredericks, *Buddhists and Christians*, 15-23.

[67] This is the response given to the question "openness to being converted ourselves?" by Terrance L. Tiessen, *Who Can Be Saved? Reassessing Salvation in Christ and World Religions* (Downers Grove, Ill.: InterVarsity, 2004), 456-57.

framework, such confidence arises not from out of ourselves but from our trusting that the God who has begun a good work in our lives "will bring it to completion by the day of Jesus Christ" (Phil 1:6).

ONE GOD, MANY RELIGIOUS ENDS: TRANSFORMING THE INTERRELIGIOUS ENCOUNTER

Up to now in this chapter I have refrained from identifying names of individual theologians in the body of the text, preferring instead to cite them in the notes as examples of those holding the positions I have been staking out. This is because many theologians of religions are not easily classifiable under either the exclusivist or inclusivist camps without significant qualification. In the rest of this chapter, however, I will focus on the work of four theologians—S. Mark Heim here, and John Hick, Raimon Panikkar, and Aloysius Pieris—although even for them we must apply the labels we use with care.

I turn here to the work of Heim because he wrote in his third book on theology of religions that he was "a convinced inclusivist."[68] Yet Heim's view actually emerged out of his criticism that the kinds of pluralistic theologies of religions we will discuss in the next part of this chapter are insufficiently pluralistic. By this, he means that the more "traditional" pluralistic theologies posit the various religious traditions as responses to the one God (or the Real or the ultimate) at different times and places. The problem with this is that pluralism remains at the level of religious phenomena (e.g., many paths up the side of the mountain) while at the level of religious ultimacy there is only the one final endpoint (e.g., one mountaintop).

Against this view, Heim has argued that the many religions actually envision different religious ends. Further, the various religious traditions have also developed practices commensurate with attaining those ends and not others. Hence, Buddhists meditate not to achieve communion with God in Christ but to escape the cycle of suffering (*dukkha*) and the never-ending circle of history (*samsara*), even as Christians strive for holiness not to experience Nirvana but to enjoy the beatific vision. So while Buddhist meditative practices nurture the devotee on the path toward the intended aims, so also Christian holiness practices shape the believer toward union with God. In other words, the many religions have many aims, many practices, and many ends. These are not equivalent with Christian salvation but they are real nonetheless.

Heim's question is whether or not he can make sense of this claim from

---

[68] S. Mark Heim, *The Depths of the Riches: A Trinitarian Theology of Religious Ends* (Grand Rapids, and Cambridge, U.K.: Eerdmans, 2001), 8. The previous two books were *Is Christ the Only Way? Christian Faith in a Pluralistic World* (Valley Forge, Pa.: Judson Press, 1985), and *Salvations: Truth and Difference in Religion* (Maryknoll, N.Y.: Orbis Books, 1995).

a Christian theological point of view. To do so, he explores the possibility of thinking about the multiplicity of religious ends in trinitarian terms. Just as the trinitarian persons retain the particularity of their identities only in relation to the others, so also the many religious ends retain their particularity only in relation to the triune God. More precisely, Heim suggests that while Christians understand eschatological salvation in terms of *interpersonal* and perichoretic communion with the triune God, the complexity of the divine Trinity also sustains other eschatological ends of the *impersonal* and the *transcendental* type that are commensurate with other sets of religious practices. In this framework, whereas Buddhist and Advaitic traditions emphasizing emptiness or Brahmanic nondualism might indeed aim for and achieve union with the impersonal dimension of the Trinity (which is common to all three persons), so also Islamic traditions that insist on divine transcendence might indeed aim for and achieve an iconic relationship with the transcendent dimension of the Trinity. Similarly, and by extension for Heim, there would be other religious traditions that aim for and achieve various levels of impersonal and iconic relationships with the triune God, but only Christians would experience full interpersonal communion with God through Christ by the Holy Spirit.[69] Heim suggests that there is precedent in the Christian theological tradition for such a vision of eschatological plenitude or diversity: in Dante's *Divine Comedy*, which posits a great diversity even within the three levels of hell, purgatory, and paradise.[70]

This is why Heim's is ultimately an inclusivist rather than pluralist view. Whereas postliberal theologies would attempt to "read the world in Christ,"[71] Heim has attempted to read the world of the religions according to the logic of the trinitarian God. In this way, we can grant the integrity and even validity of the many religions understood on their own terms, without sacrificing the trinitarian vision of God as revealed in Christ by the Holy Spirit.

What then are the interreligious practices nurtured and sustained by such a trinitarian, inclusivistic, and pluralistic theology of religious ends? Heim suggests three types of Christian practices commensurate with his theological view.[72] First, the study of other religions now belongs in the

---

[69] Heim writes, "Alternative religious ends define God essentially in terms of one dimension (other than communion) of the triune life. That is, they are rooted in authentic revelation *of* the triune God, but not revelation of God *as* triune" (*Depths of the Riches*, 275, italics in original).

[70] Note that Heim does allow for the possibility also of nonreligious ends—hells, to be blunt—which are the result of idolatry and stubborn self-indulgence resisting the being of God. In addition, there are also those who negate creation itself, whose end would be annihilation. There is indeed a dazzling array of ends in Heim's eschatological vision.

[71] Francis X. Clooney, "Reading the World in Christ: From Comparison to Inclusivism," in *Christian Uniqueness Reconsidered: The Myth of a Pluralistic Theology*, ed. Gavin D'Costa (Maryknoll, N.Y.: Orbis Books, 1990), 63-80.

[72] See Heim, *Depths of the Riches*, 291-94.

theological curriculum itself. Christians can recognize other faiths as meaningfully related to God in some respect, and theological education will be enriched with and through the perspectives afforded by learning about them. Second, Christians can earnestly honor the claims of people in other faiths, respect their views, and engage in a dialogue of genuine difference. While in one respect we are talking about the same God, there is an infinite complexity to this God that we can grow in knowledge of through the interreligious encounter of differences. Last but not least, the Christian mission can be revitalized on a more adequate footing in terms of emphasizing dialogue and proclamation, social witness and evangelism. In each of these ways and more, I suggest that Heim's trinitarian theology of religious ends is a massive illocutionary act that invites Christians to commit themselves, on the basis of their own trinitarian faith, to engage with religious differences in general and with people in other faiths more particularly.

Heim's proposals, however, have drawn criticism from both sides. Exclusivists do not think his view is biblically sustainable, and Protestant exclusivists doubt his appeal to Dante is as viable as he thinks. On the other side, however, pluralists are unconvinced that Heim's inclusivism can genuinely honor the claims of people in other faiths and respect their views because Heim has already located the beliefs and practices of other faiths at various "places" in his eschatological cartograph. So can Heim's theology of religions nurture the kind of mutual transformation I have ascribed to the inclusivist posture after all?

PLURALISTIC THEOLOGIES OF RELIGIONS: WHAT PRACTICES?

In contrast to exclusivism and inclusivism which have long had advocates in the history of the Christian tradition, pluralism is a relatively late newcomer on the theology of religions block, having emerged more or less during the last generation. It is in fact difficult to define this idea—theology of religious pluralism communicates one thing; pluralistic theology of religions communicates another; and so on—even as it has generated an enormous response that may have put forth more heat than light. Some have defined it according to a theocentric model that includes many (religious) ways or approaches toward an indefinable or ineffable center.[73] This will be at least our starting point as we engage here the ideas of John Hick before moving on to discuss in order the work of Raimon Panikkar and Aloysius Pieris. Be warned that we will not attempt any comprehensive review of these thinkers, as their work is complex, multifaceted, and many stranded. Rather, continuing with our hermeneutic of charity, we will, as in

---

[73] Paul F. Knitter, *No Other Name? A Critical Survey of Christian Attitudes toward the World Religions* (Maryknoll, N.Y.: Orbis Books, 1985), ch. 8.

the previous two sections, ask throughout what kinds of postures, attitudes, sensibilities, and practices are fostered by and nurtured through their theological views regarding the diversity of religions.

JOHN HICK AND THE COPERNICAN REVOLUTION: PRACTICES IN A PLURALISTIC WORLD

John Hick will probably be recognized as one of the most important philosophers of religion in the twentieth century. He experienced a powerful evangelical conversion during his college years, but later moved steadily away from that point of view as he wrestled with philosophical questions related to Christian faith, on the one hand, and with religious questions related to the multifaith context of Birmingham, where he lived and worked, on the other.[74] Over the course of time, Hick came to argue for what he called a "Copernican Revolution" in theology and philosophy of religion—namely, the idea that just as humanity came at one point to understand that the earth was not the center of the cosmos but that the earth and the other planets revolved around the sun, so also should people of faith come to see that their own religion is not the only or primarily true one but that each religious tradition is true in its own way insofar as it is a result of different conceptions, perceptions, and responses to the ineffable and transcendent ultimate reality (what Hick calls the Real).[75] Hick's proposal has generated an enormous response, many from critics. Our goal here is less to engage the debate than to understand what practices are implicated in this idea. I will identify and discuss three interrelated sets of practices.[76]

First, I suggest Hick's proposal emerges out of and is intended to sustain human inquiry. Hick argues that there are important senses in which the world as we experience it is religiously ambiguous. By this he means that a naturalistic interpretation of the universe is just as rationally compelling as a religious one.[77] Hick himself opts for the right to believe, following

---

[74] See John Hick, *An Autobiography* (Oxford: Oneworld, 2002); cf. Chris Hewer, "The Multireligious Multicultural Society: A Case Study of Birmingham, England," in *Theology and the Religions: A Dialogue,* ed. Viggo Mortensen (Grand Rapids, and Cambridge, U.K.: Eerdmans, 2003), 67-71.

[75] Hick first articulated this idea in his *God and the Universe of Faiths: Essays in the Philosophy of Religion* (London: Macmillan, 1973), esp. ch. 9. His most mature statement is his 1986-87 Gifford Lectures, later published as *An Interpretation of Religion* (New Haven, Conn., and London: Yale University Press, 1989).

[76] I will not identify these as specifically *Christian* practices since Hick says of his own personal faith that it is "of a more universal than exclusively Christian kind" (*An Autobiography,* 323). I will suggest later, however, that many of these practices are consistent with specifically Christian beliefs.

[77] Hick, *An Interpretation of Religion,* part 2. Terence Penelhum, "Reflections on the Ambiguity of the World," in *God, Truth and Reality: Essays in Honour of John Hick,* ed. Arvind Sharma (New York: St. Martin's Press, 1993), 165-75, argues further that on Hick's

William James,[78] even while being very careful to insist that such faith should be neither irrational nor blind, but should be vulnerable to correction. Then, in presenting his Copernican Revolution as a pluralistic "hypothesis," Hick further accentuates the speculative, and thereby revisable, character of his ideas. In an increasingly shrinking world, the point is that human beings should be open to learn about their religious neighbors, to understand the very many different beliefs and practices, to interact with others in a respectful yet inquiring manner, and to be willing to change their minds. In short, I understand Hick's epistemological position to invite and even foster human inquiry in the face of the staggering diversity of religious and nonreligious options in the world today.

But how does Hick's Copernican Revolution avoid epistemic and, worse, moral relativism? This leads, second, to his soteriological-ethical criteria.[79] Hick proposes a way to grade the religions according to two sets of norms. Soteriologically, do the religions promote saintliness and foster spiritual and politico-economic liberation? Then ethically, do the religions promote goodwill, love, and compassion? Hick observes that in the world religious traditions, there is at least a form of the Golden Rule—either in its positive form of "do unto others what you would want done to you," or in its negative form of "do not do to others what you do not wish done to you"—that serves as a basic moral criterion. I suggest these soteriological and ethical criteria combine to function normatively for Hick to judge human behavior in general and religious behavior in particular. In this way, the pluralistic hypothesis is intimately connected with moral-ethical criteria so that beliefs about the diversity of religions endorse only certain kinds of practices that can be said to be salvific. In short, religious truth is to be finally judged, at least on this side of the eschaton, according to its fruits.

This leads, third, to the suggestion that Hick's pluralistic hypothesis is designed to enable the practices of what might be called global citizenship. Here the emphasis is not only on fostering inquiry and promoting moral character but, building on these, on nurturing the attitudes, sensibilities, and skills appropriate to global participation amidst a plurality of nations, cultures, and religions. If exclusivism seems parochial (how can so many others be completely wrong?) and inclusivism seems imperialistic (what right do we have to define the beliefs and practices of others in our own terms?), then is not the pluralistic hypothesis the only reasonable explanation for the universe of faiths? Hick's Copernican Revolution is thereby intended to promote a global consciousness, one that is able to account for

---

account, religious ambiguity pertains not only to the possibility of a naturalistic interpretation of the world, but also to the impossibility of deciding which of the world's many religions is more or less truthful than others.

[78] Hick, *An Interpretation of Religion*, ch. 13 §6.

[79] Hick, *An Interpretation of Religion*, chs. 17-18.

the diversity of religions and avoid moral relativism, on the one hand, but also lapse neither into a radical incommensurability of religious language games (recalling Wittgenstein and Lindbeck) nor into an intolerant contestation of religious competition (remembering Nigeria and Sri Lanka), on the other.[80] The pluralistic hypothesis allows people to approach religious others in a way that respects their differences but is yet at the same time open to learning further about other beliefs and practices, and exploring if and how these are dissimilar from or perhaps more finally comparable to their own. More specifically, the conviction that people of other faiths may be responding in their own way to the lures of that which is ultimately transcendent opens up a common public space in and through which religiously diverse groups of people can work together for the common and global good. In short, Hick's theology of religious pluralism can be understood to advance the kinds of values and practices conducive to life in an increasingly shrinking global village.

It might be questioned whether or not Hick's Copernican Revolution is convincing. At the speculative and philosophical level, some of the most repeated criticisms of Hick's proposal are that it is not pluralistic enough or that it either assumes a modernist (Enlightenment) rationality or even a covert (Christian) monotheism.[81] At the theological level, there are certainly questions about the heterodoxy, if not outright heresy, of Hick's christology when measured according to the classical Nicene and Chalcedonian creeds.[82] I believe that we can accept the various practices related to Hick's pluralism—the need to foster inquiry, the emphasis on the moral and ethical fruits of religious traditions, and those essential for global citizenship—without embracing the theological and philosophical details of his pluralistic theory of religions. At the same time, if practices are related

---

[80] For many, the unattractiveness of the alternatives makes Hick's proposal, or something very much like it, the only live intellectual option; see, e.g., Wilfred Cantwell Smith, *Toward a World Theology: Faith and the Comparative History of Religion* (Philadelphia: Westminster, 1981); Leonard J. Swidler, ed., *Toward a Universal Theory of Religion* (Maryknoll, N.Y.: Orbis Books, 1987); John Hick and Paul F. Knitter, eds., *The Myth of Christian Uniqueness: Towards a Pluralistic Theology of Religions* (Maryknoll, N.Y.: Orbis Books, 1987); Leonard J. Swidler, *After the Absolute: The Dialogical Future of Religious Reflection* (Minneapolis: Fortress, 1990); and Ninian Smart and Steven Constantine, *Christian Systematic Theology in a World Context* (London: Marshall Pickering, 1991).

[81] See, e.g., Christopher Sinkinson, *The Universe of Faiths: A Critical Study of John Hick's Religious Pluralism* (Carlisle, U.K., and Waynesboro, Ga.: Paternoster, 2001); Paul Rhodes Eddy, *John Hick's Pluralist Philosophy of World Religions* (Burlington, Vt., and Aldershot, U.K.: Ashgate, 2002); and others. Hick responds to these and other criticisms in the "Introduction to the Second Edition" of his *An Interpretation of Religion: Human Responses to the Transcendent*, 2nd ed. (New Haven and London: Yale University Press, 2004), xvii-xlii.

[82] These are articulated in detail by Gavin D'Costa, *John Hick's Theology of Religions: A Critical Evaluation* (Lanham, Md.: University Press of America, 1987); and Gregory H. Carruthers, *The Uniqueness of Jesus Christ in the Theocentric Model of the Christian Theology of World Religions: An Elaboration and Evaluation of the Position of John Hick* (Lanham, Md.: University Press of America, 1990), among others.

to beliefs and vice versa, then the affirmation of a set of practices for a pluralistic world requires also a correlative theological vision. Here, it is worthwhile recalling David Cheetham's closing words to his study of Hick: "his work represents the most systematic and thorough attempt at constructing a harmonious pluralistic model in Western thought. In light of this, perhaps the challenge for Hick's future critics is not to find more ingenious ways of demolishing his proposals, rather it is to construct hypotheses of equal caliber."[83] In one sense the entirety of this present book can be read as one response to Cheetham's invitation.

RAIMON PANIKKAR AND RELIGIOUS HYBRIDITY: TRANSFORMING "SYNCRETISM"

Raimon Panikkar was born to a Spanish Roman Catholic mother and an Indian Hindu father. He was raised as a strict Roman Catholic, educated by the Jesuits, and then later ordained as a Roman Catholic priest in 1946, and his life journey took him throughout Europe, India, and America.[84] He achieved three doctorates, in philosophy (1946), and science (1958), both at the University of Madrid, and then in theology (1961) at the Pontifical Lateran University in Rome. It was during and then long after his theological studies that he immersed himself in Hindu and Buddhist ways of life, without ever renouncing his Christian faith.[85] Rather than try to unravel the complexity of Panikkar as one who might be called a "hybridized" religious thinker, I want to discuss, each in turn, the mystical, philosophical, and theological practices evidenced in his life.

At one level, Panikkar cannot be understood as other than a contemplative mystic. Among his earliest major books were three that focused on Christian, Buddhist, and Hindu traditions respectively, each on its own terms, while also attempting to discern how they related to one another in a pluralistic world.[86] Read according to the logic of noncontradiction,

---

[83] David Cheetham, *John Hick: A Critical Introduction and Reflection* (Burlington, Vt., and Aldershot, U.K.: Ashgate, 2003), 169.

[84] For an overview of Panikkar's life, see Joseph Prabhu, "Lost in Translation: Panikkar's Intercultural Odyssey," in *The Intercultural Challenge of Raimon Panikkar,* ed. Joseph Prabhu (Maryknoll, N.Y.: Orbis Books, 1996), 1-21.

[85] In his late seventies, Panikkar reaffirmed his Christian, Hindu, Buddhist, and secular identities; see Raimon Panikkar, "A Self-Critical Dialogue," in *The Intercultural Challenge of Raimon Panikkar,* ed. Joseph Prabhu, 227-91, esp. 262-66 (see n. 84). In another even later essay, he suggests that the questions Who is a Christian? and What is a Christian? can be answered only pluralistically: there are many answers and many different levels—e.g., at least ontologically, historically, sociologically, and ecclesiologically—and they all boil down finally to actual persons making confessions in actual communities; see Panikkar, "On Christian Identity: Who Is a Christian?" in *Many Mansions? Multiple Religious Belonging and Christian Identity,* ed. Catherine Cornille (Maryknoll, N.Y.: Orbis Books, 2002), 127-47, esp. 133-40.

[86] Panikkar's *The Unknown Christ of Hinduism* (London: Darton, Longman, & Todd, 1964) was revised as *The Unknown Christ of Hinduism: Towards an Ecumenical Christo-*

these works reflect a divided mind, with allegiances spreading out in three incompatible directions. However, read sympathetically, they reveal the profound stirrings of an existential conversation percolating deep within the soul of a cosmopolitan mystic. While not exclusive of *interreligious* interactions *between* people of various faiths, for Panikkar the *intrareligious* dialogue is more fundamental because it takes place *within* individual human hearts and lives.[87] At this level, Panikkar is best understood not as a theologian or even philosopher but as a monk, the archetypal expression of what it means to be fully human.[88] Monkhood, or full humanness, thus represents the following experiences: (1) of the breakthrough of immanence into transcendence; (2) of the primacy of being over doing or having; (3) of the primordiality of silence over speech; (4) of the womb of Mother Earth producing human fellowship; (5) of the overcoming of spatiotemporal parameters; (6) of transhistorical consciousness over historical concerns; (7) of the fullness and dynamism of persons over their individuality; (8) of the holy or the sacred in and through phenomena; and (9) of memory or recollection of the ultimate. These are features less of discursive reason than they are of Panikkar as a contemplative mystic. As monk, Panikkar does not merely hold beliefs about religious plurality but embodies in his habits, piety, and practices a religiously pluralistic way of life.

Yet, of course, Panikkar is not only a mystic, but he is also a philosopher, a lover of wisdom. But what are the central tenets of Panikkar's philosophy? Perhaps these are best summarized in his "cosmotheandric" notion. As implied by this neologism, there is a perichoretic unity between the world (*cosmos*), the divine (*theos*), and humankind (*anthropos*).[89] Hence nature, religion, and culture are bound up indissolubly even while they remain irreducible dimensions or aspect of any reality. Two points need to be emphasized from this. First, the irreducibility of these domains cannot be underestimated. This leads Panikkar to affirm not only an epis-

---

phany (Maryknoll, N.Y.: Orbis Books, 1981). Whereas the first edition was more orthodox in suggesting that the Christ of Christianity was known in Hinduism albeit in a different form, the later edition included the more radical suggestion that the Christ of Hinduism was much more expansive than imaginable by Christianity. Panikkar's *El Silencio de Dios* (Madrid: Guadiana, 1970), translated as *The Silence of God: The Answer of the Buddha*, trans. Robert R. Barr (Maryknoll, N.Y.: Orbis Books, 1989), wrestled with scientism, secularism, and atheism in dialogue with Buddhism. Then Panikkar's *The Vedic Experience* (Berkeley: University of California Press, 1977) documented his immersion into the Vedic scriptures and how they continue to speak to the globalizing world of late modernity by inviting readers to experience the world differently.

[87] Raimundo Panikkar, *The Intrareligious Dialogue* (New York: Paulist Press, 1978).

[88] Raimundo Panikkar, *Blessed Simplicity: The Monk as Universal Archetype* (New York: Seabury, 1982), 14. For more on Panikkar the contemplative mystic, see his *Invisible Harmony: Essays on Contemplation and Responsibility*, ed. Harry James Cargas (Minneapolis: Fortress, 1995).

[89] Raimon Panikkar, *The Cosmotheandric Experience: Emerging Religious Consciousness*, ed. Scott Eastham (Maryknoll, N.Y.: Orbis Books, 1993).

temological pluralism but also a pluralistic ontology and theory of truth. Any universal theory is undermined from the start and any -ology is perspectivally limited by definition.[90] But second, this radical pluralism at the level of logic (*logos*) nevertheless holds together at the level of wisdom (*sophia*). So the love of wisdom opens up to a "cosmotheandric spirituality" wherein human beings are irreducibly material, spiritual, and psychic creatures perpetually in a quest for self- and communal-understanding in a God-infused world.[91] If Hick's pluralistic hypothesis is read as an invitation toward responsible global citizenship, Panikkar's cosmotheandrism is an invitation to include human relations with and responsibility for the environment in the exercise of such citizenship, given that the earth is the womb that nurtures human culture and religiosity. For Panikkar, then, philosophy is not only a set of discursive practices but a paradoxical way of life that blends naturalism, humanism, and religion without erasing their distinctiveness.

Hence, Panikkar's cosmotheandrism means he is mystic, philosopher, *and* theologian. Arguably, Panikkar is the "God-intoxicated" philosopher of late modernity since the divine is both within and beyond the world, both incarnate and transcendent to humankind, both behind and ahead of time and history. But Panikkar is less a speculative theologian than mystical theologian: theology is but reflection on the human experience of the divine in and through the icons of creaturely, cosmic, and cultural existence.[92] It is at this level of Panikkar as a mystical theologian that the influence of the Upanishadic doctrine of nondualism shows itself most clearly. In this view, reality is considered neither in monistic nor dualistic or pluralistic terms, but rather is affirmed as *nondual*, manifest to those who are able to see. Panikkar suggests that such is also the affirmation regarding the incarnation or the Eucharist: neither merely human nor merely divine, but nondually manifest to those with the eyes of faith;[93] or with the Trinity: neither merely one nor merely three, but dynamic perichoresis of mutual subsistence; or with the God-world relationship: neither pantheism nor classic theism (emphasizing divine transcendence) but a nondual relationality.

---

[90] See Panikkar, "The Invisible Harmony: A Universal Theory of Religion or a Cosmic Confidence in Reality?" in *Towards a Universal Theology of Religion*, ed. Leonard Swidler (Maryknoll, N.Y.: Orbis Books, 1987), 118-53, esp. 124-35; and idem, "The Jordan, the Tiber, and the Ganges: Three Kairological Moments of Christic Self-Consciousness," in *The Myth of Christian Uniqueness: Towards a Pluralistic Theology of Religions,* ed. John Hick and Paul F. Knitter (1987; reprint, Maryknoll, N.Y.: Orbis Books, 1994), 89-116, esp. 109-11.

[91] Panikkar spells out his pluralistic anthropology in his *A Dwelling Place for Wisdom*, trans. Annamarie S. Kidder (Louisville, Ky.: Westminster John Knox Press, 1993), ch. 2.

[92] Raimon Panikkar, *The Experience of God: Icons of Mystery*, trans. Joseph Cunneen (Minneapolis: Fortress, 2006).

[93] For Panikkar's mature reflections on Christ and what he calls the "christic experience," see his *Christophany: The Fullness of Man*, trans. Alfred DiLascia (Maryknoll, N.Y.: Orbis Books, 2004).

Even so, if at the level of *logos* the world's religions are radically incommensurable, at the level of *mythos* they are neither all the same nor unrelated but icons, each in its own way, of the cosmotheandric harmony.

I suggest that the Panikkarian *oeuvre* can be read as an invitation to a multiplicity of contemplative practices. Panikkar himself has been deeply shaped by the contemplative traditions of Christianity, Buddhism, and Hinduism. His own life is a living hybridization of these three wisdom traditions coming together, and he speaks and writes as one who has been shaped and formed by religious plurality. Whereas syncretism as a cultural and even religious fad often results either in a careless aggregation of doctrines and ideas unrelated to practices or a naïve syncretism of practices devoid of beliefs, Panikkar's cosmotheandrism is a much deeper blend of diverse religious practices, sensibilities, and commitments. This kind of hybridized or multiple religious identity will no doubt become more prevalent in our increasingly shrinking global village. While it is undeniable that all religious traditions are syncretistic in terms of drawing from other traditions in some respect, the question Panikkar poses for Christians today is whether or not there can be a theologically responsible syncretism that nevertheless remains faithful to the gospel of Jesus Christ.[94]

It is precisely with regard to christology that the most important questions for Panikkar's project emerge vis-à-vis the Christian theological tradition. While he retains traditional Christian theological language such as Christ and Trinity, Panikkar's christology and trinitarianism seem to be defined more by Buddhist and Hindu nondualism than by classical Christian categories and commitments. Dislodged from the historicity of Christian faith, then, Panikkar's cosmotheandrism retains the form of Christian orthodoxy but not its substance. While we can appreciate his distinction between *logos* and *mythos*, it seems that the connections between these two domains are closer than Panikkar thinks, especially since the content of myths cannot be communicated except through propositions. And although it remains true that Panikkar's ideas are difficult to criticize since very few individuals have the breadth and depth of experience in multiple religious traditions to engage him, it nevertheless appears that he is ultimately caught on the horns of a dilemma: either he affirms a unity and universality of truth, which can be accomplished only on the basis of a particular theological or philosophical notion—in his case, that of Buddhistic or Advaitic nonduality—or he insists on an ultimate pluralism of religious beliefs and practices, which would then undermine the thrust of his universalistic cosmotheandric spirituality.[95]

---

[94] I take the phrase "theologically responsible syncretism" from Walter J. Hollenweger, *Pentecostalism: Origins and Developments Worldwide* (Peabody, Mass.: Hendrickson, 1997), ch. 11. We will return to discuss this question of syncretism in our final chapter.

[95] Veli-Matti Kärkkäinen, *The Trinity and Religious Pluralism: The Doctrine of the Trinity in Christian Theology of Religions* (Burlington, Vt., and Aldershot, U.K.: Ashgate, 2004),

Even if much more can and should be said about Panikkar both in terms of explication and in terms of critical assessment, our task is to understand the correlation between beliefs and practices in Panikkar's cosmotheandrism. At this level, I propose that we can adopt to a certain extent the various practices that inform Panikkar's vision without adopting the more controversial theological ideas. In particular, I think that a Panikkarian spirituality that embodies *philo-sophia*, the love of wisdom, and embraces the unity of humanity and nature (or the environment) reflects an important posture for life in the global village of the twenty-first century. To some degree, Panikkar the mystic-monk also represents a holistic way of being in the world that can inform a socially and environmentally engaged mode of human religiousness. But I am also convinced that such practices related to global citizenship in our time can be authentically grounded in Christian faith and yet remain open to others, without embracing the details of Raimundo Panikkar's cosmotheandric proposals. We will return to this issue later (see below, pp. 143-46).

ALOYSIUS PIERIS, S.J., AND ECO-SOCIAL-JUSTICE: PERFORMING LIBERATION THEOLOGY OF RELIGIONS

Like Panikkar, Aloysius Pieris, S.J., has also been shaped by multiple religious traditions. After taking vows as a Jesuit (1953), Pieris completed a Licentiate in Sacred Theology at the Pontifical Theological Faculty in Naples (1966). This was followed by a course on Buddhist meditation while pursuing a doctorate in Buddhist studies and philosophy at the University of Sri Lanka (1971), the first non-Buddhist to be awarded such a degree.[96] Over the past thirty years, he has lived and worked in Sri Lanka, founding the Tulana Research Center in Kelaniya and engaging in scholarly research and interfaith ecumenical work as a Roman Catholic priest alongside other Christians and Buddhists, even during the civil war years.[97]

Unlike Panikkar, however, I suggest that Pieris is less a contemplative and mystic (even if he is an adept both of the Ignatian Exercises and Bud-

---

128-33, and Vinoth Ramachandra, *The Recovery of Mission: Beyond the Pluralist Paradigm* (Grand Rapids: Eerdmans, 1996), ch. 3, both ask some hard questions of Panikkar from evangelical points of view; an excellent book-length critical analysis is Jyri Komulainen, *An Emerging Cosmotheandric Religion? Raimon Panikkar's Pluralistic Theology of Religions*, Studies in Christian Mission 30 (Leiden and Boston: Brill, 2005).

[96] For autobiographical notes, see Aloysius Pieris, S.J., with Georg Evers, "A Self-Portrait," in *Encounters with the Word: Essays to Honour Aloysius Pieris S.J. on His 70th Birthday 9th April 2004*, ed. Robert Crusz, Marshal Fernando, and Asanga Tilakaratne (Colombo: Ecumenical Institute for Study and Dialogue, 2004), 643-70.

[97] Pieris is only now beginning to publish in book form his ongoing philosophical, philological, text-critical, linguistic, and exegetical studies in the Pali canon, some of which date from his student days at the University of Sri Lanka. For the first of a multivolume work, see Aloysius Pieris, S.J., *Studies in the Philosophy and Literature of Pāli Ābhidhammika Buddhism* (Colombo: Ecumenical Institute for Study and Dialogue, 2004).

dhist *vipassana,* or mindfulness meditation[98]) than he is a social reformer and an advocate for the poor. For Pieris, the twin realities of the Asian context are poverty and religiousness. In the conflict-ridden situation of Sri Lanka, the Christian mission must engage the issues of poverty in dialogue and solidarity with those in other faiths. Christians missionize by embodying the life of Jesus in solidarity with the poor and by proclaiming his covenant against the principalities and powers of mammon, which are oppressive and destructive of human life and community.[99]

This theme of social liberation is articulated variously in Pieris's writings. To begin, the church cannot only speak of and preach about the Son of God in non-Christian Asian cultures; rather, going beyond the fulfillment and contextual approaches, the church is called to retrieve the Jesus of the poor in the New Testament so as to embody in the contemporary Asian church the living Christ and the covenant of God with the poor. Pieris argues that "in an Asian [or Buddhist] situation, the antonym of 'wealth' is not 'poverty' but acquisitiveness or avarice, which makes wealth antireligious. The primary concern … is not eradication of poverty, but struggle against mammon—that undefinable force that organizes itself within every person and among persons to make material wealth antihuman, antireligious, and oppressive."[100] Further, if poverty is no respecter of persons (and it isn't), and if "only the oppressed know and speak the language of liberation, the language of the Spirit, the language of true religion,"[101] then the experiences of the masses need to be not only consulted but also entered into. The truth of the gospel must be expressed in concrete spiritual and social emancipation, even as the authority of the gospel must finally be grounded and demonstrated in orthopraxis. Hence, Pieris is critical of the "Christ-against-religions" model of colonialism, neocolonialism, and crypto-colonial-Marxism which either perpetuates poverty (in the first two cases) or ignores religion (in the last case). He also rejects the "Christ-of-religions" model because it ignores the links between religion and material poverty (the gnostic tendency), between religion and structural poverty (the ashramic Christ), and between religion and liberation (the a-historical Christ). Rather, Pieris presents a Third World and Asian theology of reli-

---

[98] See Aloysius Pieris, S.J., *Fire and Water: Basic Issues in Asian Buddhism and Christianity* (Maryknoll, N.Y.: Orbis Books, 1996), ch. 17: "Ignatian Exercises against a Buddhist Background."

[99] Aloysius Pieris, S.J., *God's Reign for God's Poor: A Return to the Jesus Formula,* 2nd rev. ed. (Kelaniya, Sri Lanka: Tulana Research Centre; and Mt. Lavinia, Sri Lanka: Logos Printing, 2000); cf. Aloysius Pieris, S.J., "Political Theologies in Asia," in *The Blackwell Companion to Political Theology,* ed. Peter Scott and William T. Cavanaugh (Malden, Mass., and Oxford: Blackwell, 2004), 256-70.

[100] Aloysius Pieris, S.J., *An Asian Theology of Liberation* (Maryknoll, N.Y.: Orbis Books, 1988), 75.

[101] Aloysius Pieris, S.J., "Faith-Communities and Communal Violence: The Role of Religion and Ideology," *Dialogue,* n.s. 29 (2002): 111-31, quotation from p. 129.

gions as a theology of liberation that emphasizes a liberative and revolutionary Christ opposed to any religious system that has been coopted by the powers of mammon.

But from this, an Asian Christian theology of liberation must be informed not only by the experiences of poverty but also by the deep structures of Asian religiosity.[102] The inculturation of the gospel in Asia must also be an "enreligionization," a baptism into the mentality of Asian religious experiences. Hence, Pieris argues that the battle against poverty cannot but be an interreligious endeavor. In the Sri Lankan context, Christians must work together with Buddhists to address the challenges of war, corruption, and poverty. Christians can and must learn from the spirituality of Buddhist monks and from Buddhist monastic practices, especially those that challenge the vices of greed and lust for wealth through the embrace of voluntary, rather than forced, poverty. On the other side of the interreligious encounter, Jesus' renunciation to be poor and to be with the poor as well as his denunciation of mammon complement rather than compete against the life and teachings of the Buddha.[103] In this way, Asian religiousness engages with Asian poverty even as Asian poverty informs Asian religious beliefs and practices.

But Asian interreligious engagement and praxis liberate not only the poor in general but also women in particular.[104] Incorporating the insights of feminism into a liberation theology of religions, Pieris argues that feminism lifts up the holistic, agapeic, and sacramental or bodily aspects of religiousness and the struggle for full humanity, over and against the dualistic, gnostic, and (merely) spiritualistic emphases of patriarchal religiosity. The feminist critique, therefore, needs to be constantly appropriated in the development of a liberative interreligious theology, especially when it confronts religious traditions that have perennially abused or subordinated women. Throughout this discussion, Pieris works meticulously to draw out the ways in which Buddhism and feminism are complementary even as he points out areas where their concerns are very different.

As Pieris has drunk deeply from the Buddhist and Christian wells, his liberation theology draws almost subliminally from the ideas, practices, spiritualities, and canonical texts of both traditions. It is this commitment to a dual religious citizenship as well as his religious vows that allows him to speak with such authority of a Buddhist-Christian theology of liberation.

---

[102] This is the argument of Pieris in his *Love Meets Wisdom: A Christian Experience of Buddhism* (Maryknoll, N.Y.: Orbis Books, 1988).

[103] Hence, Pieris has long understood the Buddha and Jesus Christ as mediators of salvation understood as social liberation; see his "The Buddha and the Christ: Mediators of Liberation," in *The Myth of Christian Uniqueness*, ed. John Hick and Paul F. Knitter, 162-77 (see n. 90).

[104] The theme of the six chapters in part 1 of *Fire and Water* is titled "Women and Religion: Buddhist and Christian Appropriation of Feminist Criticism."

He is careful, however, to insist that rather than being syncretistic or synthetic, his blending of the two is *symbiotic*, by which he means that the identities of the two religious traditions are retained rather than dissolved or merged.

With regard to critical questions regarding Pieris's project, the more effective ones will be informed by prolonged and sustained engagement with poverty and interreligiosity of the kind Pieris has undertaken.[105] Yet the following critical questions still need to be posed. First, one wonders if *only* the oppressed or the poor know the language of the Spirit, as Pieris has suggested. I would prefer to say that the poor and the oppressed have essential perspectives without which Christian theological reflection would be impoverished (pun intended!). To the extent that Pieris adopts what might be called an "exclusivism of the poor," to that same degree his proposals are just as one-sided as those of which he is critical. Second, a closer reading of Pieris's theology of liberation suggests that its central features are informed more by Marxist categories than by the biblical and theological traditions; rather, the latter have been fit, in many cases not too easily, into the Procrustean bed of the former.[106] And last but not least, while there are important elements regarding the contextualization of the gospel inherent in Pieris's proposal regarding "enreligionization," is it possible for Christianity to be baptized into Buddhism, Hinduism, or other religious tradition without conceding its fundamental features, or for there to be a *symbiosis* of multiple religious traditions that is not also syncretistic? To what degree is the notion of a dual religious citizenship that does not compromise Christian faith viable? Is the only other alternative an imperialistic baptism of other faiths into the Christian framework, as Pieris's proposals would lead us to think? What about a *via media* through which there is the mutual transformation of religious traditions in ways that produce instead a deepening of each tradition without abandonment of that tradition's distinguishing characteristics?

I suggest that such a third way may indeed be present if we focused at the level of the practices emanating from Pieris's project rather than the ideas propounded in his pluralistic theology of religions. With Pieris we see theology of religions dovetailing with theology of liberation such that the interreligious engagement that emerges is focused on practices conducive to social reform and liberation. In the impoverished and multireligious context of Sri Lanka, a Christian theology of religions that is not socially lib-

---

[105] Hence, Stanley Hauerwas acknowledged not writing about the poor because it is difficult "to imagine what it would mean for us ... to be poor"; cited in Stephen C. Barton, "New Testament Interpretation as Performance," *Scottish Journal of Theology* 52, no. 2 (1999): 179-208, from p. 203.

[106] As argued by both Kenneth Fleming, *Asian Christian Theologians in Dialogue with Buddhism* (Frankfurt: Peter Lang, 2002), 279-81 and 323-24, and Vinoth Ramachandra, *The Recovery of Mission*, 49-69.

erative betrays the fundamental impulse of the gospel. This is the challenge to which Pieris's liberation theology of religions is responding,[107] and this is what any theology of religions will need to foster and motivate. The question is whether or not we can embrace some of the core practices manifest in Pieris's life without adopting the more questionable aspects of his theological proposals.

We are unable, in the scope of one brief chapter, to do justice to any of the four theologians—Heim, Hick, Panikkar, and Pieris—much less to the three types of theologies of religions we have discussed. Instead, our focus has been on describing, as sympathetically as possible, what kinds of practices are interrelated with these theological positions. We have seen how advocates of exclusivism, inclusivism, and pluralism have been shaped and formed out of different social, political, and theological contexts even as they have then gone on to promote a wider range of practices that are in principle not limited to those original contexts. Further, it is also clear that each has a "missionary" dimension that sustains different kinds of interreligious practices as well as a "dialogical" dimension that advances different forms of interreligious interactions. Clearly, as forms of interreligious practices, exclusivism, inclusivism, and pluralism make sense together, albeit they are manifest most effectively in different times and places, especially in the complex post-9/11 world of many faiths. Yet, theologically and theoretically, these various theologies of religions may be logically incompatible: it is difficult to see how all three can be true in the same respects at the same time. I suggest that what we need is a theology of religions that can redeem the many interreligious practices while being critically accepting of theological claims across the three dominant positions. The last two chapters of this book will present one possible form of such a theological vision, one shaped by a pneumatological theology of hospitality.

---

[107] I should mention that in the Western context, this is also the emphasis of Paul Knitter's theology of religions; see, e.g., Knitter's *One Earth Many Religions: Multifaith Dialogue and Global Responsibility* (Maryknoll, N.Y.: Orbis Books, 1995), and idem, *Jesus and the Other Names: Christian Mission and Global Responsibility* (Maryknoll, N.Y.: Orbis Books, 1996).

4

Performing Hospitality

Toward a Pneumatological Theology of Interreligious Engagement

So far in this book we have discussed the complexity of interreligious relations in our early twenty-first-century context (chapter 1); clarified the interconnectedness between Christian beliefs and practices and articulated a pneumatological theology of interreligious practices (chapter 2); and correlated the basic Christian theologies about other religions—exclusivism, inclusivism, and pluralism—with their related practices vis-à-vis people in other faiths (chapter 3). We have discovered that while there may be a wide range of valid, viable, and even essential practices that many if not most Christians would agree need to be cultivated and nurtured in our time, these same Christians would probably not agree about the theological positions that underwrite these practices. In these last two chapters, I will sketch a Christian theology of interreligious praxis that might provide a common platform to sustain the *theological* conversation among Christians across the exclusivist-inclusivist-pluralist spectrum of practices.

This approach of systematically linking Christian theology of religions to Christian interreligious practices is relatively new. Working from within the postliberal tradition, George Sumner has recently suggested that the kind of ad hoc apologetic engagement with other faiths prominent in Lindbeck's cultural-linguistic model (see above, pp. 50-54) invites three sets of Christian practices: proclamation, theological retrospection, and neighborliness.[1] Expanding and extending Sumner's proposal, I want to insist on a more robust and systematic, rather than merely ad hoc, approach to the interreligious encounter today. To do so, I will develop what I call a pneumatological theology of interreligious praxis in two steps: in this chapter

---

[1] George R. Sumner, *The First & the Last: The Claim of Jesus Christ & the Claims of Other Religious Traditions* (Grand Rapids: Eerdmans, 2004), esp. 53-60.

focusing on a pneumatological theology of hospitality, and then in our concluding chapter fleshing out the implications and applications for interreligious praxis of such a theological stance. My thesis, and the goal toward which the argument of this volume has been building, is that the many tongues and many practices of the Spirit of God are the means through which divine hospitality is extended through the church to the world, including the worlds of the religions, and that it is precisely through such hospitable interactions that the church in turn experiences the redemptive work of God in anticipation of the coming kingdom.

Our formulation of a pneumatological theology of hospitality in this chapter will proceed in three steps. First, I will focus on the theme of hospitality in the narrative of Luke-Acts. Second, I proceed from there to explore through the lens of hospitality the wider biblical narrative concerning the relationship between the people of God and the alien and stranger. Third, I build upon these more biblically focused exercises to sketch the main features of a pneumatological theology of guests and hosts in dialogue with contemporary theorists of hospitality, especially from the tradition of French phenomenology. Our goal will be to present a constructive pneumatological theology of hospitality that will be capable of providing sound theological justification for the various Christian practices we have identified as necessary and observed already at work.[2]

LUKE-ACTS AND THE TRINITARIAN
SHAPE OF HOSPITALITY

We begin this constructive part of the book by examining the motif of hospitality in Luke-Acts. I begin here for various reasons, not the least of which includes the fact that Luke-Acts is central to the pentecostal tradition that has shaped my own theological imagination.[3] But more importantly, the centrality of the theme of hospitality to Luke-Acts has not gone unnoticed within the guild of biblical scholarship.[4] We will draw from this

---

[2] This pneumatological perspective will constitute my distinctive contribution to the growing literature on the theology of hospitality; see, e.g., Christine D. Pohl, *Making Room: Recovering Hospitality as a Christian Tradition* (Grand Rapids: Eerdmans, 1999); Lucien Richard, *Living the Hospitality of God* (New York: Paulist Press, 2000); and Arthur Sutherland, *I Was a Stranger: A Christian Theology of Hospitality* (Nashville, Tenn.: Abingdon, 2006).

[3] For further elaboration of this point, see Amos Yong, *The Spirit Poured Out on All Flesh: Pentecostalism and the Possibility of Global Theology* (Grand Rapids: Baker Academic, 2005), 27 and 83-86.

[4] E.g., Errol M. McGuire, "Hospitality in Luke-Acts" (M.A. thesis, Abilene Christian College, 1966); David B. Gowler, *Host, Guest, Enemy, and Friend: Portrait of the Pharisees in Luke and Acts*, Emory Studies in Early Christianity 2 (New York: Peter Lang, 1991); Andrew E. Arterbury, *Entertaining Angels: Early Christian Hospitality in Its Mediterranean Setting*, New Testament Monographs 8 (Sheffield: Sheffield Phoenix, 2005), ch. 5; and other literature to be cited in what follows.

research in our outline of Jesus and hospitality in Luke, the early church and hospitality in Acts, and a basic pentecostal theology of hospitality. This first leg of our constructive proposal presumes, complements, and extends the preceding discussion on performing pneumatology in a pluralistic world (see above, pp. 57-64) by sketching a trinitarian theology of many hospitable practices.

JESUS AND HOSPITALITY

We begin with Jesus as the paradigm of hospitality because he represents and embodies the hospitality of God.[5] Indeed, as the authorized representative of God's salvific hospitality, Jesus is inhabited by and filled with the power of the Holy Spirit (Luke 4:1, 14; cf. Acts 10:38) in order "to bring good news to the poor ..., to proclaim release to the captives and recovery of sight to the blind, to let the oppressed go free, [and] to proclaim the year of the Lord's favor" (Luke 4:18b-19).[6] In the Lukan perspective, Jesus is the anointed one, the Christ, precisely as the one empowered in all aspects of his life and ministry by the Holy Spirit. It is in this sense that we can understand the entire life of Jesus, including his ministry of hospitality, as pneumatically or pneumatologically constituted. While much can be said about Jesus and his Spirit-inspired hospitality in Luke, we will focus on three motifs.

First, Jesus characterizes the hospitality of God in part as the exemplary recipient of hospitality. From his conception in Mary's womb by the power of the Holy Spirit to his birth in a manger through to his burial (in a tomb of Joseph of Arimathea), Jesus was dependent on the welcome of others. As "the Son of Man has nowhere to lay his head" (Luke 9:58), he relied on the goodwill of many, staying in their homes and receiving whatever they served (10:5-7). Thus during his public ministry, he is a guest of Simon Peter (4:38-39), Levi (5:29), Martha (10:38), Zacchaeus (19:5), and various Pharisees and unnamed homeowners (5:17; 7:36; 11:37; 14:1; 22:10-14).[7]

But it is precisely in his role as guest that Jesus also announces and enacts, through the Holy Spirit, the hospitality of God. As evidenced in one

---

[5] Brendan Byrne, *The Hospitality of God: A Reading of Luke's Gospel* (Collegeville, Minn.: Liturgical Press, 2000).

[6] That Jesus' ministry in Luke is focused on the traditionally marginalized of society is not insignificant; see Ernesto Cardenal, *The Gospel in Solentiname*, trans. Donald D. Walsh, 4 vols. (Maryknoll, N.Y.: Orbis Books, 1976-1979), passim; C. R. Hensman, *Agenda for the Poor—Claiming Their Inheritance: A Third World People's Reading of Luke*, Quest 109 (Colombo, Sri Lanka: Center for Society and Religion, 1990); and Michael Prior, *Jesus the Liberator: Nazareth Liberation Theology (Luke 4.16-30)*, The Biblical Seminar 26 (Sheffield: Sheffield Academic Press, 1995).

[7] This list can be supplemented by details in the other Gospels—e.g., Mark 3:20; 7:17, 24; 9:28; 10:10; 14:3; and Matt 9:10; 17:25; 26:6, 18.

of the last scenes in the Gospel, for example, Jesus is invited by two disciples to stay with them because the night was at hand (24:29). Yet rather than they serving him, it is he who "took bread, blessed and broke it, and gave it to them" (24:30), at which moment they recognized that it was they who had been guests in the presence of the divine all along.[8] Similarly, throughout his public ministry, Jesus as the recipient of hospitality is at the same time the one who heralds and personifies the redemptive hospitality of God. He is the "journeying prophet" of the Spirit who eats at the tables of others but at the same time proclaims and brings to pass the eschatological banquet of God for all those who are willing to receive it.[9] Those who welcome Jesus into their homes become, in turn, guests of the redemptive hospitality of God.[10]

This leads, second, to the observation that it is in the various meal scenes in the Gospel wherein we see that the most eager recipients of the divine hospitality were not the religious leaders but the poor and the oppressed. In fact, the meal scenes can be understood as pneumatically constituted speech acts through which Jesus calls for the religious leaders to repent of their self-serving interests precisely in order to "share in the meal fellowship with repentant and forgiven sinners."[11] To do so, Jesus frequently breaks the rules of hospitality, upsets the social conventions of meal fellowship (e.g., Jesus does not wash before dinner), and even goes so far as to rebuke his hosts.[12] Luke thus shows that it is Jesus, not the religious leaders, who is the broker of God's authority,[13] and it is on this basis that Jesus establishes, through the power of the Spirit, the inclusive hospitality of the kingdom. This involves not only women, children, and slaves,[14] but

---

[8] Elizabeth Rankin Geitz, *Entertaining Angels: Hospitality Programs for the Caring Church* (Harrisburg, Pa.: Morehouse, 1993), 28-32.

[9] David P. Moessner, *Lord of the Banquet: The Literary and Theological Significance of the Lukan Travel Narrative* (Minneapolis: Fortress, 1989); cf. Arland J. Hultgren, "The Johannine Footwashing (13.1-11) as a Symbol of Eschatological Hospitality," *New Testament Studies* 28 (1982): 539-46.

[10] As in Zacchaeus, who though short in stature, has received salvation as a son of Abraham; cf. Luke 19:1-9, and Mikeal C. Parsons, *Body and Character in Luke and Acts: The Subversion of Physiognomy in Early Christianity* (Grand Rapids: Baker Academic, 2006), 107.

[11] John Paul Heil, *The Meal Scenes in Luke-Acts: An Audience-oriented Approach*, SBL Monograph Series 52 (Atlanta: Scholars Press, 1999), 312.

[12] David B. Gowler, "Hospitality and Characterization in Luke 11:37-54: A Socio-Narratological Approach," *Semeia* 64, no. 1 (1993): 213-51.

[13] Anthony C. Thiselton, "Christology in Luke, Speech-Act Theory, and the Problem of Dualism in Christology after Kant," in *Jesus of Nazareth: Lord and Christ—Essays on the Historical Jesus and New Testament Christology*, ed. Joel B. Green and Max Turner (Grand Rapids: Eerdmans; and Carlisle, U.K.: Paternoster, 1994), 453-72, makes this argument about Jesus' performative speech acts representing the authority of God and thus functioning legally within this institutional framework.

[14] On this point, see Eugene LaVerdiere, *Dining in the Kingdom of God: The Origins of the Eucharist in the Gospel of Luke* (Chicago: Liturgy Training Publications, 1994), 192-93; cf. James L. Resseguie, *Spiritual Landscape: Images of the Spiritual Life in the Gospel of Luke* (Peabody, Mass.: Hendrickson, 2004), ch. 4.

also the poor, the crippled, the blind, and the lame who are the oppressed and marginalized of the ancient world (Luke 14:21).[15] Last for our purposes but not least, observe Jesus' teaching on hospitality in the parable of the Good Samaritan (10:25-37). In spite of the fact that the Samaritans had just rejected Jesus' visitation (9:51-56),[16] Jesus nevertheless presents the Samaritan as fulfilling the law, loving his neighbor, and embodying divine hospitality.[17] If the Samaritans were those of the other religion to the Jews of the first century, what implications does this parable hold regarding those in other faiths for Christians in the twenty-first century? Might people of other faiths not only be instruments through which God's revelation comes afresh to the people of God, but also perhaps be able to fulfill the requirements for inheriting eternal life (10:25) precisely through the hospitality that they show to their neighbors (which includes Christians)?[18]

Now the question for us is whether Luke intends his portrait of Jesus to be merely informative (locutionary) or commendable to and even normative for (illocutionary) his readers. Put alternatively, what does the hospitality of Jesus—that given as host and that received as guest—mean for those who confess him as Christ, the Spirit-anointed one, and Lord?[19] Part of Luke's answer comes in his follow-up volume, the book of Acts.

HOSPITALITY AND THE EARLY CHURCH

Put succinctly, the hospitality of God manifest in Jesus the anointed one in Luke is now extended through the early church in Acts by the power of

---

[15] I argue at length elsewhere that this inclusion of people with disabilities is also not marginal to the message of the Gospel; see Amos Yong, *Theology and Down Syndrome: Reimagining Disability in Late Modernity* (Waco, Tex.: Baylor University Press, 2007).

[16] For discussion of the acrimonious relations between Jews and Samaritans in the first century, see J. Massyngbaerde Ford, *My Enemy Is My Guest: Jesus and Violence in Luke* (Maryknoll, N.Y.: Orbis Books, 1984), esp. 79-83. But note that in John's Gospel, the Samaritans actually do welcome Jesus through the witness of the woman at the well; see Adeline Fehribach, *The Women in the Life of the Bridegroom: A Feminist Historical-Literary Analysis of the Female Characters in the Fourth Gospel* (Collegeville, Minn.: Liturgical Press, 1998), ch. 3.

[17] Elmer G. Homrighausen, "Who Is My Neighbor? The Christian and the Non-Christian," *Interpretation* 4, no. 4 (1950): 401-15, esp. 405-7; and Ian A. McFarland, "Who Is My Neighbor? The Good Samaritan as a Source for Theological Anthropology," *Modern Theology* 17, no. 1 (2001): 57-66.

[18] I argue these points in detail in Amos Yong, *The Spirit Poured Out on All Flesh*, 241-44.

[19] These are the questions of Edmund Arens, "Jesus' Communicative Actions: The Basis for Christian Faith Praxis, Witnessing, and Confessing," *The Conrad Grebel Review* 3, no. 1 (1985): 67-85; and Mark S. Burrows, "The Hospitality of Christ and the Church's Resurrection: A 'Performed' Christology as Social Reformation," in *In Essentials Unity: Reflections on the Nature and Purpose of the Church*, ed. M. Douglas Meeks and Robert D. Mutton (Minneapolis: Kirk House, 2001), 282-92.

the same Holy Spirit.[20] On the one hand, the Spirit is the divine guest resident in the hearts and lives of all the people of God upon whom she has been poured out; on the other hand, the Spirit empowers from within the body of Christ (the anointed ones) to bear witness to the hospitable God to the ends of the earth (see Acts 1:8). We will focus our discussion on the missionary journeys of St. Paul.

As with Jesus and Peter before him,[21] Paul is also both a recipient and conduit of God's hospitality. He was first the beneficiary of divine hospitality through those who led him by the hand, and then through Judas on Straight Street, Ananias, other followers of Jesus who helped him escape from conspiring enemies, and Barnabas (Acts 9:8, 11, 17-19, 25, 27, 30; cf. 11:25-26). Then during his missionary journeys, he is "prevailed" upon by Lydia, a new convert, to stay in her home (16:15b),[22] and then has his wounds treated by the Philippian jailer (16:32-34). Paul is also a guest of Jason of Thessalonica (17:7), Prisca and Aquilla at Corinth (18:3), Titius Justus also at Corinth (18:7), Philip the evangelist at Caesarea (21:8), Mnason in Jerusalem (21:16), and unnamed disciples at Troas, Tyre, Ptolemais, and Sidon (20:8; 21:4, 7; 27:3), staying with each varying lengths of time.

Along the way, Paul is escorted by Bereans (17:15), protected by two Roman centurions (23:23-24; 27:43), cared for by friends (24:23; 27:3), and entertained by Felix the governor (24:26). During the storm threatening the voyage to Rome, under custody, Paul hosts the breaking of bread, which itself becomes significant as a life-giving event that foreshadows the salvation of 276 people on the ship (27:33-37).[23] After the shipwreck, Paul is guest of the Maltese islanders in general and of Publius the chief official in particular (28:2-10), and then later of some brothers on Puteoli (28:14). The book of Acts closes with Paul as host, welcoming all who were open to receiving the hospitality of God (28:23-30).

This giving and receiving of hospitality is also manifested throughout

---

[20] This motif of hospitality is evident throughout Acts; see Ajith Fernando, *The NIV Application Commentary: Acts* (Grand Rapids: Zondervan, 1998), esp. 127-28, 134-35, 314-15, 324-25, 330-31, 452-53, 510-11, and passim.

[21] Due to space constraints, I pass over the ministry of Peter, who is both guest of and host to, albeit in different respects, Simon the tanner (Acts 10:6), Cornelius's servants (10:23)—note that Peter hosts Cornelius's servants while he himself is a guest of Simon the tanner!—Cornelius the centurion (10:48), and Mary the mother of John Mark (12:12-17).

[22] John Gillman notes that for both Lydia and the jailer, ritual baptism was only part of their Christian initiation and "the acceptance of hospitality in their home was also an integral part of the full initiation experience ... From a theological perspective it is important that the authenticity of a believer's faith is acknowledged not only by the believer himself/herself but in interaction with the community of the faithful"; see Gillman, "Hospitality in Acts 16," in *Sharper Than a Two-edged Sword: Essays in Honor of Professor Dr. Jan Lambrecht S.J.*, ed. Veronica Koperski and Reimund Bieringer (Louvain: Faculty of Theology Katholieke Universiteit Leuven, 1992), 181-96, esp. 194.

[23] Eugene LaVerdiere, *The Breaking of the Bread: The Development of the Eucharist according to the Acts of the Apostles* (Chicago: Liturgy Training Publications, 1998), ch. 6.

the first century church. For the early Christians, the house or home "becomes a new sort of sacred space, where the reign of God produces the community of grace, the house of God, *Beth-El*, where God dwells."[24] If the meal scenes in Luke's Gospel anticipated the eschatological banquet of God to come, in Acts they enact and realize the meal fellowship of God that marks the reconciliation of Jew, Samaritan, and Gentile, male and female, young and old, slave and free (cf. 2:17-18) in the present life of the church. Hence, the first Christians who had received the gift of God's Holy Spirit "had all things in common … , broke bread at home and ate their food with glad and generous hearts" (2:44, 46; cf. 4:32-37 and 5:42). They cared for one another and ensured a "daily distribution of food" (6:1).[25] It is within this framework of mutuality and hospitality that "day by day the Lord added to their number those who were being saved" (2:47b).[26]

What is of central import for our purposes both in the life of Jesus and in the ministry of the early church is the themes of household relationships, table fellowship, and journeying and itinerancy.[27] In all of these cases, not only is Christian life and Christian mission mutually intertwined, but we have seen that the roles of guests and hosts are fluid, continuously reversing.[28] What implications does this Lukan portrayal have for a theology of hospitality?

PENTECOST, HOSPITALITY, AND THE TRINITARIAN ECONOMY OF GOD

I suggest from the foregoing that a Lukan theology of hospitality reflects the trinitarian character of the hospitable God. The God who invites

---

[24] Carisse Mickey Berryhill, "From Dreaded Guest to Welcoming Host: Hospitality and Paul in Acts," in *Restoring the First-Century Church in the Twenty-First Century: Essays on the Stone-Campbell Restoration Movement,* ed. Warren Lewis and Hans Rollmann (Eugene, Ore.: Wipf & Stock, 2005), 71-86, quotation from p. 85.

[25] Brian Capper, "Reciprocity and the Ethic of Acts," in *Witness to the Gospel: The Theology of Acts,* ed. I. Howard Marshall and David Peterson (Grand Rapids, and Cambridge, U.K.: Eerdmans, 1998), 499-518, notes that after Acts chapter 6, this theme of mutual communion is replaced by almsgiving—e.g., 9:36; 10:2, 4, 31; 11:27-30; 20:35; 24:17—and suggests that "to restrict community of property to a past withdrawn from the present experience of the Church is also for Luke to postpone it to the eschatological future and not to demand its full realization in the present community" (p. 511).

[26] Donald Wayne Riddle, "Early Christian Hospitality: A Factor in the Gospel Transmission," *Journal of Biblical Literature* 62, no. 2 (1938): 141-54.

[27] This theme of journeying has recently been studied in Luke-Acts by Octavian D. Baban, *On the Road Encounters in Luke-Acts: Hellenistic Mimesis and Luke's Theology of the Way* (Milton Keynes, U.K., and Waynesboro, Ga.: Paternoster, 2006), although Baban's focus is specifically on the disciples on the road to Emmaus, Philip on the road to Gaza, and Saul on the road to Damascus. For more on hospitality understood within the framework of journey and pilgrimage, see K. M. George, *The Silent Roots: Orthodox Perspectives on Christian Spirituality,* Risk Book Series 63 (Geneva: World Council of Churches, 1994), ch. 3.

[28] John Koenig, *New Testament Hospitality: Partnership with Strangers as Promise and Mission,* Overtures to Biblical Hospitality 17 (Philadelphia: Fortress, 1985), 91-103.

humanity to experience his redemptive hospitality in Christ by the Holy Spirit is the same God who receives the hospitality of human beings as shown to Christ and as manifest through those who welcome and are inhabited by the Holy Spirit. In this trinitarian framework, Jesus is the normative, decisive, and eschatological revelation of the hospitable God, the Son of God who goes into a far country, to echo the words of Karl Barth.[29] Luke's portrait of the journey of the Son of God confirms his humiliation, his taking the form of a slave in obedience to the Father by the power of the Spirit, even to the point of death. Yes, he was rejected by many, perhaps even by most, but not by all. To those who were hospitable to receive Jesus, they are now empowered by the same Spirit to walk in the footsteps of his filial obedience, to journey themselves into the far countries at the ends of the earth, and to bear witness to the redemptive hospitality of God. Hence, trinitarian hospitality as manifest through the body of Christ is not only christomorphic but also empowered by the Holy Spirit.

What then are the central features of this redemptive and pneumatological hospitality of God? If the Day of Pentecost signifies the gift of God, the Holy Spirit that produces many tongues, and if many tongues open up the life of the church's ministry to many practices (see above, pp. 62-64), then the redemptive and pneumatological hospitality of God must also involve many hospitable practices. We can flesh out this idea conceptually along three lines.

First, the Lukan presentation of the life of Christ and the lives of the earliest Christians is not only descriptive but also normative: his readers are informed about the Holy Spirit's empowering Jesus and the early Christians so as to be invited also to extend the story of the hospitality of God to the ends of the earth and to the end of the ages. The twentieth-eighth chapter of the book of Acts is not the end of the story of the church; rather, the story continues through to our time as the followers of Jesus attempt to discern, by the power of the Spirit, how to enact creatively and faithfully the next chapters of the life of the body of Christ based on the Lukan script. Such creative fidelity requires many practices of hospitality to be continually adapted rather than one set of practices to be routinely performed. Hence, depending on what is seen to be happening in different parts of the earth and what is read as the signs of those specific times, the discernment of the Spirit is needed to determine how to best enact the hospitality of God.

Second, the church is the fellowship of the Holy Spirit that makes available and embodies the hospitality of God through the practices of its individual members. Each member of the body of Christ, following the lives of Jesus and the early Christians, is a recipient of and a conduit for the hos-

---

[29] Karl Barth, *Church Dogmatics*, vol. 4, part 1, trans. G. W. Bromiley (London and New York: T & T Clark, 1956), §59.1.

pitality of God, and that precisely through ever-shifting sets of human interrelationships. As we have seen, there is not only a continual reversal of roles, such that hosts become guests and vice versa, but, sometimes, we play both roles simultaneously, discerning through the Holy Spirit how best to respond and react in each case. So on the one hand, we receive the hospitality of God through the welcome of others, but, on the other hand, we enact the hospitality of God to our hosts. Now insofar as there are distinct protocols for hosts and guests (see also pp. 122-26 below), to that degree, those who have been recipients of the hospitality of God and are now invited to represent that hospitality to others must be flexible and adept in the many different types of practices of giving and receiving relevant to various situations. There are better and worse ways to be hosts and guests, and we need to be sensitive to the Spirit's leading to determine if and when the social conventions of hospitality prevalent in any particular place and time are to be appropriately upset.

Finally, many tongues require many hospitable practices because the life of the church includes its mission in a pluralistic world. But to be more precise, believers in Jesus are sustained by the hospitable God not only because they have been born again by the Holy Spirit into a new community (the body of Christ), but also because the Spirit drives them into the world, even to the ends of the earth (Acts 1:8), to interact with and receive the hospitality, kindness, and gifts of strangers of all sorts, even Samaritans, public or governmental officials, and "barbarians" (from βάρβαροι in Acts 28:2)! Now some might object here that the hospitality of the earliest Christians was primarily, if not exclusively, directed toward other Christians.[30] I would counterquestion with the words of Matthew (5:47): "Do not even the Gentiles do the same?" Further, in the New Testament, the love of neighbor is never confined only to believers.[31] Finally, it is precisely Christianity that extended the ancient Roman conception of hospitality so as to include the hospitable treatment of strangers.[32] More to the point, the many practices of hospitality are unavoidable and even essential for the church that does not neglect its mission. Insofar as the Son of God has indeed journeyed into the far country, and insofar as the people of God have also been carried

---

[30] Thus Andrew Arterbury notes, "In reality Christian hosts typically offered hospitality only to Christian travelers" (*Entertaining Angels*, 132); cf. Abraham J. Malherbe, *Social Aspects of Early Christianity*, 2nd enlarged ed. (Philadelphia: Fortress, 1983), ch. 4; and Steve Wilkins, *Face to Face: Meditations on Friendship and Hospitality* (Moscow, Id.: Canon Press, 2002), ch. 6.

[31] Victor Paul Furnish, "Love of Neighbor in the New Testament," *Journal of Religious Ethics* 10, no. 2 (1982): 327-34, esp. 330-31, cites Gal 6:10; 1 Thess 5:15; Rom 12:14-21; James 2:2ff.; and Matt 5:10-12, 43-48.

[32] Thus, the ancient Hellenistic xenophobia was gradually overcome by the indiscriminate application of the Golden Rule and the conviction regarding the common "brotherhood" (better: humanity) of all; for argument, see Ladislaus J. Bochazy, *Hospitality in Early Rome: Livy's Concept of Its Humanizing Force* (Chicago: Ares, 1977), esp. ch. 3.

into far countries by the power of the Spirit, to that same extent the lines between those who are near and those who are far off have now been bridged through the economy of God. Many tongues and many hospitable practices not only open up to but also result from the access all humans beings have through Christ, in the Spirit, to the Father (cf. Eph 2:18).[33]

HOSPITALITY, THE PEOPLE OF GOD, AND THE STRANGER

We are still not yet ready, however, to leave the biblical narrative. This is not only to assuage those who might be suspicious about developing a full-blown trinitarian theology of hospitality out of the Lukan account, but also because we have yet to more fully unpack how the many hospitable practices of the church meets, encounters, and engages the many cultures (and religions) of the world. To do so, I now want to pay further attention to the scriptural depictions of how the people of God interacted with the alien and the stranger. We will quickly present an overview of hospitality in ancient Israel, the inclusive vision of the Hebraic wisdom literature, and developments in the wider Christian diaspora of the first century CE. Throughout this central section of this chapter, our emphasis will be on what might be suitably called the multicultural (and multireligious) experiences and practices of the ancient Hebrews and the early Christians.

THE ALIEN AND THE STRANGER: HOSPITALITY IN ANCIENT ISRAEL

The springboard for our discussion of ancient Israelite hospitality derives from St. Stephen's speech in Acts 7.[34] Here he recites the journeys of the forefathers of Israel: of Abraham, who was told, "Leave your country and your relatives and go to the land that I will show you" (7:3); of Joseph, who was sold into Egypt (7:9); of Moses, who was adopted by Pharaoh's daughter into his household (7:21-22) and later "became a resident alien in the land of Midian" (7:29); and of the descendents of Abra-

---

[33] On this point, see Jean-Jacques Suurmond, *Word and Spirit at Play: Towards a Charismatic Theology*, trans. John Bowden (Grand Rapids: Eerdmans, 1994), 198-203; Maria Clara Lucchetti Bingemer, "The Holy Spirit as Possibility of Universal Dialogue and Mission," in *Christian Mission and Interreligious Dialogue*, ed. Paul Mojzes and Leonard Swidler, Religions in Dialogue 4 (Lewiston, Queenston, and Lampeter: Edwin Mellen Press, 1990), 34-41; and Ulrich Dehn, "Life and Spirit: A New Approach to a Theology of Religions," in *Theology and the Religions: A Dialogue*, ed. Viggo Mortensen (Grand Rapids, and Cambridge, U.K.: Eerdmans, 2003), 457-62.

[34] This connection is made also by Aldebert Denaux, "The Theme of Divine Visits and Human (In)Hospitality in Luke-Acts: Its Old Testament and Graeco-Roman Antecedents," in *The Unity of Luke-Acts*, ed. J. Verheyden, Bibliotheca Ephemeridum Theologicarum Lovaniensium 142 (Leuven: Peeters and Leuven University Press, 1999), 255-79, esp. 262.

ham, Isaac, and Jacob, who were "resident aliens in a country belonging to others" (7:6). What happens when we revisit the history of ancient Israel through the lens of hospitality?

For starters, we find that it is Abraham (the "founding father" of the three Western monotheistic religions[35]) and his relatives (Lot and Laban) and descendents (Isaac and Jacob) who are at the center of the paradigmatic hospitality narratives for the ancient Hebrews (Gen 18, 19, 24, 29).[36] If hospitality in the Hebrew Bible "enhances the host's publicly recognized honor,"[37] then the stature of the forefathers of the ancient Israelites involves the hospitality they offered, and then received in turn. Arguably, it is Abraham, the sojourner-recipient of the hospitality of the Canaanites, the Egyptians, those in the Negeb and at Bethel, even of Melchizedek, king of Salem (Gen 14:18-19, of which more in a moment), who is able in turn to render hospitality to the three strangers (Gen 18).[38]

Yet the Abraham narrative is significant not only because of his exemplary hospitality but because his life served as an archetype for ancient Israel's nomadic, national, and exilic experiences.[39] He was the "wandering Aramean" who "went down into Egypt and lived there as an alien" (Deut 26:5; cf. Gen 12:10; 17:8; 20:1; 21:34; and 23:4). Hence, the ancient Hebrews were portrayed as *gērîm* (sojourners) especially during the period prior to the Canaan settlement. As such they were found more at the bottom half of the social hierarchy than at the top, and their immigrant or migrant status brought with it all of the discriminatory attitudes and behaviors usually displayed against *gērîm*. But it was precisely for this reason that they were chosen by YHWH. In fact, with Abraham and his descendents, dependent as they were on the hospitality of others, this may have represented "the first time in human history in which the divine world was seen to side with 'outlaws, fugitives and immigrants' rather than with the

---

[35] See F. E. Peters, *Children of Abraham: Judaism, Islam, and Christianity* (Princeton: Princeton University Press, 1982); cf. Joan Chittister, O.S.B., Murshid Saadi Shakur Chishti, and Rabbi Arthur Waskow, *The Tent of Abraham: Stories of Hope and Peace for Jews, Christians, and Muslims* (Boston: Beacon, 2006).

[36] T. Desmond Alexander, "Lot's Hospitality: A Clue to His Righteousness," *Journal of Biblical Literature* 104, no. 2 (1985): 289-91, esp. 290, reminds us that "Lot's hospitality is a mark of his righteousness" (cf. Pet 2:7); see also Scott Morschauser, "'Hospitality,' Hostiles and Hostages: On the Legal Background to Genesis 19.1-9," *Journal for the Study of the Old Testament* 27, no. 4 (2003): 461-85; and Stuart Lasine, "Guest and Host in Judges 19: Lot's Hospitality in an Inverted World," *Journal for the Study of the Old Testament* 29 (1984): 37-59.

[37] T. R. Hobbs, "Hospitality in the First Testament and the 'Teleological Fallacy,'" *Journal for the Study of the Old Testament* 95, no. 1 (2001): 3-30, quotation from p. 28.

[38] Andrew E. Arterbury, "Abraham's Hospitality among Jewish and Early Christian Writers: A Tradition History of Gen 18:1-16 and Its Relevance for the Study of the New Testament," *Perspectives in Religious Studies* 30, no. 3 (2003): 359-76.

[39] Thomas M. Bolin, "'A Stranger and an Alien among You' (Genesis 23:4): The Old Testament in Early Jewish and Christian Self-Identity," in *Common Life in the Early Church: Essays Honoring Graydon F. Snyder*, ed. Julian V. Hills (Harrisburg, Pa.: Trinity Press International, 1998), 57-76.

political structures whose policies and use of power made such social types inevitable."[40]

This also puts into perspective the many laws given to remind Israel, once she settled into Canaan, of her responsibilities to the aliens and strangers in her midst: Israel is now no longer merely guest but host to others.[41] Often discussed with the widows and orphans, the sojourner (*gēr* or *gērîm*) is considered, in light of Israel's early history, to be vulnerable as a resident alien without status in a strange land.[42] From their deliverance from Egypt comes an ethic toward slaves and sojourners (Exod 22:21; 23:9; Lev 19:33-34; Deut 15:15; 16:12; 24:17-18, etc.): "You shall also love the stranger, for you were strangers in the land of Egypt" (Deut 10:19).[43] More to the point, Israel remains ever a group of sojourners in the eyes of God, as it is God who also owns the land and all that is in it that is given to Israel (Lev 25:23). And as perpetual sojourners, Israel not only had the responsibility to care for the strangers in her midst, but also the opportunity to receive, even the blessings of YHWH, from them.[44]

But over time, the sojourners welcomed into their midst became residents who had shed their "alien" status. Hence, we see Israel accommodating these further developments so that there are laws regarding the poor, the temporary resident, and those who have now been sufficiently assimilated into Israel so as to have attained certain rights and privileges as "insider" community members.[45] The *gēr* have shifted from ethnic out-

---

[40] Frank Anthony Spina, "Israelites as *gērîm*, 'Sojourners,' in Social and Historical Context," in Carol L. Meyers and M. O'Connor, eds., *The Word of the Lord Shall Go Forth: Essays in Honor of David Noel Freedman in Celebration of His Sixtieth Birthday* (Winona Lake, Ind.: Eisenbrauns, 1983), 321-35, quote from 332; see also Spina's intriguing book-length study, *The Faith of the Outsider: Exclusion and Inclusion in the Biblical Story* (Grand Rapids: Eerdmans, 2005).

[41] Bernhard A. Asen, "From Acceptance to Inclusion: The Stranger (gēr) in Old Testament Tradition," in *Christianity and the Stranger: Historical Essays*, ed. Francis W. Nichols (Atlanta: Scholars Press, 1995), 16-35.

[42] Donald E. Gowan, "Wealth and Poverty in the Old Testament: The Case of the Widow, the Orphan, and the Sojourner," *Interpretation* 41, no. 4 (1987): 341-53.

[43] "Israel's conduct with the stranger or sojourner is both an *imitatio dei*, a reflection of God's way with sojourners, and the primary specific Old Testament manifestation of the Great Commission to love the neighbor"; see Patrick D. Miller, "Israel as Host to Strangers," in Patrick Miller, *Israelite Religion and Biblical Theology*, JSOTSup 267 (Sheffield: Sheffield Academic Press, 2000), 548-71, quote from 569, italics in original.

[44] Naomi Patricia Franklin, "The Stranger within Their Gates (How the Israelite Portrayed the non-Israelite in Biblical Literature)," (Ph.D. diss., Duke University, 1990), shows how individuals like Eliezer, Jethro, Rahab, Uriah, Hushai, and Ebed-Melech were mediatorial instruments of YHWH's *hesed* to ancient Israel. Lois Evans, with Jane Rubietta, *Stones of Remembrance: A Rock-Hard Faith from Rock-Hard Places* (Chicago: Moody, 2006), also discusses Rahab alongside other women such as Puah and Shiphrah, Pharoah's daughter, and Zipporah, who were hospitable in different ways to the people of God.

[45] Christiana van Houten, *The Alien in Israelite Law*, JSOT 107 (Sheffield: JSOT Press, 1991), ch. 5.

siders to national outsiders, and a few might have actually even succeeded in "getting ahead" enough so that they are in a position to employ Israelite laborers (Lev 25:47-54).[46] There were also those who had become cultic insiders and participate as proselytes with Israel in the worship of YHWH.

At the same time, Israel's openness to the stranger was not unrestrained. Of course, YHWH's prohibition against idolatry meant that there is a "far less welcoming attitude toward those termed foreigners, *Nochrim*, the idolatrous nations."[47] This exclusive posture is later retrieved in the postexilic period, and especially is visible in the remnant communities of Ezra and Nehemiah.[48] The concerns of these communities over foreign marriages reflect at least in part concerns to maintain ethnic purity as well as the social conditions of being threatened by hostile outsiders.[49]

But this exclusivist trajectory represents only one side of the postexilic memory of the stranger in ancient Israel. On the other side, we see further that the God whose redemptive hospitality was first made known to Abraham and his descendents through their sojourns in strange lands and their interactions with foreign hosts continues to speak to a postexilic community dispersed throughout the wider ancient Near Eastern world. And it is this multicultural character of ancient Israelite hospitality that is seen more clearly in the Hebraic wisdom literature.[50]

---

[46] Rolf Rendtorff, "The *Gēr* in the Priestly Laws of the Pentateuch," in *Ethnicity and the Bible*, ed. Mark Brett, Biblical Interpretation Series 19 (Leiden: E. J. Brill, 1996), 76-87, esp. 80-81.

[47] Rabbi Sheila Peltz Weinberg, "Stranger, Guest, Neighbor: Paradoxical Views of the Other in Our Traditions," *The Drew Gateway* 58, no. 3 (1989): 39-46, esp. 41.

[48] See Daniel Smith-Christopher, "Between Ezra and Isaiah: Exclusion, Transformation, and Inclusion of the 'Foreigner' in Post-Exilic Biblical Theology," in *Ethnicity and the Bible*, ed. Mark Brett, 117-42 (see n. 46).

[49] This more exclusionary perspective is also seen in the rabbinic Judaism of the post–second-temple period. There, in the pages of the Mishnah-Tosefta, "The claims of 'chosenness' implied in the discussion of the gentile, YHWH's Land, his Residence, and the like can be seen as typical expressions of ethnicity and not as *uniquely* Israelite attempts to establish their religious superiority"; rather, "the treatment of the gentiles in Mishnah-Tosefta parallels, in general and in particular terms, the ways in which any ethnic group treats those outside its unit. The Israelites' description of the gentile as expressed in Mishnah-Tosefta is decidedly common-place, when viewed from the perspective of the interaction of ethnic units throughout the world and throughout history." See Gary G. Porton, *Goyim: Gentiles and Israelites in Mishnah-Tosefta*, Brown Judaic Studies 155 (Atlanta: Scholars Press, 1988), 10-11 and 299, italics in original.

[50] Here I am extending Robert C. Stallman's work—e.g., "Divine Hospitality in the Pentateuch: A Metaphorical Perspective on God as Host" (Ph.D. diss., Westminster Theological Seminary, 1999), and idem, "Divine Hospitality and Wisdom's Banquet in Proverbs 9:1-6," in *The Way of Wisdom: Essays in Honor of Bruce K. Waltke*, ed. J. I. Packer and Sven K. Soderlund (Grand Rapids: Zondervan, 2000), 117-33—to argue that God is host not only to Israel but also, through Israel, to the world.

HOSPITALITY IN MANY TONGUES: THE WISDOM OF THE ANCIENTS

I propose here that ancient Israelite wisdom not only foreshadows the multicultural character of divine hospitality declared through the many tongues of the postexilic experience but also provides bridges for understanding how such hospitality is pertinent to the contemporary interfaith encounter. This thesis flows from the now widespread recognition that the canonical wisdom sayings reflect the influence of the ancient Near Eastern cultures, especially of Mesopotamia, Egypt, and Canaan, on the mindset of Hebrew sages.[51] There have long been comparisons between the book of Job and the Babylonian *I Will Praise the Lord of Wisdom* (ca. 2000-1500 BCE), and *The Dialogue about Human Misery* (ca. 1000 BCE). Scholars have also compared *The Dialogue of Pessimism* with the Preacher's Ecclesiastes, as well as noticed the influence of Hellenistic wisdom (*sophia*) on Qohelet, Sirach, and the Wisdom of Solomon.

Turning more explicitly to the book of Proverbs, there are parallels to *The Counsels of Wisdom*, a Mesopotamian collection of moral exhortations dating back to at least 1200 BCE that includes proverbs, admonitions, and maxims. More directly influential is the Egyptian *Instruction of Amenemope* (ca. 1100 BCE) on the "Sayings of the Wise" in Proverbs 22:17-24:22, and the Akkadian "wisdom" text *Ahiqar* (seventh century BCE), on the personification of Wisdom in Proverbs 1-9. There is also a cryptic reference assigning some proverbs (Proverbs 30) to Agur son of Jakeh, who may have been from Arabia. Finally, there is a wide range of Egyptian instructional material, primarily from kings, their scribes, or sages in the royal courts, that contain numerous sayings similar to what is found in Proverbs.

While direct dependence of the biblical authors on these ancient Near Eastern texts cannot be definitively established, there is no doubt, at least at the canonical level, that the wisdom material was collected and preserved by a postexilic community coming to terms with its diasporic situation. Hebrew Bible scholar Ronald Clements notes that it was "this uniquely international origin of wisdom, its claim to express universally valid truths, and not least to present a teaching about life that knew no national boundaries, nor based itself upon a single revelatory act of the past, that made wisdom so important to Israel in the post-exilic period"; hence, this wisdom "could address its promised benefits to Jews who found themselves part of a wider, and often scattered, community who inhabited

---

[51] Some of this material is reproduced in Derek Kidner, *The Wisdom of Proverbs, Job & Ecclesiastes: An Introduction to Wisdom Literature* (Downers Grove, Ill.: InterVarsity, 1985), appendix 1: "Some International Reflections on Life," 125-41. See also the discussion in Roland E. Murphy, *The Tree of Life: An Exploration of Biblical Wisdom*, 2nd ed. (Grand Rapids, and Cambridge, U.K.: Eerdmans, 1996), 151-79; and Richard J. Clifford, *The Wisdom Literature* (Nashville, Tenn.: Abingdon, 1998), ch. 2.

a God-created universal order."[52] Was this not also the experience of the early Christian diaspora as well as of our own global village today?

It is not surprising, then, that the wisdom material opened up the Israelite view of God's salvation history toward the wider scope of creation history itself.[53] This expanded theological vision that embraced the many ancient Near Eastern cultures and wisdom languages anticipates the many tongues of the Day of Pentecost made possible by the outpouring of the Spirit on all flesh (Acts 2:17). Here it is important to retrieve the Hebrew Bible witness to the work of the Spirit throughout all of creation. The Spirit of God fills the world and holds all things together (Ps 139:6; Wis. 1:7). The outpouring of the Spirit transforms deserts into fertile fields and forests (Isa 32:15). All the creatures of God's creation—wild donkeys, birds, storks, goats, lions, the fish of the sea, etc.—are fed by YHWH and nourished by his breath, apart from which "they die and return to their dust"; but, "When you send your Spirit, they are created; and you renew the face of the ground" (Ps 104:29-30; cf. Judith 16:14). And, as with the Priestly creation narrative when the *ruah* of God "swept over the face of the waters" (Gen 1:2) and the world was spoken into existence, so also is God's ongoing providential, sustaining, and creative work accomplished by the divine *ruah* and Word: "By the word of the LORD the heavens were made, and all their host by the breath of his mouth" (Ps 33:6).

I therefore suggest that the wisdom of ancient Israel opens up to the many tongues of the contemporary interreligious encounter in a variety of ways. First, there are meaningful points of contact between the biblical wisdom materials and the world religions that provide a common platform for discussion, interaction, and perhaps even evangelism.[54] The "vanity" (*hebel*) of Qohelet, for example, provides windows into the Buddhist notion of disease (*dukkha*).[55] Both notions present fundamental analyses of the human condition that enable dialogue across religious lines.

---

[52] Ronald E. Clements, *Wisdom for a Changing World: Wisdom in Old Testament Theology* (Berkeley, Calif.: Bibal Press, 1990), 18 and 20. Elsewhere, Clements suggests that the wisdom of ancient Israel was honed and developed in and through the "liminal" conditions of their exilic, postexilic, and diasporic experiences; see Clements's *Wisdom in Theology: The Disbury Lectures 1989* (Grand Rapids: Eerdmans; and Carlisle, U.K.: Paternoster, 1992), 26-31.

[53] Leo G. Perdue, *Wisdom and Creation: The Theology of Wisdom Literature* (Nashville, Tenn.: Abingdon, 1994).

[54] E.g., Michael Pocock, "Selected Perspectives on World Religions from Wisdom Literature," in *Christianity and the Religions: A Biblical Theology of World Religions*, ed. Edward Rommen and Harold Netland, Evangelical Missiology Society Series 2 (Pasadena, Calif.: William Carey Library, 1995), 45-55.

[55] See, e.g., Michal Solomon Vasanthakumar, "An Exploration of the Book of Ecclesiastes in the Light of Buddha's Four Noble Truths," in *Sharing Jesus Holistically with the Buddhist World*, ed. David Lim and Steve Spaulding (Pasadena, Calif.: William Carey Library, 2005), 147-77; and Seree Lorgunpai, "The Books of Ecclesiastes and Thai Buddhism," *Asia Journal of Theology* 8, no. 1 (1994): 155-62.

Second, there are also more general comparative studies of the wisdom material that are possible. If the sages of ancient Israel were willing to learn from the surrounding cultures, would they not also have been willing to entertain the wisdom of those more distant, perhaps even that of the ancient Confucian sages farther east?[56] Or how might the contemplatives of Hebrew wisdom have understood their tradition in dialogue with Islamic Sufis, Jewish mystics, or Indian *rishis*?[57] Might not these more dialogical exercises enrich Christian self-understanding, even as they provide opportunities for mutual transformation?[58]

Finally, there is always the straightforward question about the mutual practice of hospitality between and across wisdom (religious) traditions.[59] Christians do not corner the market of hospitality, and an interreligious dialogue on hospitality would seem to flourish amidst the mutuality of hospitable practices. Inasmuch as the ancient Israelites were willing to be hospitable to and perhaps even instructed by the wisdom traditions of their neighbors, might we not also profitably adopt this same posture today? Was this not the experience of the early Christians?

Each of these parallel observations should be taken merely as initial bridges for the dialogue between biblical wisdom and the wisdom traditions of the Eastern world. Further explorations and discussion will reveal many discontinuities and even incompatibilities. The point being made here, however, is that there are possibilities for interreligious dialogue opened up through the ancient Hebraic categories of hospitality and wisdom, not that these ideas in the Hebrew mind are synonymous with similar notions in Eastern religious and philosophical traditions. How far the comparisons go can be determined only over the long haul of the interreligious encounter, so it is dispositions toward the latter that must be cultivated.

---

[56] Xinzhong Yao, *Wisdom in Early Confucian and Israelite Traditions* (Burlington, Vt., and Aldershot, U.K.: Ashgate, 2006).

[57] John Eaton, *The Contemplative Face of Old Testament Wisdom in the Context of World Religions* (London: SCM; and Philadelphia: Trinity Press International, 1989).

[58] In the words of an Islamicist: "In reading and studying the Qur'an over the years, 'I received insights that included an apperception that the Qur'an was reading me as much as I was reading it ... That realization did not frighten or 'spook' me; rather it inspired me and engendered trust in the text's goodness and power. I wondered if this experience was a prelude to conversion or simply an awareness of divine hospitality to a guest who has been honored with a share in its open secret of revelation"; see Frederick M. Denny, *The Spiritual-Intellectual Hospitality of Islam and Muslims: Reflections of a Christian Scholar*, Youngstown Papers in Islamic Religion, History, and Culture 1 (Youngstown, Ohio: Center for Islamic Studies, Youngstown State University, 2005), 12.

[59] E.g., Ven. Master Hsing Yun, *Humble Table, Wise Fare: Hospitality for the Heart*, 2 vols., trans. Tom Manzo and Shujan Cheng (Hacienda Heights, Calif.: Fo Guang Shan International Translation Center, and Hsi Lai University Press, 1999); Mariasusai Dhavamony, "Hindu Hospitality and Tolerance," *Studia Missionalia* 39 (1990): 303-20; or, with regard to sub-Saharan African hospitality, Mercy Amba Oduyoye, *Introducing African Women's Theology* (Cleveland, Ohio: Pilgrim; and Sheffield, U.K.: Sheffield Academic Press, 2001), ch. 7, on "Hospitality and Spirituality."

HOSPITALITY, THE CHRISTIAN DIASPORA, AND THE RELIGION OF MELCHIZEDEK

Note that it was also amidst a diasporic experience that the earliest Christians practiced hospitality. There are references throughout the New Testament to the Christian scattering (Acts 8:1-4; 11:19-20), to the "twelve tribes in the Dispersion" (James 1:1), and to the "exiles of the Dispersion in Pontus, Galatia, Cappadocia, Asia, and Bithynia" (1 Pet 1:1).[60] These Christians inevitably found themselves in marginal situations of shame, unrest, and even persecution. Hence while seeing themselves as missionaries, the early Christians nevertheless recognized their status as aliens and strangers, guests who needed to conduct themselves in an honorable and blameless manner amidst their hosts (e.g., 1 Pet 2:12).[61] Perhaps it was precisely because of this precarious situation that they took hospitality seriously (e.g., 1 Pet 4:9; cf. 1 Tim 5:10).[62]

Yet as already noted, Christian hospitality was not directed only to fellow believers but also to strangers. While Paul's injunction to "extend hospitality to strangers" in Romans 12:13 occurs in the broader context of blessing one's persecutors and doing good to one's enemies (12:14-21), the author of the letter to the Hebrews explicitly admonishes, "Do not neglect to show hospitality to strangers, for by doing that some have entertained angels without knowing it" (Heb 13:2). It is not surprising that the early Jewish-Christians (most likely the original audience of this letter) had donned the mindset of the forefathers of Israel, recognizing themselves like Abraham, Isaac, Jacob, and their descendents as wanderers in search of the rest of God (Heb 4) and the heavenly city.[63] In fact, their lives were modeled after that of the heroes of faith who had set out according to the call and promises of God to places that they did not know, and who confessed themselves as "strangers and foreigners on the earth" (Heb 11:13). They were pilgrims on a journey, called to follow after Jesus their great high priest while living at peace with everyone (Heb 12:14).[64]

---

[60] Reinhard Feldmeier, "The 'Nation' of Strangers: Social Contempt and Its Theological Interpretation in Ancient Judaism and Early Christianity," in *Ethnicity and the Bible*, ed. Mark Brett, 241-70 (see n. 46).

[61] See Aiyenakun P. J. Arowele, "Diaspora-concept in the New Testament: Studies on the Idea of Christian Sojourn, Pilgrimage and Dispersion according to the New Testament" (D.Th. diss., Bayerischen Julius-Maximilians-Universität Würzburg, 1977), ch. 7, on the Petrine diaspora, esp. 401-9, on their public behavior and civic obligations.

[62] Amy Oden, "God's Household of Grace: Hospitality in Early Christianity," in *Ancient and Postmodern Christianity: Paleo-orthodoxy in the 21st Century—Essays in Honor of Thomas C. Oden*, ed. Kenneth Tanner and Christopher A. Hall (Downers Grove, Ill.: Inter-Varsity Press, 2002), 38-48.

[63] Emily Jeptepkeny Choge, "An Ethic for Refugees: The Pilgrim Motif in Hebrews and the Refugee Problem in Kenya" (Ph.D. diss., Fuller Theological Seminary, 2004), ch. 5.

[64] Joseph M. Shaw, *The Pilgrim People of God: Recovering a Biblical Motif* (Minneapolis: Augsburg, 1990).

It is also in this letter to the Hebrews that we have the reference to the enigmatic Melchizedek. He is first cited from the Psalms with regard to Christ, of whom it is said, "You are a priest forever, according to the order of Melchizedek" (5:6; 6:20-7:25; cf. Ps 110:4).[65] The main point for the Hebrews is precisely that Jesus fulfills the greater Melchizedekian rather than the lesser Levitical high priesthood because (1) Levi himself paid tithes through Abraham (the former being in the loins of the latter when he gave his gift) to Melchizedek (7:2); (2) both Jesus and Melchizedek are (of supernatural origins) without proper genealogy (7:3); and (3) both Jesus and Melchizedek have an eternal (rather than temporal) priesthood "through the power of an indestructible life" (7:16). For our purposes, however, I suggest that Melchizedek also potentially represents the religion of the stranger that prefigures and is now incorporated into the salvation history of the people of God.

The plausibility of this reading derives from the original reference to Melchizedek's hospitality to Abram.[66] After Abram returned from retrieving Lot and his family from their kidnappers, we are told,

> King Melchizedek of Salem brought out bread and wine;
> he was priest of God Most High [*El 'Elyon*]. He blessed him and said,
> "Blessed be Abram by God Most High,
>   maker of heaven and earth;
> and blessed be God Most High,
>   who has delivered your enemies into your hand!"
> And Abram gave him one-tenth of everything. (Gen 14:18-20)

Now, although identified as king of Salem and as priest of *El 'Elyon*, little is known about the identity of Melchizedek. Some have suggested based on the citation in the Psalms that he was retrieved by the Hasmonean dynasty to justify the leadership of Simon during the Maccabean revolt, while others proffer that his appearance in the literature of Qumran as an angelic being is in the background to the references in Hebrews about his supernatural origins and immortality (and, might I suggest, also in the background of the possibility that hospitality could be shown to angels in

---

[65] The definitive study on Melchizedek is Fred L. Horton, Jr., *The Melchizedek Tradition: A Critical Examination of the Sources to the Fifth Century A.D. and in the Epistle to the Hebrews* (Cambridge: Cambridge University Press, 1976). See also Birger A. Pearson, "Melchizedek in Early Judaism, Christianity, and Gnosticism," in *Biblical Figures Outside the Bible*, ed. Michael E. Stone and Theodore A. Bergren (Harrisburg, Pa.: Trinity Press International, 1998), 176-202; and John G. Gammie, "Loci of the Melchizedek Tradition of Genesis 14:18-20," *Journal of Biblical Literature* 50, no. 4 (1971): 385-96.

[66] James L. Kugel, *The Bible as It Was* (Cambridge, Mass., and London: Belknap Press of Harvard University Press, 1997), ch. 8, on Melchizedek, esp. 152.

13:2?).[67] More important, Melchizedek is priest of *El 'Elyon* long before the establishment of the ancient Israelite cultus. As worshiper of *El*, Melchizedek was patron and priest to a well-known henotheistic God in the Canaanite background of the second millennium BCE.[68] It was in his role of priest-king of *El* that Melchizedek played host to Abram.

Two theological conclusions can be tentatively drawn from the reception of the Melchizedek tradition in Hebrews. First, inasmuch as in Hebrews the pilgrim people of God experience God's redemptive hospitality through the high priesthood of Christ, such hospitality is prefigured in the Genesis narrative's account of the hospitality received by Abram through the high priesthood of Melchizedek. In turn, Abram is transformed into a paradigm of hospitality, both in his receiving of the divine guests (Gen 18) and in his mediating God's redemptive hospitality ultimately (eschatologically) to all the nations of the world (Gen 12:2-3). The implications for world Christians today in a world of many faiths, following in the footsteps of the pilgrim people of God (the original readers of Hebrews), of Abraham the wandering Aramean, and of those who have experienced the redemptive hospitality of God in Christ, can be extrapolated.

Second, inasmuch as Melchizedek was priest of *El 'Elyon*, can it also be said he was "the High-priest of the cosmic religion,"[69] and in that way have represented and foreshadowed how the religious longings and perhaps even beliefs and practices of all people are oriented toward God? Might we even be able to go further and suggest that Melchizedek's "eternal priesthood, consummated in the ministry of Christ, lies behind the church's calling as a witnessing community among and for—not against—other witnessing communities"?[70] Can Melchizedek symbolize the stranger with whom we have more affinity than we realize, and can his religion be the religion of the stranger that is preserved, however obliquely, in the wisdom of the cultures and traditions of the ancient Near East and that anticipates the religion of Christ witnessed to in the many tongues of the Spirit?

---

[67] E.g., Jakob J. Petuchowski, "The Controversial Figure of Melchizedek," *Hebrew Union College Annual* 28, no. 1 (1957): 127-36; Joseph A. Fitzmyer, "Further Light on Melchizedek from Qumran Cave 11," *Journal of Biblical Literature* 46, no. 1 (1967): 25-41; A. J. Bandstra, "*Heilsgeschichte* and Melchizedek in Hebrews," *Calvin Theological Journal* 3, no. 1 (1968): 36-41; and Richard Longenecker, "The Melchizedek Argument of Hebrews: A Study in the Development and Circumstantial Expression of New Testament Thought," in *Unity and Diversity in New Testament Theology: Essays in Honor of George E. Ladd*, ed. Robert A. Guelich (Grand Rapids: Eerdmans, 1978), 161-85.

[68] Joseph A. Fitzmyer, "'Now This Melchizedek …' (Heb 7,1)," *Catholic Biblical Quarterly* 25, no. 3 (1963): 305-21, esp. 315.

[69] Jean Daniélou, *Holy Pagans of the Old Testament*, trans. Felix Faber (Baltimore: Helicon Press, 1957), 104. Previously, Daniélou had suggested understanding Melchizedek as high priest of God's covenant with the natural universe; see Daniélou, *Advent*, trans. Rosemary Sheed (New York: Sheed & Ward, 1951), ch. 2.

[70] T. K. Thomas, "Melchizedek, King and Priest: An Ecumenical Paradigm?" *Ecumenical Review* 52, no. 3 (2000): 403-9, quotation from p. 409.

PRACTICING HOSPITALITY: TOWARD
A PNEUMATOLOGICAL THEOLOGY OF GUESTS AND HOSTS

We have in this chapter so far traversed the biblical text—beginning with Luke-Acts and then going backward to the Abrahamic narratives through the wisdom literature and returning to the experiences of the early Christian diaspora—in search of a theology of hospitality. Along the way, I have suggested a pneumatological theology of hospitality shaped by the economy of God. In this final part of the chapter, we need to flesh out such a vision with greater conceptual rigor by engaging contemporary philosophical discussions on hospitality. My goal is to draw out the connections between the hospitality of God and what I call a pneumatological theology of guests and hosts for the postmodern and pluralistic world of the twenty-first century. If the gifts of many tongues equals the empowerment toward many hospitable practices, then Christian hospitality today remains, paradoxically, both unlimited and yet constrained—unconditional and yet conditioned—by the trinitarian economy and hospitality of God.

UNCONDITIONALITY AND THE ABUNDANT HOSPITALITY OF GOD

I argue first that because Christian hospitality proceeds from the magnanimous hospitality of God, it is founded on the incarnational and pentecostal logic of abundance rather than that of human economies of exchange and of scarcity. My primary dialogue partner on this point is the continental philosopher of deconstruction Jacques Derrida (1930-2004).

Derrida's reflections on hospitality were themselves developed in conversation with the philosophical tradition from Immanuel Kant through Søren Kierkegaard, Edmund Husserl, and especially Emmanuel Levinas.[71] Kant wrote on hospitality in the context of his discussing the conditions for peace between states.[72] For Kant, "*hospitality* means the right of a stranger not to be treated with hostility when he arrives on someone else's territory"; by the same token, strangers must behave peaceably, and while they cannot claim "right of guest," they can claim "right of resort" because "all men are entitled to present themselves in the society of others by virtue of their right to communal possession of the earth's surface."[73] It is against

---

[71] For overviews, see James K. A. Smith, *Jacques Derrida: Live Theory* (New York and London: Continuum, 2005), ch. 3; and Mark Dooley, "The Politics of Exodus: Derrida, Kierkegaard, and Levinas on 'Hospitality,'" in *Works of Love*, ed. Robert L. Perkins, International Kierkegaard Commentary 16 (Macon, Ga.: Mercer University Press, 1999), 167-92.

[72] Immanuel Kant, "Perpetual Peace: A Philosophical Sketch," in *Kant: Political Writings*, ed. Hans Reiss; trans. H. B. Nisbet, 2nd enlarged ed. (Cambridge: Cambridge University Press, 1991), 93-115.

[73] Here the discussion is in "Perpetual Peace," article 3: "Cosmopolitan right shall be limited to conditions of universal hospitality," 105-8; quotations from pp. 105 and 106.

this background that Derrida sees hospitality as a set not merely of inter-personal affairs but of political relations.[74]

The Kantian reference to the treatment of hospitality rather than hostil-ity is shifted in Levinas, who points out that hospitality involves, from the point of view of the "host," a divesting of one's own concerns so as to be a "hostage" to the guest.[75] But since for Levinas, the face of the Other "orders" and "ordains" me, placing me under (even infinite) obligation—it is Levinas who argues that first philosophy is ethics—the host is perpet-ually hostage to the Other.[76] From the point of view of the guest, Levinas was also concerned, with Kant, about the human quest for peace. While symbolized finally in the longing for Zion, peace, justice, and righteousness are also prefigured in the "cities of refuge" that are set aside as places of hospitality for guests (exiles) who were responsible but not culpable for killing others.[77] I would add that these cities are types of our journeys as aliens and strangers in this world since we are never quite guiltless, never quite "at home," always guests on the roam (Heb 11). Hence we conclude to two impossibilities: that on the part of the host (explicitly thematized by Levinas), who can never fulfill his or her obligation to provide hospitality to others, and that on the side of the guest (extrapolated from Levinas), who both is undeserving of unconditional hospitality on the one hand and is also never quite able to find perpetual peace and rest on the other.[78]

Derrida's work on hospitality builds precisely on these Kantian and Lev-inasian ideas. To begin, Derrida recognizes with Kant that peace and jus-tice involve the question of foreigners, immigrants, refugees, etc. Derrida's context includes the human rights debates (involving activists) in Prague; apartheid in South America; the "Algerian" question; and controversies

---

[74] Note also that for Derrida, friendship is also a political set of relations; see the discus-sion of hospitality in ch. 5 of Derrida's *Politics of Friendship*, trans. George Collins (London and New York: Verso, 1997).

[75] Emmanuel Levinas, "Responsibility for the Other," in *Ethics and Infinity: Conversa-tions with Philippe Nemo,* trans. Richard Cohen (Pittsburgh: Duquesne University Press, 1985), 100.

[76] See Levinas's *magnum opus, Totality and Infinity,* trans. Alphonso Lingis (The Hague: M. Nijhoff, 1979), and elsewhere throughout his corpus. Note that Derrida calls Levinas's *Totality and Infinity* "an immense treatise *of hospitality*"; see Derrida, *Adieu to Emmanuel Levinas,* trans. Pascale-Anne Brault and Michael Naas (Stanford, Calif.: Stanford University Press, 1999), 21, italics in original.

[77] The relevant biblical texts are Num 35:6-34; Deut 4:41-43; and Josh 20. Levinas's dis-cussion of the cities of refuge is most concentrated in his *Beyond the Verse: Talmudic Read-ings and Lectures,* trans. Gary D. Mole (Bloomington and Indianapolis: Indiana University Press, 1994), ch. 3.

[78] Lest we get the view that Levinas's is a thoroughly pessimistic anthropology, I should note that his thinking is rabbinically shaped so as to presume an original peace (rather than the Kantian original violence) to which Zion retrieves and holds forth as the messianic promise. For a Christian reading of Levinasian hospitality, see David F. Ford, *Self and Salva-tion: Being Transformed* (Cambridge: Cambridge University Press, 1999), ch. 2, "Enjoyment, Responsibility and Desire: A Hospitable Self."

about immigration and amnesty in France. (I would add, from our survey in the first chapter, the Tamil diaspora, displaced Nigerians, the long history of American immigrants, and globalization, all combined to force Kant's question upon us in unprecedented ways.) Going beyond Kant, however, original violence is that such people have to ask for hospitality to begin with and that in a language not their own.[79] But things get worse because the secondary violence toward strangers is that the reception of hospitality itself creates an obligation on the part of guests to repay their hosts. Hence, the offering of hospitality under the conditions of the economy of exchange sets in motion a never-ending cycle of indebtedness.

This leads to Derrida's observations about the impossibility of hospitality. It is not just that we have infinite obligations to others (*pace* Levinas), but that insofar as we are caught up in the economy of exchange, there can be no true hospitality that is not already tainted by debts and obligations.[80] What is owed or obligated cannot be freely given.[81] The paradox of hospitality is that it is continually threatened if not deconstructed by what might be called the logic of indebtedness. This is because even to say "I invite you" places you under obligation to reciprocate my invitation.[82]

Derrida hence distinguishes between absolute hospitality that is freely given and the conditional hospitality of reciprocity. The latter is structured by the economy of exchange and the logic of gratitude, depending in many ways on the conventions of place and time. The former cannot depend on the "invitation," over which "we" retain control—whom to invite, under what conditions, etc.—but must be beholden to the "visitation." The visitation implies "the arrival of someone who is not expected, who can show up at any time. If I am unconditionally hospitable I should welcome the visitation, not the invited guest, but the visitor. I must be unprepared, or

---

[79] Jacques Derrida, *Paper Machine*, trans. Rachel Bowlby (Stanford, Calif.: Stanford University Press, 2005), 68; and Jacques Derrida and Anne Dufourmantelle, *Of Hospitality*, trans. Rachel Bowlby (Stanford, Calif.: Stanford University Press, 2000), 15. Thus in *Acts of Religion*, ed. Gil Anidjar (New York and London: Routledge, 2002), 401, Derrida suggests that "the hôte or stranger is holy, divine, protected by divine blessing."

[80] What Derrida calls the logic of exchange is described in first-century terms of benevolent reciprocity by Stephen Charles Mott, "The Power of Giving and Receiving: Reciprocity in Hellenistic Benevolence," in *Current Issues in Biblical and Patristic Interpretation: Studies in Honor of Merrill C. Tenney Presented By His Former Students*, ed. Gerald F. Hawthorne (Grand Rapids: Eerdmans, 1975), 60-72; cf. Marcel Mauss, *The Gift: Forms and Functions of Exchange in Archaic Societies*, trans. Ian Cunnison (New York: Norton, 1967).

[81] Hélène Cixous, "Sorties: Out and Out: Attacks/Ways Out/Forays," in *The Logic of Gift: Toward an Ethic of Generosity*, ed. Alan D. Schrift (New York and London: Routledge, 1997), 148-73, identifies the "masculine" fear of loss as central to the economy of exchange focused on profit, and, against this, unfolds a "feminine" economy that is truly generous, seeking not profit and based not on reciprocity, but on relationship, modeled after maternal giving. While this division of economies is a bit too simplistic, I will later provide a trinitarian logic for precisely the type of economic generosity Cixous seeks to articulate.

[82] Derrida, *Acts of Religion*, 398.

prepared to be unprepared, for the unexpected arrival of *any* other."[83] With the visitation, it is the guest who is in charge, to arrive whenever he, she, or even it, wishes.[84] In fact, the Levinasian transformation of the host into the hostage is extended: the guest takes my place, even holds the keys to "my" house. Derrida thus writes of the homeowner or master

> awaiting his guest as a liberator, his emancipator ... This is always the situation of the foreigner, in politics too, that of coming as a legislator to lay down the law and liberate the people or the nation by coming from outside, by entering into the nation or the house ... [It is] *as if*, then, the stranger could save the master and liberate the power of his host; it's *as if* the master, *qua* master, were prisoner of his place and his power, of his ipseity, of his subjectivity (his subjectivity is hostage).[85]

The Derridean reversal is now also clear: the host is hostage even as the guest now hosts the host/age's salvation, redemption, and liberation.[86]

I suggest that the realization of Derrida's absolute hospitality presumes if not requires a theological dimension that we might call the trinitarian logic of abundance. Amidst the conditions of finitude, the impossibility of hospitality parallels the impossibility of the gift, structured as both are under the logic of exchange, reciprocity, and scarcity: both hospitality and gifts (1) are never unconditional—witness our "much obliged!"; (2) even from the giver's perspective, they pat themselves on the back for being charitable; and, finally, (3) once the gift is taken, it is now a possession, not a gift. Precisely here we see why a works/righteousness that is based on the economy of exchange cannot finally save. What we need, as biblical scholar Theodore Jennings argues in dialogue with Derrida, are excess and abundance, for example, the "much more" of Romans 5, which responds to the human need for redemptive and gracious hospitality constrained by the law in

---

[83] Richard Kearney and Mark Dooley, eds., *Questioning Ethics: Contemporary Debates in Philosophy* (London: Routledge, 1999), ch. 6, "Hospitality, Justice and Responsibility: A Dialogue with Jacques Derrida," quotation from p. 70, italics in original; cf. Penelope Deutscher, *How to Read Derrida* (London: Granta, 2005), 66.

[84] Derrida, *Acts of Religion*, 362; in the next few pages, Derrida argues that hospitality's total openness must include neighbors, strangers, even nonhumans (such as the animals in Noah's ark), so that "Hospitality is the deconstruction of the at-home" (p. 364).

[85] Derrida and Dufourmantelle, *Of Hospitality*, 123, italics in original. Derrida's concrete examples are Mary, whose hospitality involved the "invasion" and transformation of her inmost being, and Abraham, whose guests so overwhelmed their host to the point of even changing his name! See Derrida, *Acts of Religion*, 372; cf. Cleo McNelly Kearns, "Mary, Maternity, and Abrahamic Hospitality in Derrida's Reading of Massignon," in *Derrida and Religion: Other Testaments*, ed. Yvonne Sherwood and Kevin Hart (New York and London: Routledge, 2005), 73-94.

[86] Derrida and Dufourmantelle, *Of Hospitality*, 124.

Romans 1-4.[87] In this light we see that Paul's exhortation to practice hospitality to strangers (Rom 12:13) includes the call to go beyond repayment (12:17) and insists on welcoming those who have other eating/meal practices (Romans 14), which in effect amounts to welcoming the religious stranger. Jennings concludes, "What Paul was attempting in his own time was the creation of something like a new politics that stood in contrast to the dominant political orders within which he worked as both a Pharisee and as a citizen of Rome ... Paul was concerned to foster the emergence of a new kind of society or sociality that would instantiate justice outside the law and so bring to expression the duty beyond debt that he called love."[88]

CONDITIONALITY AND THE REDEMPTIVE HOSPITALITY OF GOD

Jennings's proposal needs to be given further theological articulation. But before we do so, we must attend to an all-important question: What if the visitor is not only a stranger, but also an enemy, or worse, the devil himself?[89] This is not just an abstract question.[90] Derrida recognizes that while hospitality must always welcome the stranger, it must also address the stranger, even ask about the stranger's name, "all the while trying to prevent this question from becoming a 'condition,' a police interrogation, an inquest or an investigation, or a simple border check."[91] Because there is never only a "general" stranger that is welcomed, but always a particular individual or group, "real hospitality would consist of ... the necessity of welcoming someone in particular, someone with a proper name and not just some vague Nobody ... Between the welcoming question, 'Hey you there, what's your name?' and the police interrogation, 'Hey you there, what's your name?,' the difference is subtle but fundamental—a difference between two *inflections*."[92] In short, for Derrida, hospitality involves risks

---

[87] Theodore W. Jennings, Jr., *Reading Derrida/Thinking Paul: On Justice* (Stanford, Calif.: Stanford University Press, 2006), 88-91.

[88] Jennings, *Reading Derrida/Thinking Paul*, 126.

[89] Thus Jean-Luc Marion has suggested that a true gift can be given only to an enemy, "the one who does not love in return and therefore permits one to love freely (without reservation) ... The enemy thus becomes the ally of the gift and the friend becomes the enemy of the gift"; see Jean-Luc Marion, "Sketch of a Phenomenological Concept of Gift," in *Postmodern Philosophy and Christian Thought*, ed. Merold Westphal (Bloomington and Indianapolis: Indiana University Press, 1999), 122-43, from p. 138.

[90] Rosemarie Freeney Harding with Rachel Elizabeth Harding, "Hospitality, Haints, and Healing: A Southern African American Meaning of Religion," in *Deeper Shades of Purple: Womanism in Religion and Society*, ed. Stacey M. Floyd-Thomas (New York: New York University Press, 2006), 98-114, esp. 101-2, recollect unconditional "southern" (African American) hospitality practices, to the point of opening their home to peddlers, gamblers, thieves, and homeless streetwalkers.

[91] Cited in Michael Naas, *Taking on the Tradition: Jacques Derrida and the Legacies of Deconstruction* (Stanford, Calif.: Stanford University Press, 2003), 160.

[92] Naas, *Taking on the Tradition*, 164-65, italics in original.

and rides the tension between absolute unconditionality and conventional constraints: "Calculate the risks, yes, but don't shut the door on what cannot be calculated, meaning the future and the foreigner."[93] Is this Derridean discussion of the limits to hospitality sufficient?

I suggest that there are at least two further approaches to discussing the limits or conditions of hospitality: that related to the host and that related to the guest. From the perspective of the former, one might argue at various levels. At the philosophical level, it could be argued that hospitality and boundaries go together: "unless we draw a line—a boundary—and say that something lies outside its domain, then we can speak about nothing that lies inside with real meaning ... Without boundaries, there will be no system into which anyone could be invited; without hospitality, the system will dry up, will turn in on itself and die."[94] Put alternatively, without home ownership, "there cannot be hospitality."[95]

Biblically, there are of course warnings against idolatry, yoking with the enemy, and the distinctions between the church and the world.[96] Commenting on the latter—for example, the boundaries established by the Jerusalem Council (Acts 15)—Christine Pohl writes, "Boundaries are an important part of making a place physically and psychologically safe."[97] Hospitality needs to preserve the alterity of the other in at least two senses: in recognizing the distinctiveness with which the other represents the image of God and in rejecting the attempts of the unholy other to overwhelm and destroy the self.

Practically, it might also be said that Christian practices of hospitality are baptismally and eucharistically conditioned such that for some Christian groups, the "open table" is quite offensive (see below, pp. 134-37). Further, there is also what Hans Boersma calls "penitential hospitality": "Without penance, our sins exclude us from the community of reconcilia-

---

[93] Derrida, *Paper Machine*, 67.

[94] N. Lynne Westfield, *Dear Sisters: A Womanist Practice of Hospitality* (Cleveland: Pilgrim Press, 2001), xi-xii. While insisting on not confusing "welcome" with politically correct notions of "inclusion," Westfield proceeds to suggest that the lines between "inside" and "outside" are perhaps articulated best through stories and narratives, and concludes by urging "insiders" to be willing to be transformed through interacting with "familiar voices" and other neighbors.

[95] Rosemary L. Haughton, "Hospitality: Home as the Integration of Privacy and Community," in *The Longing for Home*, ed. Leroy S. Rouner (Notre Dame, Ind.: University of Notre Dame Press, 1996), 204-16, quote from p. 215. Haughton does go on to ask, however: home ownership toward what end? The answer she provides is: hospitality.

[96] Henry F. Knight, "Coming to Terms with Amalek: Facing the Limits of Hospitality," in *Post-Shoah Dialogues: Re-Thinking Our Texts Together,* ed. James F. Moore (Lanham, Md.: University Press of America, 2004), 195-207, esp. 202, writes: "Amalek is that other whom hospitality cannot welcome because Amalek's identity denies the validity of hospitality even when it welcomes Amalek."

[97] Pohl, *Making Room*, 140. While Pohl nicely discusses the abuses of hospitality, she also insists that we must be open to discerning God's working in any situation so that boundaries may be redrawn.

tion and turn us into strangers exiled from home ... Forgiveness without penance means hospitality without boundaries and an invitation to Satan, sin, and death to take over the community of grace."[98] In each of these ways, hospitality is conditioned by convictions about what Christian identity means (see above, pp. 73-76), and about what Christian identity resists. As Boersma notes elsewhere, "Hospitality is an art that is impossible to practice when we refuse to challenge evil."[99]

The conditions of hospitality, however, can also be approached from the perspective of the guest. Kant's universal hospitality, which insisted that the stranger does not have the right to be a "permanent visitor," echoes the protocols of guest behavior widespread among many cultures. In the ancient Near Eastern and Hellenistic worlds, hosts could infringe on the laws of hospitality by (1) insulting rather than honoring the guest; (2) failing to protect the guest; and (3) providing what is less than the best for the guest. But as important, guests could also infringe on the laws of hospitality variously by (1) insulting rather than honoring the host; (2) usurping the role of the host; (3) refusing what is offered; (4) asking the host for more than what is minimally needed; and (5) asking personal questions of the host.[100] Clearly, there is a distinction between those strangers (*xenoi*) who knew how to behave as guests in the Greco-Roman world, and those who did not (*barbaroi*).[101]

From a theological point of view, I argue that the Christian condition of being aliens and strangers in this world means both that we are perpetually guests, first of God and then of others, and that we should adopt the postures appropriate to receiving hospitality even when we find our-

---

[98] Hans Boersma, "Liturgical Hospitality: Theological Reflections on Sharing in Grace," *Journal for Christian Theological Research* 8 (2003) [http://www.luthersem.edu/ctrf/JCTR/default.htm]: 67-77, quote from p. 76.

[99] Hans Boersma, *Violence, Hospitality, and the Cross: Reappropriating the Atonement Tradition* (Grand Rapids: Baker Academic 2004), 35. In another essay—"Irenaeus, Derrida and Hospitality: On the Eschatological Overcoming of Violence," *Modern Theology* 19, no. 2 (2003): 163-80, esp. 168-69—Boersma registers his conviction that Derrida's open hospitality cannot exclude anyone, even the devil, and suggests instead grounding human hospitality in God's eschatological hospitality that is more capable of resisting evil and evoking trust and hope for a better future. I share Boersma's concerns. Yet, while he rightly points out that Derrida's absolute hospitality is incapable of excluding the devil, I am not as pessimistic about the practices related to Derrida's conditional hospitality.

[100] See Julian Pitt-Rivers, "The Stranger, the Guest and the Hostile Host: Introduction to the Study of the Laws of Hospitality," in *Contributions to Mediterranean Sociology: Mediterranean Rural Communities and Social Change*, ed. J.-G. Peristiany, Publications of the Social Sciences Centre Athens 4 (Paris and The Hague: Mouton, 1968), 13-30, esp. 25-29; and Victor H. Matthews, "Hospitality and Hostility in Judges 4," *Biblical Theology Bulletin* 21, no. 1 (1991): 13-21, esp. 13-15.

[101] Bruce J. Malina, "The Received View and What It Cannot Do: III John and Hospitality," in *Social-scientific Criticism of the New Testament and its Social World*, ed. John H. Elliott (Decatur, Ga.: Scholars Press, 1986), 171-94, at 183.

selves as hosts.[102] If the first shall be last, and the follower of Christ is the servant of all, then a Christian theology of guests and hosts emerges out of and is shaped by a theology of exile. In his *The Religion of the Landless*, Mennonite scholar Daniel Smith suggests a theology of exile, by which he means living as did deported Israel in "Babylon" and thereby rejecting the power of the nation-state and of the right to go to war.[103] Now Smith also insists that adopting a posture of countercultural resistance and nonconformity means not socioethical disengagement, but exactly the opposite: "The theology of exile affirms the separation from conformity, the preservation of culture in a minority, the unique needs of exiled or refugee peoples, in a manner that Exodus theology cannot understand."[104] I agree with the broad strokes of Smith's theology of exile and wish to embrace such an exilic posture as central to a theology of hospitality in a postmodern and pluralistic world. At the same time, I suggest that the requisite posture is much more paradoxical in affirming both countercultural opposition and hospitable openness.[105] What is more important, whereas Smith's theology of exile cautions against Christian complicity with the modern nation-state, my focus is on how to live as aliens in a strange land. In this case, countercultural opposition means maintaining a distinctively Christian communal identity, but hospitable openness means interacting with rather than isolating ourselves from our neighbors. In this case, the instructions given to the exilic community through the prophet Jeremiah remain apropos: "But seek the welfare of the city where I have sent you into exile, and pray to the LORD on its behalf, for in its welfare you will find your welfare" (Jer 29:7).

How might we seek the welfare of the cities wherein which Christian exiles find themselves today? We do so, I suggest, through the practices of hospitality on the margins. It is at the margins, Christine Pohl reminds us, where Christian hospitality has been most vibrantly practiced.[106] Hospitality is transformed, in effect taken out of the economy of exchange, when it is associated with hosts who are liminal, marginal, and on the underside of the social order. Hospices, hospitals, and orphanages work most effectively when serviced not by those existing within a system of salary and remu-

---

[102] Graham Ward, "Hospitality and Justice towards 'Strangers': A Theological Reflection," paper presented at the "Migration in Europe: What are the Ethical Guidelines for Political Practice?" symposium, Katholische Akademie, Berlin, 27-29 November 2003 [available at http://www.katholische-akademie-berlin.de/Veranstaltungen/ 2003112729/Ward_pdf.pdf] (accessed 29 September 2006).

[103] Daniel L. Smith, *The Religion of the Landless: The Social Context of the Babylonian Exile* (Bloomington, Ind.: Meyer-Stone Books, 1989).

[104] Smith, *The Religion of the Landless*, 213.

[105] As suggested by another Anabaptist scholar, Peter C. Blum, "Totality, Alterity, and Hospitality: On the Openness of Anabaptist Community," *Brethren Life and Thought* 48, no. 3/4 (2003): 159-75.

[106] Pohl, *Making Room*, ch. 6

neration, but by hosts who respect their guests and "have a sense of their own alien status."[107] In these cases, the lines between guests and hosts are blurred, and the conditions for giving and receiving hospitality apply to both sides, even if in (subtly) different respects.

THE SPIRIT OF HOSPITALITY: TRINITARIAN BELIEFS— PNEUMATIC PRACTICES

It is now time to present the basic features of the pneumatological theology of guests and hosts that has been our goal in this chapter. I do so through presenting the following four theses.

Thesis 1—For Christians, Jesus Christ is not only the paradigmatic host representing and offering the redemptive hospitality of God, but he does so as the exemplary guest who went out into the far country. In this regard, Abraham is the prototype of guest transformed into host who always remains guest. Paul followed in their footsteps and urges us to do the same. Christian life enacts the hospitality of God precisely through our embodying, paradoxically, both the exclusively christomorphic shape of the *ecclesia,* on the one hand, and, on the other, the inclusively incarnational *koinonia* of God at work in aliens in a strange land.[108]

Thesis 2—For Christians, the gift of the Holy Spirit signifies the extension of God's economy of abundant hospitality into the whole world. As we have seen, the outpouring of the Spirit enabled the continued reenactment of Jesus' habits of meal-fellowship to include Samaritans and gentiles, and empowered the expansion of Jesus' journeying into the far country through his followers to the ends of the earth. As John Koenig reminds us, "The Spirit moves to create 'grace-grace' situations, that is, communions or *koinōnias* in which all parties 'deny' themselves but also receive, and *expect* to receive, 'good measure, pressed down, shaken together, running over' (Luke 6:38). Grace abounds because God multiplies both the giving and receiving (2 Cor 9:8-11)."[109] The Spirit who is divine guest in the lives of those who receive her is also the divine host who dispenses the economy of God's hospitality.

Thesis 3—For Christians, the practices of hospitality therefore embody the trinitarian character of God's economy of redemption. In the economy of God, the unconditional gifts of God in Christ and the Holy Spirit mean that there is never any lack of hospitality to be offered and received. Rather, the grace of God overturns the world's economy of exchange so that there

---

[107] Pohl, *Making Room*, 124.

[108] Bernard P. Prusak, "Hospitality Extended or Denied: *Koinonia* Incarnate from Jesus to Augustine," in *The Church as Communion*, ed. James H. Provost; Permanent Seminar Studies 1 (Washington, D.C.: Canon Law Society of America, 1984), 89-126.

[109] Koenig, *New Testament Hospitality*, 134-35.

is only an endless giving and receiving that now characterizes the relationship of the church and the world. This is because what is being given and what is being received is not any *thing* but the triune God as manifest in the body of Christ and animated by the power of the Spirit.

I want to pause further to emphasize this point in light of our dialogue with Derrida. If what is needed is the redemption of the economy of exchange and reciprocity, then the answer might be found in such a trinitarian theology of mutuality. Rather than an excessive giving that would be taken as squandering if conceived within an economy of scarcity, the trinitarian life of God reveals instead the abundance of an excessive God whose gifts are extravagant, inexhaustible, free, and undeserved (completely gratuitous), but yet simultaneously directed nonsuperfluously toward equality and justice on the one hand, and the creation of a community of mutual givers on the other. The trinitarian logic that entails God as Giver, Given, and Giving—a truly perichoretic hospitality—initiates, sustains, and solicits, rather than requires, by law or otherwise, our own giving.[110] In this scheme of things, receivers do not return to givers out of any incurred indebtedness dictated by an economy of scarcity; rather, receivers allow the gifts received to overflow through their lives into those of others because of the boundless hospitality of an excessively gracious God.[111]

Thesis 4—For Christians, then, the redemptive economy of the triune God invites our participation as guests and hosts in the divine hospitality revealed in Christ by the power of the Holy Spirit. From the preceding discussion, I insist we take seriously our always being both guests and hosts, albeit in different respects in different contexts and relationships. As guests and hosts, sometimes simultaneously, we are obligated only to discern the Spirit's presence and activity so that we can perform the appropriate practices representing the hospitable God. Which tongues we speak and what practices we engage in will depend on where we are, who we are interacting with, and what the social, political, and economic structures are that give shape to our encounter. In a postmodern and pluralistic world after 9/11 that includes situations like Sri Lanka, Nigeria, the United States, and innumerable other locations of interreligious tension, no one set of practices suffices.

---

[110] This is the argument of Stephen H. Webb, *The Gifting God: A Trinitarian Ethics of Excess* (New York: Oxford, 1996), esp. 90; see also Robert Vosloo, "Identity, Otherness and the Triune God: Theological Groundwork for a Christian Ethic of Hospitality," *Journal of Theology for Southern Africa* 119 (2004): 69-89.

[111] Calvin Schrag, *God as Otherwise Than Being: Toward a Semantics of the Gift* (Evanston, Ill.: Northwestern University Press, 2002), 119-20. Schrag also writes, "A genuine gift will need to issue from an economic region. The dynamics of the gift comes into view only in the wake of the suspension of the 'law (*nomos*) of the *oikos*,' understood as the rules, regulations, and requirements that govern the organization of the family, household, the mundanity of the familiar and quotidian practices of everyday life. The gift transgresses law" (p. 109).

When set in a pneumatological perspective, such a theology of hospitality points to the dynamic rather than static aspect of our witness such that we can never be too comfortable in any one role. Rather, we are participants in the redemptive hospitality of God, even while we are conduits of this hospitality to the world, albeit from its margins as aliens and strangers. Hence, we find ourselves in a paradoxical state of being guests in a strange land on the one hand, even as we embody the divine hospitality on the other. But in either case, we are caught up in the excessive hospitality of God that has been revealed in his Son and poured out through his Spirit upon us and even upon all flesh.

We have now arrived at a resting place in our journey halfway through the constructive part of our argument. In this chapter I have not developed a full-blown theology of hospitality; instead, I have attempted to contribute some pneumatological (and trinitarian) perspectives toward such a theological vision. More precisely, however, the theology of hospitality sketched here is intended to provide a vigorous theological platform that can sustain a flexible and relevant theology of interreligious practices for our time. Such a Christian theology is resolutely christomorphic in establishing Jesus as the paradigmatic guest and host representing the hospitable God; at the same time, I have also presented a robust pneumatological perspective which argues that the divine economy inaugurated on the Day of Pentecost overcomes the economies of exchange and scarcity, thus making it possible for us to participate as guests and hosts, to speak in many strange tongues, and engage in a multiplicity of practices. In the next and last chapter of this book, we complete the second part of our constructive argument by fleshing out how such a pneumatological theology of many interreligious practices is enacted in a pluralistic world of diverse cultures, traditions, and religions.

5

The Welcoming Spirit

Theology of Hospitality and Interreligious Practices

We have set forth to explore and defend one major and two minor theses in this book. The latter have been to establish the interconnections between Christian beliefs and practices on a sound pneumatological platform and to articulate a Christian theology of hospitality within a more robust pneumatological and trinitarian framework. These tasks we have attempted to fulfill in chapters 2 and 4 above. Both minor theses, however, are formulated in the service of the major objective of this book: in response to the complexities surrounding interfaith relations in the twenty-first century (chapter 1), we have set forth to develop a Christian theology of religions commensurate with the many kinds of practices constitutive of the contemporary interreligious encounter (chapter 3). My central argument, teasing out the pneumatological perspective on beliefs and practices and the pneumatological theology of hospitality, is that the Christian encounter with the religions today is witnessed to by the many tongues enabled by the Spirit and engaged through the many hospitable practices empowered by the same Spirit.

In this final chapter, I will fill out the details of this central thesis by explicating what kinds of interreligious practices are consistent with the theology of hospitality presented in the preceding pages. We will explore, respectively in each of the following three main sections, what it means to perform Christian mission, to seek after peace and justice, and to engage in interreligious dialogue in a religiously plural world. I will argue that Christian mission in a postmodern, pluralistic, and post-9/11 world is constituted by evangelism, social witness, and interreligious dialogue and that evangelism and proclamation always involve social engagements and interreligious dialogues of various kinds.

Be warned that the following discussion does not map exactly on to the typology of exclusivism, inclusivism, and pluralism. Rather, even as I had earlier acknowledged that these are three irreducible positions from a logical point of view, at the same time I present the following in the quest to go beyond the impasse that reads these theologies as mutually exclusive. I argue that there are central practices and correlating beliefs related to these classic positions that need to be retrieved for all forms of Christian witness in our time, and that this is possible within the framework of the pneumatological theology of interreligious hospitality offered here because it provides an interpretive grid that preserves the valid insights of and is enriched by each approach. Hence, a theology of interreligious hospitality is neither exclusivistic nor inclusivistic nor pluralistic in any straightforward sense; however, I will suggest that a pneumatological theology of hospitality and interreligious practices is also exclusivistic, inclusivistic, and pluralistic in different respects insofar as it is informed by elements of these three views. Might it be that a theology of interreligious hospitality provides not necessarily a fourth theological proposal but an integrative framework for redeeming and theologically grounding the most important Christian practices for our time?

PERFORMING CHRISTIAN MISSION: ECCLESIAL PRACTICES AND THE HOSPITABLE GOD

Given the interrelationship between beliefs and practices that we have already established, we can now recognize that being the church—the body of Christ—is defined not only by who we are but also by what we do. The latter involves bearing witness to the Christ, whose disciples we are. Hence, in a world of many faiths, there is no denying this missionary aspect of our ecclesial identity. So the question is not whether to bear witness, but how; and this is an especially urgent one in a pluralistic world after 9/11. In this section I sketch a pneumatological theology of mission by expanding on the *missio Dei* concept prominent in missiology circles, specifying its ecclesial shape, and suggesting some modes of implementation in places like Sri Lanka, Nigeria, and the United States.[1] Throughout, we ask how the church participates in God's economy of hospitality by focusing on the need to discern the contexts, tongues, and practices relevant to the *missio Dei* in a religiously plural world.

---

[1] Here, I build on previous attempts in pneumatological theologies of mission, as in John V. Taylor, *The Go-Between God: The Holy Spirit and Christian Mission*, 2nd ed. (London: SCM, 2004); Veli-Matti Kärkkäinen, *Toward a Pneumatological Theology: Pentecostal and Ecumenical Perspectives on Ecclesiology, Soteriology and Theology of Mission*, ed. Amos Yong (Lanham, New York, and Oxford: University Press of America, 2002); and Andrew Lord, *Spirit-Shaped Mission: A Holistic Charismatic Missiology* (Milton Keynes, U.K., and Waynesboro, Ga.: Paternoster, 2005).

WELCOMING OTHERS: *MISSIO DEI* AND THE HOSPITALITY OF GOD

"*Missio Dei*" is a summary phrase for Protestant theologies of mission coming out of the International Missionary Conference's meeting at Willingen, Germany, in 1952.[2] Three interrelated themes are emphasized in *missio Dei*. (1) Christian mission belongs first and foremost to God rather than to the church; God is the principal protagonist of missionary activity and the church participates in the mission of God. (2) The mission of God is fully trinitarian in shape: God the Father reconciles the world to himself by sending the Son by the power of the Spirit; the focus is on the universal fatherhood and spiritual presence of the first and third divine persons rather than on the Sonship of the second as proclaimed through the body of Christ. (3) The presence and activity of God's mission are to be found throughout the created order, even in the "secular" and "non-Christian" realms, and the goal of the *missio Dei* is the ushering in of the kingdom of God rather than the enlargement of the church. Fully recognizing the dangers in this scheme, which sees everything as mission and leaves nothing distinctive about Christian mission,[3] I nevertheless wish to build on the *missio Dei* concept in conjunction with a theology of hospitality along the following lines.

To begin, the Christian mission is nothing more or less than our participation in the hospitality of God. God is not only the principal "missionary" but also the host of all creation who invites the world to "God's banquet of salvation."[4] Evangelization is in this scheme of things nothing more or less than our having experienced God's redemptive hospitality and our inviting others to experience the same.

Hence, the Christian mission involves the reconciliation of aliens and strangers (ourselves) to God, and our making available this reconciliation to other aliens and strangers by becoming reconciled to them. The *missio Dei* is in this sense a "stranger-centered" theology that follows in the footsteps of Jesus: the Son of God became a stranger, coming into a far country, even to the point of death.[5] Here, Christian mission is the embodiment of divine hospitality that loves strangers (*philoxenia*), to the point of giving up our lives on behalf of others as to be reconciled to them, that they might in turn be reconciled to God.

---

[2] See David J. Bosch, *Transforming Mission: Paradigm Shifts in Theology of Mission* (Maryknoll, N.Y.: Orbis Books, 1991), 389-93; and Carlos F. Cardoza-Orlandi, *Mission: An Essential Guide* (Nashville, Tenn.: Abingdon, 2002), ch. 2.

[3] A set of articles revisits and assesses the *missio Dei* theme for contemporary theology of mission in *International Review of Mission* 92, no. 367 (October 2003).

[4] John Navone, "Divine and Human Hospitality," *New Blackfriars* 85 (2004): 329-40; cf. Andrew E. Arterbury and William H. Bellinger, Jr., "'Returning' to the Hospitality of the Lord: A Reconsideration of Psalm 23,5-6," *Biblica* 86, no. 3 (2005): 387-95.

[5] Kosuke Koyama, "'Extend Hospitality to Strangers': A Missiology of *Theologia Crucis*," *Currents in Theology and Mission* 20, no. 3 (1993): 165-76.

Such a "stranger-centered" (rather than church-centered) theology of hospitality produces the following missionary practices in an interreligious context. First, hospitality opens up a "free space," where people of other faiths can enter, where strangers, even enemies, might be transformed into friends, where hosts do not dictate how guests must change but rather provide a safe forum for changes to occur.[6] Focus here is not on who the host is or what the host has to offer, but on the relationship with guests and on respecting the integrity of the guests.

Second, Christian mission in terms of hospitality means not only hosting people of other faiths but risking being guests of such strangers. Thomas Ogletree writes, "My readiness to welcome the other into my world must be balanced by my readiness to enter the world of the other ... The universal claims which are implicit in my perspective are offset by the universal claims residing in the perspective of the stranger. In short, the ramifications of hospitality are not fully manifest unless I also know the meaning of being a stranger."[7] Remembering that hospitality involves a set of relationships between guests and hosts, and that Christian mission inevitably involves us as both guests and hosts, we must recognize that our embracing strangers of other faiths involves them also doing the same. Hence, our desire for them to embrace our beliefs and enter into our practices must be matched by our willingness to do the same.

This means, third, that Christian mission conceived in terms of hospitality involves not only the risk of our interacting with strangers of other faiths but also the risk of our being vulnerable to and with them.[8] This is fully consonant with the theology of exile we developed earlier (see above, pp. 122-26), such that Christian mission occurs not out of a centrist ecclesial identity (as in the Christendom era) but out of a marginal and ambiguous status (as in our postcolonial and post-Christendom situation). Having said this, I insist that such a posture is not only commendable for Christians who find themselves as religious minorities, such as in the Sri Lankan case, but that it is precisely such a self-understanding that is all the more important in places like America so that the church is not seduced into confusing the political power she has access to with the spiritual power of the gospel. When Christian mission is conducted from the vantage point of being guests of those of other faiths, then not only do we defer to our hosts

---

[6] Charles Maahs, "Hospitality, Power, and Missio: A Review of the Writings and Leadership of Roger W. Fjeld," *Currents in Theology and Mission* 30, no. 3 (2003): 168-72, esp. 168.

[7] Thomas W. Ogletree, *Hospitality to the Stranger: Dimensions of Moral Understanding* (Philadelphia: Fortress, 1985), 4.

[8] Anthony J. Gittins, "Beyond Hospitality? The Missionary Status and Role Revisited," *Currents in Theology and Mission* 21, no. 3 (1994): 164-82. In what follows I draw also from Gittins's book-length argument, *Gifts and Strangers: Meeting the Challenge of Inculturation* (New York, and Mahwah, N.J.: Paulist Press, 1989), esp. chs. 4-5.

(even in the American context), but we also receive from them as aliens in a strange land. Hence, Christian missionaries (or ministries, in the American scene) should be of the mentality that they are not only givers but also receivers of the gifts borne by those in other faiths.[9] This means recognizing that if the gospel is not being welcomed, perhaps it is because we are being disagreeable guests who have broken the protocols for hospitality in a foreign environment.

I need to be clear that what I am not advocating is any naïve "conversion" of Christians to other faiths. But I am saying that taking the incarnational and pentecostal principles seriously results in a missiological contextualization that includes the mutual transformation of faith traditions. The result, however, is not a blurry syncretism but a deepening of the home tradition as enriched by the gifts of others. Thomas Reynolds puts it this way: "Hospitality is a fruitful metaphor for the being-with of relational differentiation. Differences here are not swallowed into the home-dwelling, but rather preserved in their uniqueness as they are welcomed and taken in, thus enlargening and enriching the scope of the resonance created by the 'us' now dwelling together more inclusively, extending the frontiers of that dwelling field of semantic power and becoming more complex and beautiful because of it."[10]

At the same time, I should also note that one can be a "disagreeable guest" unintentionally or intentionally. Christians should avoid giving needless offense. When we realize we have given needless offense, we should apologize, and sensitize ourselves to avoiding repeating such disapprobative behavior in the future. Sometimes, however, there is no evading the offence that the gospel itself presents (1 Cor 1:18ff.). There will be occasions when the protocols of hospitality are deemed broken by our guests and hosts of other faiths, but only because of the scandal of the gospel. In these instances, the integrity of Christian witness can be preserved if the scandal of the *evangelion* is communicated with love, kindness, and compassion. The *how* of hospitable practices, both in giving and receiving hospitality, should always provide an opening for the gospel, even if on occasion the *what* of the Christian witness may be disagreeable to others.

---

[9] Graham Ward, *Christ and Culture* (Malden, Mass.: Blackwell, 2005), 82, writes, "There is no superiority between host and guest. For to host is to allow the guest to be as oneself; and to be a guest is to receive the host as oneself. True justice only operates in obedience to the economy of faithful response that recognizes the question in every encounter, 'Who is the stranger?,' and realizes the answer is: 'Neither of us—while we have each other.' This is the economy of love—that aims always at the perfection and righting of relation."

[10] Thomas E. Reynolds, *The Broken Whole: Philosophical Steps toward a Theology of Global Solidarity* (Albany: State University of New York Press, 2005), 131.

EMBRACING OTHERS: ECCLESIAL HOSPITALITY AND
THE NEW EVANGELISM

We turn now from more individual and interpersonal practices of hospitality to its communal forms as manifest in the church. What are the concrete ecclesial practices of such a stranger-centered theology of hospitality and mission? I will sketch responses at the levels of congregational and liturgical practices.

To begin, congregational hospitality involves at least the following elements: a visible and welcoming public face, a dialogical posture, and a commitment to public servanthood. These are minimal aspects of a congregational ministry that is oriented toward welcoming, including, and reconciling strangers.[11] People with the requisite gifts need to be mobilized to interact with strangers, not only on the "home turf" of the church grounds but in public and even private spaces where more genuine dialogue, interchange, and interaction occur. In such contexts "away from home," Christian mission involves the gifts or graces (*charisms*) of listening to and receiving from others.

When engaging people in other faiths, however, even more intentional strategies are needed. At the congregational level, it is unlikely that whole congregations are going to interact across faith lines. One suggestion might be to look for opportunities to work together toward common causes (see below, pp. 146-50). Anticipating such interfaith ventures, what about the possibility of having neighborhood meals together where we can envision and plan such joint projects? To be sure, such eating together (cf. above, chapter 4, pp. 100-105) is usually facilitated by congregational leaders who have already had the opportunity to experience hosting or being guests of members of the other congregation. Because food plays an important role in hospitality, eating together is already a major accomplishment that symbolizes the establishment of sufficient bonds of trust across interreligious lines. Further, meal occasions are not only acts of friendliness but serve the processes of socialization and negotiation of religious identity.[12] When people of different faiths come together around the meal table, the boundaries between adversaries break down, ritual practices are expanded, and a public space of mutual transformation is potentially established.

---

[11] See Elizabeth Rankin Geitz, *Entertaining Angels: Hospitality Programs for the Caring Church* (Harrisburg, Pa.: Morehouse, 1993); Delia Halverson, *The Gift of Hospitality in the Church, in the Home, and in All of Life* (St. Louis, Mo.: Chalice Press, 1999); and Thomas Carvel Edward Lobaugh, "Setting the Captives Free: Hospitality's Liberating Power of Reconciliation between Church and Neighborhood" (D.Min. project, Columbia Theological Seminary [Decatur, Ga.], 2004).

[12] Conrad Lashley, "Towards a Theoretical Understanding," in *In Search of Hospitality: Theoretical Perspectives and Debates*, ed. Conrad Lashley and Alison J. Morrison (Oxford and Boston: Butterworth-Heinemann, 2000), 1-17.

This raises the question: What role, if any, does the Christian liturgy play in the church's practices of hospitality? Naturally, people committed to other faiths would find few reasons to attend a Christian service or liturgy. People of nominal faith, however, may in fact be visitors. Is the Christian liturgy only for the purposes of nurturing Christian discipleship or also for evangelism? Patrick Keifert suggests both, by insisting on an inclusive liturgy that emphasizes God as the host and the church as the minister of public worship.[13] He recognizes that the church's hosting strangers is risky, requiring decentering, vulnerability, and the readiness to have tables turned so we become guests instead. These attitudes and sensibilities can be nurtured only by our continual repentance, conversion, and transformation. Such congregations will be sensitive to the strangers in their midst, to the point of undertaking architectural rearrangement, liturgical reorganization, and even ritual adjustment to accommodate, include, and engage their ever-shifting audiences.[14] These shifts suggest there are no hard and fast lines between "insiders" and "outsiders" since the church itself will be a "company of strangers" shaped by the works (*poiemata*) of the Spirit (see chapter 2 above, pp. 59-62).[15]

But can such shifts be made with regard to specific liturgical events such as the sacraments of baptism and the Eucharist? Of course, people of other faiths would not be active participants in baptism understood as a rite of Christian initiation. But the case of the Eucharist is less straightforward. On the one side, some (including the Orthodox and the Roman Catholic churches) would point to the early church's example, when catechumens and any others not fully initiated through water baptism were dismissed before the congregational celebration of the Lord's Supper. For these traditions, the eucharistic meal reenacts the consummatory act of bonding between the bridegroom, who is Christ, and the bride, who is the church of Christ. When understood in this way, there is a sacredness, privacy, and intimacy around the Eucharist that clearly demarcates where "insiders" belong and where "outsiders" remain. Such a posture is not meant to demean "outsiders" or those in other faiths, but is an important act of Christian self-definition and identification (see chapter 3 above, pp. 73-76), especially for more high-church ecclesial traditions. The parallel here would be that there are various other (non-Christian) religious practices that are accessible only to those who have undertaken the appropriate ritual initiations, with some of the chief concerns having to do with unin-

---

[13] Patrick R. Keifert, *Welcoming the Stranger: A Public Theology of Worship and Evangelism* (Minneapolis: Fortress Press, 1992).

[14] Cf. Michael Kwatera, *Come to the Feast: Liturgical Theology of, by, and for Everybody* (Collegeville, Minn.: Liturgical Press, 2006), 12-23.

[15] Keifert, *Welcoming the Stranger*, 88-91. Also, Paul Westermeyer, "Tradition, Liturgy, and the Visitor," *Word and World* 13, no. 1 (1993): 76-84, esp. 79, writes, "We are all visitors, all strangers, all sojourners … all guests."

formed "outsiders" being unable to appreciate or engage that which is only embraceable by "insiders."

On the other hand, there are also Christian communions that have more open expressions of communion table fellowship. John Wesley understood the Supper as a "converting ordinance" that was in principle not closed to sinners seeking repentance, and many Wesleyan churches continue to practice an open, although not casual, communion table.[16] Free Church traditions, postdenominational movements, the wide range of Emerging churches, and other like contemporary Christian expressions all tend to be more flexible in their practices of the Lord's Supper.

I believe that especially for Free Church traditions (of which I am most familiar), the Wesleyan conviction of an "open table" can be reappropriated for the purposes of developing what might be called a liturgically shaped set of hospitable interreligious practices. There are two steps to this proposal. First, I think there is an undeniable "open table" in general to which all people are invited to enjoy the hospitality of God. While in the Lukan rendition of the parable of the Great Banquet the commandment is given to "Go out at once into the streets and lanes of the town and bring in the poor, the crippled, the blind, and the lame" (Luke 14:21), the Matthean version reports that "those slaves went out into the streets and gathered all whom they found, both good *and bad*" (Matt 22:10, my italics). Clearly, the hospitality of God is extended unconditionally and gratuitously to all, and "there are no barriers to Jesus' table except self-imposed ones."[17]

Second, recall that in the earliest Christian communities, this breaking of bread occurred on a daily basis, from home to home, and in a dynamical process in and through which "outsiders" were initiated into the fellowship of believers (Acts 2:42-47). Following this model, might this notion of the "open table" be a bridge through which Christians can practice a form of liturgical hospitality in their encounter with those in other faiths? This does not require a formal enactment of the eucharistic sacrament; it only needs the informal but essentially hospitable practices of sharing meals with one another with gladness and generous hearts. It is precisely in such contexts that the many tongues of the Spirit may yet speak forth and reveal the presence of God to save the lost and transform the disciples of Jesus ever closer into his image.

Our suggestions here for Christian mission in a religiously plural world are focused on the North American ecclesial context. In this situation, we

---

[16] Such openness is meant to accommodate not only sinners but also children and individuals with learning disabilities, even as the seriousness of the open table meant that "members" were excluded if they neglected the life of discipleship or refused to keep the (Wesleyan) Rules of the Society; see Mark W. Stamm, *Let Every Soul Be Jesus' Guest: A Theology of the Open Table* (Nashville, Tenn.: Abingdon Press, 2006).

[17] Cathy C. Campbell, *Stations of the Banquet: Faith Foundations for Food Justice* (Collegeville, Minn.: Liturgical Press, 2003), 87.

must emphasize, "Evangelism in the context of hospitality is crucial in a post-Christendom society."[18] Yet evangelistic hospitality is something we do not in addition to but *in and through* our worship, liturgical, or sacramental practices. Or put another way, it is in and through these ecclesial practices that the redemptive hospitality of God is accomplished by the powerful works (*poiemata*) of the Spirit. The key is to be discerning of who is present in the midst of the congregation and in the midst of the congregational community. Participation in the hospitality of the *missio Dei* requires discernment that seeks to identify how the Spirit might mediate the christomorphic character of the church's practices to engage the dynamics of the public sphere.

DISCERNING MISSION: MANY PRACTICES IN A PLURALISTIC WORLD

In this section, I want to focus our attention more specifically on discerning the *missio Dei* in religiously plural contexts such as we have seen in Sri Lanka and Nigeria. As we recognize that Christian mission and evangelism are primary characteristics of Christian discipleship, the questions here are not if but how to bear Christian witness. As suggested so far in this book, I invite us to think about how many tongues are interrelated to many practices in the Christian encounter with other faiths.

In a context like Sri Lanka, for example, we have a multifaith society— including Buddhists, Hindus, Muslims, and Christians, even though Christians are a minority group. In this situation, Christians are more guests than hosts, although in more interpersonal domains roles might certainly go in both directions. Hence, Christian witness is borne not only or even necessarily through proclamation, but inevitably by respecting the protocols of being guest to hosts of other faith traditions. When Paul was cast away to Malta, the hospitality of God was mediated instead through the hospitality of the Maltese islanders (Acts 28:2, 10). I would argue that it was precisely amidst such a reversal of roles through which Paul "visited him [Publius] and cured him by praying and putting his hands on him" (Acts 28:8b).

The Christian mission in the Sri Lankan context must be sensitive to the interreligious, political, and economic dynamics of Sinhala-Tamil relations. In some contexts, Christians find themselves as hosts, in others as guests; but in every situation, they represent, offer, and embody the redemptive hospitality of God even as they are recipients of such hospitality through their interactions with religious others. And where there is concern about the persecution of Christians (and there is), or about Christian rights and freedoms in a Buddhist-dominated state (and there is), then the way for-

---

[18] Joon-Sik Park, "Hospitality as Context for Evangelism," *Missiology* 30, no. 3 (2002): 385-95, quotation from p. 385.

ward is Christian interface with the issues according to the social conventions and political rules of engagement. This requires dialogue across religious lines since it is only through such interaction that progress can be made on these kinds of matters.[19]

What about evangelistic rallies, revivals, or crusades? In the Sri Lankan context, efforts should be made to minimize the occasion for charges of unethical conversions (although it is unforeseeable that anything less than Christian withdrawal from the public square would be acceptable to Sinhala Buddhist nationalists). On the other hand, large-scale Christian meetings are as unlikely in Sri Lanka as large-scale Muslim, Buddhist, Hindu, or Jewish meetings would be in the United States. In principle, in a democratic secular society like the United States, all faith groups are free to organize such events; demographically, economically, and politically, however, we are still perhaps half a generation away before non-Christian religious groups in America begin to organize such mass religious gatherings. The reverse probably holds true in the Sinhalese context. In other words, various local factors constrain evangelistic strategies even as they invite a diversity of Christian mission practices.

What then if we switched to a place like Nigeria, where there are equal numbers of Christians and Muslims, even if they are unevenly distributed in the south and north respectively? On the issue of evangelistic crusades, we have already observed (see chapter 1 above, pp. 18-19) how such have precipitated interreligious hostility and violence. I do not think that prohibiting evangelistic crusades is the right answer, especially since Nigeria is constitutionally structured as a democratic and secular country. Yet constitutional secularity does not give any religious group license to knowingly act in ways that might antagonize people of other faiths. Hence, Christians in Nigeria—I will leave it to Nigerian Muslims to speak for themselves—need to be circumspect about if, when, where, and how to hold such mass evangelistic endeavors, keeping in mind always their participation in the redemptive hospitality of God.

I would insist, however, that the practices of interreligious hospitality are key both to the flourishing of Nigeria as a nation and the reconciliation of its citizens across religious lines. We have already seen instances of interreligious hospitality practiced between Nigerian neighbors to those in other faiths (see p. 19), even amidst occasions of interreligious violence. The question, then, is how to further cultivate such forms of interreligious practices so that hospitality can become the norm rather than the exception to religious violence. From the Christian side, this must be developed out of the Christian conviction that "We can grow in Christian faith and discipleship

---

[19] Thus the editors note in their introduction that interreligious dialogue "can be a useful tool in lowering the hostilities between people of different faith groups"; see Harold D. Hunter and Cecil M. Robeck, Jr., eds., *The Suffering Body: Responding to the Persecution of Christians* (Milton Keynes, U.K., and Waynesboro, Ga.: Paternoster, 2006), xxi.

through getting to know ordinary Muslims!"[20] The goal must be mutual hospitality that empowers mutual transformation.

Yet we also realize that Christian-Muslim relations on the ground in places like Nigeria are inevitably shaped by the media and its presentation of Christian-Muslim relations elsewhere. So here the question is how we might encourage Christian media to give more attention to news of inter-religious hospitality, such as that between Pastor James Movel Wuye and Imam Ustaz Muhammad Nurayn Ashafa (see chapter 1, pp. 28-29), or that represented by pentecostal minister Aril Edvardsen, who has long been involved in Christian-Muslim dialogue.[21] Raising Christian awareness of these kinds of hospitable practices is essential in the Islamic context where American military initiatives are often interpreted as acts of Christian aggression against the Muslim world.[22] In our shrinking global village, "bad news" is liable to stir up interreligious tensions. But then, on the other side of this same coin, why could we not expect that "good news"—for example, the gospel of the hospitable God as manifest in the practices of those who bear God's name—might even facilitate the healing and recon-ciliation of Christians and Muslims in Nigeria and elsewhere?

Clearly the Nigerian context focuses our attention on the fact that Chris-tian witness is constituted by sociopolitical engagement and interreligious dialogue. Here we cannot be fooled into thinking that these activities are important only for the Nigerian situation. Rather, the volatility of the Nigerian case allows us to identify these tasks as essential to the Christian mission rather than as accidental. It is in this sense that the remainder of this chapter's discussion on the social and dialogical aspects of Christian mission be understood not as alternatives to but as core features of bearing witness to the gospel.

PERFORMING PEACE AND JUSTICE:
KINGDOM PRACTICES AND
ESCHATOLOGICAL HOSPITALITY

I have argued so far in this chapter that the church best fulfills the *mis-sio Dei* when she discerns the many tongues and enacts many hospitable practices relevant to the different situations in which she finds herself. In this section, I want to say more about the fact that Christian witness in a

---

[20] Bill A. Musk, *Touching the Soul of Islam: Sharing the Gospel in Muslim Cultures* (Oxford, U.K., and Grand Rapids: Monarch, 2004), 14.

[21] Oddbjørn Leirvik, "Charismatic Mission, Miracles and Faith-Based Diplomacy: The Case of Aril Edvardsen," in *Spirits of Globalization: The Growth of Pentecostalism and Expe-riential Spiritualities in a Global Age,* ed. Sturla J. Stålsett (London: SCM, 2006), 131-44.

[22] See the discussion in David L. Johnston, "Loving Neighbors in a Globalized World: U.S. Christians, Muslims, and the Mideast," in *Anxious about Empire: Theological Essays on the New Global Realities,* ed. Wes Avram (Grand Rapids: Brazos, 2004), 59-77.

religiously plural world necessarily involves a social dimension. We will begin with the question about religion and violence since that is raised so forcefully by our case studies in chapter 1. From there, I will suggest that the hospitality of God involves the in-breaking of the coming kingdom on the social and political domains of historical life, and that such redemptive hospitality is enacted in part by the practices of interfaith ecumenism. Be reminded that my theology of interreligious practices assumes that focusing on the church's social witness is not in lieu of fulfilling the Great Commission but is constitutive of that very task. In this case, however, Christian mission participates in what I call the eschatological hospitality of God that anticipates the redemption of every nation, tribe, tongue, and people. Hence, Christian mission engages in the practices of the kingdom of God. What counts here is not only the orthodoxy of Christian proclamation but the orthopraxis through which the Spirit of God accomplishes the eschatological transformation of the world.

RELIGION AND VIOLENCE IN THE LATE MODERN WORLD

The connections between religion and violence run deep, and there are too many theories attempting to explain the relationship for us to do justice to the topic in such a short space. My focus, however, is to ask what kinds of practices best respond to the interreligious violence of our time. With this question in view, I venture the following observations.

It seems plausible that religion is caught up with violence for some of the same reasons that absolute hospitality, gift giving, and forgiveness are impossible: because they are all bound up within an economy of exchange, scarcity, and reciprocity. If violence is the result in part of real or perceived scarce resources, and if religion perpetuates this perception through the identification of additional scarcity—whether of sacred space or land, group privilege, limited access to divine blessing or favor, etc.[23]—then it is understandable how religion fuels rather than resists violence. Whether Muslim jihad, the Protestant wars of religion, the medieval crusades, or the Hebrew conquest of Canaan, religious wars seem in many instances to be intimately bound up with the logic of scarcity.[24] Recent or contemporary wars in which religion predominates or figures significantly—whether between Tamils and Sinhalese in Sri Lanka; the West and the Muslim world; Christians and Muslims in Nigeria, the Philippines, Indonesia, or Ethiopia-Somalia; Orthodox Russians and Muslim Chechnyans; Orthodox Serbs, Catholic Croats, and Muslim Slavs/Bosnians in the Balkans; Israelis and Palestinians; Catholics and Protestants in Ireland;

---

[23] As argued by Hector Avalos, *Fighting Words: The Origins of Religious Violence* (Amherst, N.Y.: Prometheus Books, 2005), esp. chs. 4-5.

[24] See James A. Aho, *Religious Mythology and the Art of War: Comparative Religious Symbolisms of Military Violence* (Westport, Conn.: Greenwood, 1981), part 2.

or India and Pakistan, etc.[25]—are waged in part because religious convictions have exacerbated tensions rather than served the cause of reconciliation. And in a post-9/11 context, the verdict is still out about whether or not religion will be a force for peace or for the final conflagration.[26]

On the one side, there are those who believe that the most appropriate responses to the crises represented by 9/11 involve the restoration of religious commitments to the public square. Modernity is collapsing, secularism is bankrupt, and globalization is dissolving the nation-state; humans are adrift in the postmodern and postsecular world, and only religion can produce what the "gods" of the modern world have promised.[27] Motivated by religious convictions, the powers that be in this camp have no doubt both that *to not act* is to abnegate responsibility and unleash destructive forces that will threaten the very foundations of civilization as we know it, and that *to act* requires the kind of courageous engagement with the forces of evil that only religious faith can successfully engage. Hence, religion is not necessarily called on to justify violence per se, but religious beliefs are often called on to sustain war efforts determined just on other grounds.

On the other side are also committed religious people who are convinced that violence simply breeds violence, and that only a pacifist mode of engagement can bring about the healing and reconciliation of a divided world. After all, can we ever be in the position of having sufficient information to justify war? Further, the nonviolent stance should not be dismissed as weakness or passivity; rather, nonviolence is a resisting force, even if it does not use or condone violence.[28] Finally, from a specifically Christian point of view, insofar as war can be declared only by nation-states, Christian "aliens" and "strangers" have to be political atheists and heretics who refuse to worship the god of "our" nation.[29]

At the theological level, the debate boils down to what one thinks is the best way to reject violence. Are we to disassociate violence completely from God so that God's followers cannot justify violence by emulating God, or

---

[25] See the overview discussion in Chalres Selengut, *Sacred Fury: Understanding Religious Violence* (Walnut Creek, Calif.: AltaMira Press, 2003), ch. 4; this list does not include civil wars such as those in Burundi, Senegal, Liberia, Sudan, Iraq, Kashmir, and Uganda, even if religious elements are also in play in many of them.

[26] Ken Booth and Tim Dunne, eds., *Worlds in Collision: Terror and the Future of Global Order* (New York: Palgrave Macmillan, 2002).

[27] Gerald A. Arbuckle, *Violence, Society, and the Church: A Cultural Approach* (Collegeville, Minn.: Liturgical Press, 2003), chs. 7-8, talks about "pro-order movements" such as neocapitalism and the New Right that are intent on restoring control and rationality in a postmodern world.

[28] G. Simon Harak, S.J., ed., *Nonviolence for the Third Millennium* (Macon, Ga.: Mercer University Press, 2003).

[29] Daniel Smith-Christopher, "Political Atheism and Radical Faith: The Challenge of Christian Nonviolence in the Third Millennium," in *Subverting Hatred: The Challenge of Nonviolence in Religious Traditions*, ed. Daniel Smith-Christopher (Cambridge, Mass.: Boston Research Center, 1998), 141-65.

are we to insist that only God can justify God's own violence (e.g., through resurrection) so that we have to commit ourselves as historical beings to pursue peace nonviolently?[30] On the whole, I think we are on more speculative biblical ground in preferring the latter. Hence, I find myself in less agreement with, for example, Timothy Gorringe, who represents the former pacifist trajectory, than with, for example, Hans Boersma (see my discussion in chapter 4, pp. 122-26).[31] At one level, it is difficult to disagree with Gorringe's argument that the New Testament shifts from an economy of retribution (exchange) to an economy of forgiveness (grace) since I have embraced a version of this argument in this book. However, I am unsure that this concludes with an absolute pacifism.

Rather, I submit that absolute hospitality remains an eschatological ideal and norm even as we adjudicate historical situations in anticipation of the redemptive hospitality of God. The redeeming work of God includes the rejection of evil, and an absolutistic form of pacifism can in some situations turn out to be itself demonic.[32] Absolutizing anything removes it from the realm of the historical and, in cases of moral wrong, may render our engagement with it, or even the possibility of our future prevention of it, problematic. But while my proposal does not depend on a pacifist stance, I nevertheless am convinced that the pacifist question cannot and should not be avoided, namely, how should we respond to the question of religion and violence as followers of Jesus Christ in the power of the Holy Spirit?

Let me propose three sets of practical guidelines in response to this question. First, Christians should look for every opportunity to be mediators of peace in a world of violence. One of the ways in which Christians can mediate the hospitality of God is to be arbitrators of peaceful resolutions to the conflicts of the world. Second, violence should not be invoked except in the absolutely last resort, and then only when the full extent of just-war criteria have been consulted and found to apply. Even when war has to be waged, it is always understood as being the lesser of two evils. And amidst the horrors and tragedies of warfare, every precaution must be taken so that innocent people, especially women and children, are not targeted, and every opportunity should be embraced to manifest acts of kindness, compassion, and hospitality. Finally, the quest for peace has to be accompanied by acts of justice because there can be no reconciliation, harmony, or tran-

---

[30] This is the question posed by Henri Atlan, "Founding Violence and Divine Referent," trans. Mark R. Anspach, in *Violence and Truth: On the Work of René Girard*, ed. Paul Dumouchel (Stanford, Calif.: Stanford University Press, 1988), 192-208.

[31] Cf. Hans Boersma, *Violence, Hospitality, and the Cross: Reappropriating the Atonement Tradition* (Grand Rapids: Baker Academic, 2004); and Timothy Gorringe, *God's Just Vengeance: Crime, Violence, and the Rhetoric of Salvation* (Cambridge: Cambridge University Press, 1996).

[32] See Lloyd Steffen, *The Demonic Turn: The Power of Religion to Inspire or Restrain Violence* (Cleveland: Pilgrim Press, 2003), ch. 4.

quility wherever there is injustice. But what does it mean for justice to prevail?

HOSPITALITY, SHALOM, AND THE REIGN OF GOD

The beginning of any response to this question must hold forth the absolute hospitality of God manifest in the eschatological reign. Here, I am referring not only to the great banquet and its poor, crippled, blind, and lame guests from the highways and byways (Luke 14:21)—note that those not present had excused themselves because they had other priorities and commitments—but also the promise that, in these last days, God pours out his Spirit afresh upon all flesh. Hence, "your sons and your daughters shall prophesy, and your young men shall see visions, and your old men shall dream dreams" (Acts 2:17). This in itself calls attention to the fact that the redemptive hospitality of God restores to women what patriarchy has taken away, even as it empowers the youth who are otherwise under subjection to gerontocracies. In addition, God's redemptive hospitality brings to fulfillment the words of the prophet Joel, who spoke both about the judgment of the nations that had been inhospitable to Israel and about the restoration of fortunes of the people of God lost to the plague of locusts and other calamities.

It is in this wider eschatological framework, then, that we see that the hospitality of God involves not just interpersonal relationships but also the structural relations of a common humanity. The prophet Isaiah also spoke about the restoration of the kingdom in similar terms:

> … until a spirit from on high is poured out on us,
>   and the wilderness becomes a fruitful field,
>   and the fruitful field is deemed a forest.
> Then justice will dwell in the wilderness,
>   and righteousness abide in the fruitful field.
> The effect of righteousness will be peace,
>   and the result of righteousness, quietness and trust for ever.
> My people will abide in a peaceful habitation,
>   in secure dwellings, and in quiet resting-places.
> The forest will disappear completely,
>   and the city will be utterly laid low.
> Happy will you be who sow beside every stream,
>   who let the ox and the donkey range freely. (Isa 32:15-20)

Three observations are pertinent. First, the eschatological hospitality of God involves peace, justice, and righteousness. This is the *shalom* of the reign of God made possible by the gift of the Spirit poured out on all flesh. Second, the forest that will disappear symbolizes the threats of the unknown, while the city that will be laid low represents the mechanisms of a people caught up in their own selfish affairs rather than caring for the poor and providing hospitality to strangers. The eschatological hospitality of God thus judges inhospitality and banishes inhospitable elements from the kingdom. The practices of violence therefore call forth, even demand, repentance before such practitioners are rendered "fit" for the coming kingdom. Finally, the "all flesh" clearly includes not only sons and daughters but all creatures, including the ox, the donkey, and others that have the breath of life. The *shalom* of God, in other words, touches the whole creation, including the environment, of which the apostle Paul wrote is groaning in anticipation of the redemption of the cosmos (Rom 8:19-24; cf. chapter 3 above, pp. 90-94). Thus God's eschatological hospitality will bring to fulfillment the radical hospitality unleashed in creation and the redemptive hospitality manifest in the coming of the Son of God into the world.

Given the eschatological outpouring of the Spirit at Pentecost, we now live in some sense under the norms and ideals of the absolute hospitality of the kingdom. Hence, the spiritual reconciliation between individuals that involves love and forgiveness has an undeniable social dimension.[33] The healing of interpersonal relations cannot but involve social reconciliation as well; without social reconciliation—which includes repentance and restitution—worship becomes ritualistic escapism, and Christian mission is incomplete. God's redemptive hospitality inevitably includes the peace, justice, and righteousness—*shalom*—foretold by the prophets. At this level, Pentecost not only brings into existence a new people of God but empowers this community of the redeemed to perform the practices of peace, justice, and righteousness.[34]

But what does this mean for interreligious practices today? I suggest that the Christian encounter with other religions cannot neglect engaging the issues hindering the realization of peace, justice, and righteousness. This involves, minimally, dealing with the realities of economic and class disparity on the one hand, and social ecological and environmental unsustainability on the other.[35] In other words, the interreligious encounter needs

---

[33] See Riggins R. Earl, Jr., "Under Their Own Vine and Fig Tree: The Ethics of Social and Spiritual Hospitality in Black Church Worship," *Journal of the Interdenominational Theological Center* 14 (Fall 1986-Spring 1987): 181-93; and Caroline A. Westerhoff, *Good Fences: The Boundaries of Hospitality* (Cambridge, Mass.: Cowley Publications, 1999), ch. 5.

[34] This argument is fleshed out in Paul Valliere, *Holy War and Pentecostal Peace* (New York: Seabury, 1983). See also Donald Gee, *The Pentecostal Movement: Including the Story of the War Years (1940-1947)*, rev. and enlarged ed. (London: Elm Publishing Co., 1949), 103-5 and 196-97, for discussion of how modern pentecostals were conscientious objectors to both world wars, even to the point of being incarcerated because of their pacifist convictions; cf. Paul Alexander, "Spirit Empowered Peacemaking: Toward a Pentecostal Peace Fellowship," *Journal of the European Pentecostal Theological Association* 22 (2002): 78-102.

[35] See, e.g., John B. Cobb, Jr., and Herman E. Daly, *For the Common Good: Redirecting the Economy toward Community, the Environment, and a Sustainable Future*, 2nd ed.

to develop an interreligious ethic to frame the task of global citizenship in our time.[36] I suggested earlier (see chapter 3, pp. 87-90 and 94-98) that we can and should take up the relevant aspects of John Hick's and Aloysius Pieris's projects, without needing to embrace the entirety of their theological proposals.

The way forward is to develop an interfaith platform to address these international economic, sociopolitical, and environmental issues. Religion is manifest violently, after all, only when allied with political means and mechanisms capable of mobilizing its powers in violent ways.[37] This is not to blame interreligious violence on politics. It is to recognize the intertwining of religion and politics and the complexities involved in the work of peace and justice. In each of these areas—economics, politics, the environment—only interreligious alliances can accomplish what needs to be done. Humanity's "big problems" in the twenty-first century require the concerted and collaborative efforts of all peoples across religious lines. In an interdependent and globally shrinking village, local groups of people addressing local concerns from out of common religious commitments are important but insufficient to address global challenges. The webs of violence, the complicity of responsibility, and the interdependence of causes, effects, and benefits all suggest the importance of multireligious engagement on these issues. Put alternatively, we're all in this together, and need to work as such for the common good. Allow me to very briefly enumerate just a few of the interreligious practices conducive to the tasks of global citizenship, world peace, and international justice.

Regarding a just society: (1) Support and empower groups and especially religious organizations committed to providing for the basic needs—for example, accessible and affordable housing, clean water, basic health care, and living wages—of impoverished, marginalized, and vulnerable groups of people, including women, children, and people with disabilities. (2) Sponsor international educational partnerships that will allow students to travel in and learn from other social, cultural, ethnic, and religious groups; this will promote international understanding, interaction, and hospitality. (3) Encourage interreligious, crosscultural, and international

---

(Boston: Beacon Press, 1994); Paul F. Knitter and Chandra Muzaffar, eds., *Subverting Greed: Religious Perspectives on the Global Economy* (Maryknoll, N.Y.: Orbis Books, and Boston: Boston Research Center for the 21st Century, 2002); and Ulrich Duchrow, ed., *Faith Communities and Social Movements Facing Globalization: International and Interfaith Colloquium 2000 on Faith-Theology-Economy* (Geneva: World Alliance of Reformed Churches, 2002).

[36] E.g., Hans Küng, *Global Responsibility: In Search of a New World Ethic*, trans. John Bowden (New York: Continuum, 1993); and John D'Arcy May, *After Pluralism: Towards an Interreligious Ethic* (Münster: LIT, 2000).

[37] Robert McAfee Brown, *Religion and Violence: A Primer for White Americans* (Philadelphia: Westminster Press, 1973), ch. 3; and Samuel P. Huntington, "Religious Persecution and Religious Relevance in Today's World," in *The Influence of Faith: Religious Groups and U.S. Foreign Policy*, ed. Elliott Abrams (Lanham, Md.: Rowman & Littlefield, 2001), 55-64.

dialogue on identifying and eradicating corruption, especially in the domains of corporate business, government, and politics.

Regarding the global economy: (1) Formulate strategies to promote the exchange of ideas, goods, and services across international lines, with special attention to involving small businesses and newly emergent groups and religious organizations. (2) Focus our dialogical energies at multiple levels on developing just policies and workable practices for alleviating international debt, especially for impoverished nations or regions of the world. (3) Encourage and support international migration, especially for exiles and refugees (see also discussion below, pp. 153-56).

Regarding a sustainable environment: (1) Find ways to involve the international community in projects to recycle consumer goods consistently, replant deforested regions, and restore environmentally threatened areas, etc. (2) Draw the global community into discussion about what kind of cooperative ventures are essential in order for us to leave the environment in better shape for our children than what we had inherited. (3) Connect local communities across international and religious lines so that they can engage collaboratively as neighbors in projects having global ecological significance.

As a theologian rather than a political scientist, economist, or ecologist, I am hardly capable of spelling out a comprehensive plan of action along each of these fronts. Yet I believe the above suggestions for promoting interpersonal and international hospitality are important components that can contribute to a just and peaceful world. But even to enact some of these proposals calls for courage, vision, and faith. There is, as Denis Carroll puts it, "no easy certitude" for the pilgrim people of God on the path of faith.[38] But we are not alone in following the footsteps of Christ with his indwelling Spirit as aliens in a strange land. On this journey, we need to pray for a fresh outpouring of the Spirit, who is the harbinger and source of shared life, healing relationships, and just partnerships.[39] Will not the Spirit who inspired many tongues so long ago also today inspire the many hospitable practices needed to redeem the world?

INTERRELIGIOUS ECUMENISM: MANY TONGUES, HEALING PRACTICES

The signs portending this impossible possibility of interfaith ecumenism have been building over the last two generations. Arguably, interfaith ecumenism is a logical if not unavoidable extension of intra-Christian ecumenism.[40] Similarly, interfaith hospitality is also an extension of

---

[38] Denis Carroll, *A Pilgrim God for a Pilgrim People* (Wilmington, Del.: M. Glazier, 1989), ch. 1.

[39] Thomas R. Hawkins, *Sharing the Search: A Theology of Christian Hospitality* (Nashville, Tenn.: Upper Room, 1987), ch. 5.

[40] E.g., Peter C. Phan, ed., *Christianity and the Wider Ecumenism* (New York: Paragon

intra-Christian hospitality.[41] In eschatological perspective, the original hospitality of God shown to Abraham is also promised through him to all nations, decisively expanded in the incarnational and pentecostal events to include the gentiles, and anticipated to include all peoples, tongues, tribes, and nations before the throne of God in the end.

As enumerated in the preceding discussion, the Christian mission can and should be appropriately recalibrated so that various forms of interfaith ecumenism and practices can be focused on achieving peace and justice. At this level, conventional modes of evangelism give way to nonconventional modes of interreligious interactions that can provide the kinds of safe public spaces through which the hard work of peace and justice can be carried out. This is not to neglect the preaching of the gospel, but it is to recognize that the salvation offered by God is holistic.[42] In the public square, many different types of practices sensitive to specific goals related to the common good—for example, feeding the hungry, clothing the naked, visiting the sick, meeting the needs of the imprisoned, or transforming the circumstantial situations of the poor, the marginalized, and the oppressed—are essential for the embodiment and offering of God's redemptive hospitality to the world.

Yet it is also important to insist that interfaith ecumenism neither replaces Christian ecumenism nor is intended to produce a more universal expression of faith. I suggest that Christians ride out the tension between an explicitly Christian identity and interfaith ecumenism by recognizing the eschatological horizon within which their journey is unfolding. So on the one hand, ours is a vision of the absolute hospitality of God as revealed at the eschatological banquet; on the other hand, it is constrained by the conditional hospitality of finite beings attempting to be faithful participants in the unfolding of the divine drama.

How this tension plays out in interfaith ecumenism can be more concretely albeit briefly articulated with regard to the practices of the monastic interreligious dialogue and of interfaith prayer. The former is much more prominent in Roman Catholic circles, obviously so because of the

---

House, 1990); and Edward Idris Cardinal Cassidy, *Ecumenism and Interreligious Dialogue* (New York, and Mahwah, N.J.: Paulist Press, 2005). Yet in saying this, I don't want to lose sight of the fact that these two ecumenical tasks, while related, remain distinct, and should not be collapsed together; on this point, see Michael Kinnamon, *The Vision of the Ecumenical Movement and How It Has Been Impoverished by Its Friends* (St. Louis, Mo.: Chalice Press, 2003), ch. 8.

[41] Diane C. Kessler, ed., *Receive One Another: Hospitality in Ecumenical Perspective* (Geneva: WCC Publications, 2005), 73-76. For a specific case study of interfaith hospitality, see Thomas E. Reynolds, "Welcoming without Reserve: A Case in Christian Hospitality," *Theology Today* 63, no. 2 (2006): 191-202.

[42] Elizabeth R. Geitz, *Fireweed Evangelism: Christian Hospitality in a Multi-faith World* (New York: Church Pub., 2004), ch. 2, rightly insists that such approaches in a multicultural and multireligious world do not need to abandon historic Christian understandings of incarnation and Trinity.

developed contemplative traditions that provide bridges, especially with Hindu and Buddhist traditions.[43] Formal dialogues have been organized over the last several decades, and the results have been published.[44] In light of the intertwined histories of monasticism and hospitality in the Christian tradition,[45] it is not surprising that Christian monastics have found inter-religious dialogue partners with contemplative interests. Insofar as the monastic setting opens up space for individuals to be with one another in the presence of transcendence, it both preserves the distinctiveness of the parties and yet creates a dialogical environment of mutuality.

Both of these aspects are important since the goal of the monastic inter-religious dialogue is always focused on a deepened relationship with God (for Christians) rather than on the formation of a more universal religion. Further, the central feature of the monastic interreligious dialogue is the practice of contemplative sitting. Since this is most often done in silence, there is no concerted effort to confuse or conflate the religious beliefs of participants.[46] Finally, within the eschatological framework of our discussing interfaith ecumenism, we always recognize that the mutuality of dialogue is not equivalent to the identity of religious tradition or experience. Rather, the precise nature of the eschatological unity around the great banquet remains an open question. On this side of the eschaton, however, we can hope and even pray that our dialogue partners will be at that table, even as we are.

This raises the profoundly important question regarding interfaith prayer. Rather than engaging the issues in depth,[47] let me focus on inter-

---

[43] With regard to the Christian-Hindu encounter, I am thinking here of the work of Bede Griffiths, Henri Le Saux (Swami Abhishiktananda), Sara Grant, and others.

[44] E.g., Susan Walker, ed., *Speaking of Silence: Christians and Buddhists on the Contemplative Way* (New York, and Mahwah, N.J.: Paulist Press, 1987); Patrick G. Henry and Donald K. Swearer, eds., *For the Sake of the World: The Spirit of Buddhist and Christian Monasticism* (Minneapolis: Fortress; and Collegeville, Minn.: Liturgical Press, 1989); Gilbert G. Hardy, *Monastic Quest and Interreligious Dialogue* (New York: Peter Lang, 1990); Donald W. Mitchell and James A. Wiseman, eds., *The Gethsemani Encounter: A Dialogue on the Spiritual Life by Buddhist and Christian Monastics* (New York: Continuum, 1997); and Bruno Barnhart and Joseph Wong, eds., *Purity of Heart and Contemplation: A Monastic Dialogue between Christian and Asian Traditions* (New York: Continuum, 2001).

[45] See Daniel Homan, O.S.B., and Lonni Collins Pratt, *Radical Hospitality: Benedict's Way of Love* (Brewster, Mass.: Paraclete Press, 2002); and Leslie A. Hay, *Hospitality: The Heart of Spiritual Direction* (Harrisburg, Pa.: Morehouse, 2006).

[46] Pierre-François de Béthune, *By Faith and Hospitality: The Monastic Tradition as a Model for Interreligious Encounter*, trans. Mary Groves (Leominster, U.K.: Gracewing, 2002), ch. 5, presents three criteria for discerning the monastic interreligious encounter: the authenticity of the spiritual experience as testified to by the dialogue partners; the authority of the traditions represented by the participants; and the mutual hospitality that is shown across religious lines.

[47] For discussion of some of the issues, see Christopher Lamb, "The Experience of Interfaith Prayer," *The Way Supplement: Interfaith Spirituality* 78 (1993): 81-88; the essays on "Interreligious Prayer," in *Pro Dialogo* 98:2 (1998); Gilbert Meilaender, "Interfaith 'Prayer,'" *Christian Century* 119, no. 22 (23 October-5 November 2002): 32-37; and Gavin D'Costa, *The Meeting of Religions and the Trinity* (Maryknoll, N.Y.: Orbis Books, 2000), ch. 5.

faith prayer as one aspect of interfaith ecumenism considered in terms of the eschatological hospitality of God. In this perspective, three sets of comments suffice. First, Christians must wrestle with the apostolic teachings that, on the one hand, "there is no God but one" (1 Cor 8:4), which suggests that all genuinely offered prayers, if heard, are heard by none other than this one God; and on the other hand, "what pagans sacrifice, they sacrifice to demons and not to God" (1 Cor 10:20), which suggests that non-Christian religious rituals may have other transcendent referents of which Christians are cautioned against partaking. At this level, we are wise to be cautious about participating in religious activities, even interfaith prayer sessions, that might be understood as endorsements of or even collusions with powers antithetical to the God of Jesus Christ.

But second, as aliens and strangers in a foreign land, we often find ourselves as guests hosted by others with their rites, conventions, and ceremonies, all of which are oftentimes laden with religious meaning and significance. At this level, interfaith prayer is not a formal religious ritual but part and parcel of what it means to practice and receive hospitality one with the other. When considered in eschatological perspective, such interfaith ecumenism represents our participation in the redemptive hospitality of God in anticipation of the grand banquet when and where we will be surprised both by seeing those around the table who we did not think would be there, and missing the presence of others whom we presumed we'd see.

Hence, third, the following concrete proposals for participation in interfaith prayer are presented for further reflection and discussion. (1) In interpersonal contexts in which two or more people of different faiths have opportunities to interact, neither should impose prayer on the other without the other's consent; if consent is given, such consent should be understood to allow the prayer to be made according to the conventions of the one doing the praying, even while the one who prays should not take advantage of this as further opportunity to "preach" to the one who is listening. (2) Multireligious institutional settings—for example, public schools, community boardrooms, or congressional meetings—should respect the fact that authentic religious prayer usually occurs either in the privacy of individual lives or in the congregational context of a religious community's moments of worship; at the same time, there may be agreed upon "moments of silence" during which private prayers are offered that may also serve as palpable public symbols of the interior, religious, and spiritual dimensions of human lives that are never too far removed from our public activities and practices. (3) The public prayers of hospital or especially military chaplains wrestle with the following tension: on the one hand, religiously generic prayers are theologically vacuous and spiritually unengaging, but, on the other hand, religiously specific prayers may alienate rather than engage people of other faith traditions in those sacred moments; I hypothesize that chaplains who are intentional about getting to know their constituency will be more trusted and given greater latitude in fulfilling the duties and responsibilities of their office, which includes at various moments the giving of prayer. (4) There may be occasions such as national tragedies (recall 9/11) that prompt multifaith gatherings and collective action; these will be occasions for leaders across religious lines to come together and earnestly explore if and how it is possible to mutually construct the shape of public religious life that neither waters down the spiritual and theological elements that are important to the life of faith nor flippantly parades such core practices in the public sphere in ways that demean their meaning to the faithful. For each of these domains, the significance of prayer for people of faith is too great to ignore or dismiss simply because of the many complexities involved in the interreligious context.

PERFORMING INTERRELIGIOUS DIALOGUE: CHRISTIAN PRACTICES IN "THE BETWEEN"

We have so far in this chapter sketched a vision of ecclesial practices vis-à-vis those in other faiths understood as participation in the *missio Dei* and extended this to consider the church's social witness understood as shaped by and participating in the eschatological hospitality of God. Our goal has been to explore how the many tongues of the Spirit open up to many hospitable practices. In this final section, I want to bring the discussion to a close by elaborating on the many practices at the more personal level of the interreligious encounter in these times between the cross/Pentecost and the eschaton. We will do so by formulating a theology of the love of neighbor understood as the religious other, suggesting a theology of friendship appropriate to our globalized situation, and sketching a theology of interreligious dialogue understood as the heart of Christian practice in a religiously plural world. This discussion presumes the fundamental conviction that Christian identity is expressed in Christian mission, but that Christian mission is inclusive of rather than an alternative to the work of social justice and interreligious dialogue. But the focus now prescinds from that of ecclesial and social practices to the more pointed personal question: What should we as individual Christians do "in this between" time of our postmodern and pluralistic situation as we celebrate the redemptive hospitality of God revealed in Christ and yet await the eschatological hospitality of God to be ushered in finally by the Spirit?

Loving God and Neighbor in a World of Many Faiths

We launch out on this last leg of our journey by sketching a theology of the love of God and of neighbor and attending to the interfaith implications of such a theological conviction.[48] Our starting point will be to retrieve the parable of the Good Samaritan for our further consideration (see also chapter 4 above, pp. 101-3).

In his discussion of the love and praise of God, Karl Barth comments at some length on the first and second great commandments and on this parable.[49] While arguing that the love of neighbor participates and is grounded in the absoluteness of God's love and our responsive love for God, Barth also recognizes that in the Good Samaritan the love of God is revealed to us precisely through the love of others who are not only neighbors but actually strangers. In fact, it is these others who help us to see our own needs; hence, "My neighbour is my fellow-man acting towards me as a benefactor ... I must be ready to obey the summons to go and do likewise, that is, to be myself a benefactor, if I am to experience as such the emergence of a fellow-man as my benefactor, and therefore to see and have him as my neighbour" (*CD* I/2: 420). For this reason, Barth was willing to consider the strange neighbor even as a "brother": "What man is there who might not one day meet us as a messenger of the Word of God, a witness to the resurrection?" (*CD* I/2: 427).[50]

Barth takes seriously the contribution of the neighbor (represented by the foreign Samaritan) to the household of faith. We are ordained by God not to be alone in this world but to be, unavoidably, with our neighbors. In this sense, "Whether willingly and wittingly or not ..., my neighbour acquires for me a sacramental significance" (*CD* I/2: 436). Hence the import of a passage that deserves to be reproduced at greater length:

> In my testimony I cannot follow out the plan of trying to invade and alter the life of my neighbour. A witness is neither a guardian nor a teacher. A witness will not intrude on his neighbour. He will not "handle" him. He will not make him the object of his activity, even witness the best intention. Witness can be given only when there is respect for the freedom of the grace of God, and therefore respect for the other man who can expect nothing from me but everything from God. (*CD* I/2: 441)

For Barth, it is precisely the neighbor who is an alien and a stranger who reveals to us the redemptive hospitality of God.

---

[48] For an overview, see Garth L. Hallett, *Christian Neighbor-Love: An Assessment of Six Rival Versions* (Washington, D.C.: Georgetown University Press, 1989).

[49] Karl Barth, *Church Dogmatics*, vol. 1, part 2, trans. G. T. Thomson and Harold Knight (Edinburgh: T & T Clark, 1956), esp. 417-50. Other references to this discussion will be made parenthetically as *CD* in the text.

[50] In this way, as Kierkegaard says, the neighbor is our equal, and true agapeic love of neighbor is unconditional (versus erotic love, which is given out preferentially); see Søren Kierkegaard, *Works of Love*, trans. Howard and Edna Hong (New York: Harper, 1962), 72.

Jesus' teachings as recorded by the Matthean parable of the sheep and the goats are congruent with Barth's reading of the Good Samaritan. The sheep and the goats are judged according to the hospitality shown to Jesus as represented in the poor, the hungry, the naked, and those in prison. Some would argue that "the least of these who are members of my family" (Matt 25:40; cf. 25:45) refers to fellow Christians—including those in prison for proclaiming the gospel—rather than to the hungry, naked, stranger, and imprisoned in general. Given that the context of this passage is the final judgment scene involving "all the nations" (25:32), I read this reference more inclusively than as limited to Christian believers.[51] Further, I suggest that this reading fits better with the earlier Matthean reference to the invitation extended to "both good and bad" (22:10, which is absent from the Lukan parallel in 14:15-23) to fill up the banquet seats refused by the other invited (Jewish) guests, so that it involves the gentiles as a whole.[52]

What are the principles to be drawn from the preceding for interreligious practices? First, Christian mission is not only about bringing Christ to our neighbors of other faiths, but may also serve the important purpose of our meeting Christ in them. In fact, the early church's hospitality to strangers was based on the realization that Christ may be present in our guests and that if so, then our guests become our hosts through Christ.[53] This is, of course, the principle of the reversibility of guests and host in the redemptive hospitality of God. But perhaps more important, I suggest that rather than thinking that Christian mission is about proclaiming the judgment that threatens those who resist the offer of God's hospitality, those bearing the witness to Christ should also be open to Christ's appearing in the religious other as one bringing grace or judgment on the missionary.[54] In fact, it is precisely the judgment of the goats that awaits the priest and the Levite for passing on the other side rather than showing hospitality to the man fallen at the hands of robbers. In this case, the love of neighbor becomes not just a guide for Christian practice but also a norm that judges Christian un/belief.[55]

---

[51] See also W. D. Davies and Dale C. Allison Jr., *A Critical and Exegetical Commentary on the Gospel according to Matthew* (Edinburgh: T. & T. Clark, 1997), 418-29.

[52] For further discussion defending this broader interpretation, see Hendrikus Boers, *Theology Out of the Ghetto: A New Testament Exegetical Study Concerning Religious Exclusiveness* (Leiden: E. J. Brill, 1971), ch. 3; and George Gay, "The Judgment of the Gentiles in Matthew's Theology," in *Scripture, Tradition, and Interpretation: Essays Presented to Everett F. Harrison by His Students and Colleagues in Honor of His Seventy-fifth Birthday*, ed. W. Ward Gasque and William Sanford LaSor (Grand Rapids: Eerdmans, 1978), 199-215. Thanks to my graduate assistants Christopher Emerick and Doc Hughes for research on these texts.

[53] Amy Oden, ed., *And You Welcomed Me: A Sourcebook on Hospitality in Early Christianity* (Nashville, Tenn.: Abingdon, 2001), 51.

[54] This is articulated nicely by Michele Hershberger, *A Christian View of Hospitality: Expecting Surprises* (Waterloo, Ont., and Scottsdale, Pa.: Herald Press, 1999), 227, 230-32.

[55] Similarly, Scott J. Jones, *The Evangelistic Love of God and Neighbor: A Theology of*

I propose that Barth's notion of our meeting with, loving, and being loved by strangers being sacramental moments of encountering God is a thoroughly pneumatological idea. If the love of God is poured out into our hearts through the Holy Spirit (Rom 5:5), then not only is our loving our neighbors the means through which the love of God is given to them, but our being loved by our neighbors, including those of other faiths, is also the means through which the love of God is given to us. In this way, I suggest, the practices of hospitality—of being hosts as well as guests—become the concrete modalities through which the gifts of the Holy Spirit are poured out on all flesh.

BEFRIENDING STRANGERS AND NEIGHBORS: GUESTS, HOSTS, AND THE HOLY SPIRIT

What then are the implications of a theology of neighborly hospitality for the interreligious encounter today? In what follows, I want to very briefly suggest three concrete scenarios for practicing interreligious friendship pertinent to our contemporary experience of globalization: regarding the immigrant or migrant, the exile, and the refugee. Each case, I would argue, is pertinent to the broad scope of the American experience.

I propose that the phenomenon of immigration or migration provides us the opportunity to not only develop and articulate as many intercultural theologies as there are forms of such experiences[56] but also to think through the implications of the such experiences for a theology of religions and interreligious practices. (Note that by "immigration" or "immigrants," I am including both the experiences of those who move more or less permanently from one country to another [immigrants proper] and those who have a home base but who follow the crops and the seasons—sometimes across national borders—as migrant [usually farm] workers; these are very different, albeit related, experiences.) All too often, we think of immigrants either as "strangers" or as "workers," but less often as "neighbors" who may even be members of other faiths. The church and her theologians have actually given very little thought to a theology of immigration.

I suggest that any theology of immigration must attend to the religious diversity that is encountered through this experience. As Alfred Ancel writes, immigrants should be received "not as strangers *but as brothers*, with respect for their nationality and their own culture and with no discrimination whatever"; as important, in keeping with the theology of hos-

---

Witness and Discipleship (Nashville, Tenn.: Abingdon, 2003), 179-80, suggests that loving the neighbor becomes for Christians the norm for our evangelistic witness.

[56] On this point, see Peter C. Phan, *Christianity with an Asian Face: Asian American Theology in the Making* (Maryknoll, N.Y.: Orbis Books, 2003), ch. 1, "The Experience of Migration as Source of Intercultural Theology in the United States."

pitality to neighbors developed here, "when a local Church comes into contact with people who profess other religions, it is called upon to show them Christ's countenance in all its purity and to establish relations of friendship with them in a brotherly and sisterly spirit. Normally the local church, through this contact, is enriched by certain religious or human values by which these people order their lives."[57] In this way, the experience of immigration itself serves as what Nancy Bedford calls an "epistemological rupture" for theology since now the perspective from the margin or the underside becomes the starting point for theological reflection.[58]

The difference between the experiences of immigrants and those of exiles/refugees is their voluntary versus involuntary character. Yet the exile (or asylum seeker) is usually an individual person or family, whereas the refugee is part of a larger group of displaced persons. These experiences are similar yet also very different. Exilic existence, Edward Said (a Palestinian exile to New York City) reminds us, is marginal, cut off from personal, familial, and national roots, land, and past tradition.[59] More forcefully, exilic existence is always provisional: "Exile is life led outside habitual order. It is nomadic, decentered, contrapuntal; but no sooner does one get accustomed to it than its unsettling force erupts anew."[60] There is a sense in which the exile is the contemporary nomad, always drifting between a nomadic and settled existence, longing to return home although unable to do so, and also yearning to make a new home, although also incapable of realizing this aspiration.[61] Even more than refugees and other forcefully displaced people, exiles are at risk because they may be wanted by the authorities of the land from which they have fled.[62]

On the other hand, refugees—among whom I include people displaced by war, famine, or other socioeconomic-political factors—are at risk because in most situations they find themselves uprooted from their homes and forcibly removed to a strange land practically empty-handed.[63] There

---

[57] Alfred Ancel, *Theology of the Local Church in Relation to Migration* (Staten Island, N.Y.: Center for Migration Studies, 1974), 13.

[58] Nancy E. Bedford, "To Speak of God from More Than One Place: Theological Reflections from the Experience of Migration," in *Latin American Liberation Theology: The Next Generation*, ed. Ivan Petrella (Maryknoll, N.Y.: Orbis Books, 2005), 95-118, esp. 110-13.

[59] Edward W. Said, *Reflections on Exile and Other Essays* (Cambridge, Mass.: Harvard University Press, 2000), esp. ch. 17.

[60] Said, *Reflections on Exile*, 186.

[61] Edith Wyschogrod, "Dwellers, Migrants, Nomads: Home in the Age of the Refugee," in *The Longing for Home*, ed. Leroy S. Rouner (Notre Dame, Ind.: University of Notre Dame Press, 1996), 187-203.

[62] For more on the risk factors attending the immigration, exilic, and refugee experiences, see Gioacchino Campese and Pietro Ciallella, eds., *Migration, Religious Experience, and Globalization* (New York: Center for Migration Studies, 2003).

[63] Peter Kanyandago, "Who is My Neighbor? A Christian Response to Refugees and the Displaced in Africa," in *Moral and Ethical Issues in African Christianity: Exploratory Essays in Moral Theology*, ed. J. N. K. Mugambi and A. Nasimiyu-Wasike (Nairobi, Kenya: Initiatives Publishers, 1992), 171-84.

are also pressing questions about the legal status of refugees (and of immigrants), of assimilation, of transnationalistic connections, of language proficiency (or lack thereof), of fiscal and ethical responsibility, of the availability of and eligibility for social services, etc.[64] These are all complex matters, which I have neither the time nor the expertise to comment on at length. In principle, however, I concur with Dana Wilbanks, who concludes,

> Christians are disposed to see and respond to migrants through the lenses of their narrative faith. Images of hospitality and inclusive community are to shape the moral practice of churches and Christians. In our current nationalistic ethos, Christians are called to relativize the authority of the state and qualify the claims of the national community. Yet Christians may also participate in shaping the character of the national community. We may affirm the values of government and the existence of genuinely diverse national communities.[65]

My point is to remind us that our concerns for the immigrant, exile, and refugee are in the interest of fostering interreligious relations. Let us face the fact that we live in a continually shifting and increasingly globalized world, and that the cross-fertilization of religions that has been occurring throughout human history will only accelerate in the next century with ever-intensifying patterns of immigration and forced movements. Let us also be reminded that immigrants, exiles, and refugees are by no means only those who belong to non-Christian religious traditions; all too often, those who have moved or been forced to move are Christians, in these cases being doubly so aliens in strange lands. In the early church, these were the ones of the diaspora who were responsible for spreading the gospel to the ends of the earth (see chapter 4, pp. 115-18). Today, this phenomenon means that immigrants, exiles, and refugees are both Christians and people of other faiths, alternatively and sometimes simultaneously, guests and hosts, each having something of religious significance to offer others. Hence is it not in fact true that it is immigrants, exiles, refugees, and displaced persons who are the living theologians of exile and the norm of Christian discipleship in a multireligious world (see chapter 4, pp. 122-26)?

I am suggesting that while we cannot dispense with political theologies that address the structural issues impacting the lives of immigrants, exiles,

---

[64] I discuss many of these matters in my "Asian American Religion: A Review Essay," *Nova Religio: The Journal of Alternative and Emergent Religions* 9, no. 3 (2006): 92-107.

[65] Dana W. Wilbanks, *Re-Creating America: The Ethics of U.S. Immigration and Refugee Policy in Christian Perspective* (Nashville, Tenn.: Abingdon, 1996), 123. In this book, Wilbanks argues for an inclusive and generous immigration policy especially "given America's immigrant history and its privileged position in a world of appalling inequalities," with the goal of building a "just multicultural national community" (pp. 142, 209).

and refugees, the Christian mission also includes the dialogical moments when aliens and strangers come together as guests and hosts around the table of friendship and fellowship.[66] These are some of the most profound moments of the contemporary interreligious encounter because it is here that both find themselves caught up by the redemptive hospitality of God's Spirit who has been poured out on all flesh.

LIVING AND SEEKING THE TRUTH: INTERRELIGIOUS DIALOGUE AS CHRISTIAN PRACTICE

By now it should be clear that by "interreligious dialogue" I mean not only the more formally organized discussions between academics about comparative religious and theological topics (although more on this momentarily) but the dialogue of life focused on matters related to the common good and to the flourishing of all of us who find ourselves as pilgrims in strange lands and as sojourners in difficult and different times. How does the practice of interreligious friendship play out in a world of immigrants, exiles, refugees, and strangers? Let me identify some concrete features of the interreligious practice of hospitality, friendship, and dialogue.

First, aliens and strangers sometimes need basic accommodations. The hospitality offered in such cases is palpable, and God's redemptive gifts are felt rather than heard. Here it is orthopraxis that bears witness, not orthodoxy.[67] Second, the coming together of aliens and strangers is the appropriate occasion for exchanging stories, learning to live together, and, out of this basic sharing, envisioning the future together.[68] On these occasions, Christians can nurture their listening capabilities even as they share their own life narratives with people of other faiths. Along the way, interreligious apologetics may be engaged, but only as they arise ad hoc and are grounded in the mutual interchange of narratives.[69] Third, and recalling

---

[66] Combining both moments in a theoretically dense formulation results in, e.g., Slavoj Žižek, Eric L. Santner, and Kenneth Reinhard, *The Neighbor: Three Inquiries in Political Theology* (Chicago and London: University of Chicago Press, 2005). A much more accessible read for an interreligious theology of friendship is Kenneth Cracknell, *In Good and Generous Faith: Christian Responses to Religious Pluralism* (Peterborough, U.K.: Epworth, 2005), ch. 3.

[67] On this point, I build on the work of David and Ruth Rupprecht, *Radical Hospitality* (Phillipsburg, N.J.: Presbyterian and Reformed Publishing Company, 1983), especially in their conviction that there is a need for Christian homes to welcome those who have been deeply wounded by life's twists and turns, and who need space for healing rather than sermons demanding decisions.

[68] Vera Duncanson, Brian Johnson, and Stefanie Weisgram, eds., *Stories from Christian Neighbors: A Heart for Ecumenism* (Collegeville, Minn.: Liturgical Press, 2003).

[69] Richard Kearney, "Thinking after Terror: An Interreligious Challenge," in *Religion and Violence in a Secular World: Toward a New Political Theology*, ed. Clayton Crockett (Charlottesville, Va., and London: University of Virginia Press, 2006), 206-28, esp. 222-25.

our earlier discussion about the liturgical aspect of Christian mission, we need to develop moments, places, and spaces that address the pains and hurts that all immigrants, exiles, and refugees carry in their hearts. This may occur in specific ecclesial and liturgical contexts,[70] but I think it possible also that they occur amidst the sacred space opened up by the Spirit's outpouring on interreligious relations and friendships.

It is out of such practices that common causes are established and common projects are initiated. Here I am thinking not only about how Christians can reach out to and serve people from other faiths who are immigrants, exiles, refugees, etc., whether that be through the establishment of "welcome ministries," "friendship centers," employment and social service agencies, child care facilities, or adjustment and relief assistance.[71] All of these are important and need to remain central to the Christian mission.[72] However, we need to go beyond this to work with people of other faiths so that such ministries can be jointly envisioned, owned, and operated. Only in this way will actual rather than projected or stereotyped needs be met. Further, now interreligious dialogue becomes meaningful practice whereby we learn from and are transformed precisely through the mutual give-and-take of engaging the public square. In this way, each is a "Good Samaritan" to the religious other in a genuinely dialogical relationship.[73] To be sure, we may still be a long way from such genuinely dialogical and jointly owned interfaith ministry projects—the complexities attending to this stagger the imagination, at least in some social and political contexts around the world—but perhaps we can hold these forth as ideals that guide the practices of a just and hospitable world.

Yet the dialogue of life includes rather than is separate from the more formal interreligious dialogues characteristic of the Western academy. In fact, here is one area in which the academy may have something to teach the church about life in the public domain insofar as the academic task and process involves the ethical commitment to providing at least intellectual hospitality to the ideas of strangers, even those with whom one might not necessarily agree.[74] Academics of all people, especially those in the public university context, (should!) know about being charitable with those with

---

[70] E.g., Ruth C. Duck, "Hospitality to Victims: A Challenge for Christian Worship," in *The Other Side of Sin: Woundedness from the Perspective of the Sinned Against,* ed. Andrew Sung Park and Susan L. Nelson (Albany: State University of New York Press, 2001), 165-80.

[71] Roy Oksnevad and Dotsey Welliver, eds., *The Gospel for Islam: Reaching Muslims in North America* (Wheaton, Ill.: Billy Graham Center and Evangelism and Missions Information Service, 2001).

[72] Thus Luke Bretherton, *Hospitality as Holiness: Christian Witness amid Moral Diversity* (Burlington, Vt., and Aldershot, U.K.: Ashgate, 2006), talks about hospitality as a moral responsibility.

[73] Claudius Ceccon and Kristian Paludan, *My Neighbour—Myself: Visions of Diakonia* (Geneva: WCC Publications, 1988), ch. 3.

[74] John B. Bennett, "The Academy and Hospitality," *Cross Currents* 50, no. 1/2 (2000): 23-35.

whom one disagrees, about developing collegiality with those on opposite ends of the political, intellectual, and even religious spectrum, and about modeling to students an authentic posture of lifelong learning that is open to the process of inquiry wherever it may lead. Within this academic context, interreligious dialogue becomes an essential virtue, indeed a concrete expression of hospitality.[75]

Now to be sure, there are many types of formal interreligious dialogues at the academic level, with many different modes, forums, and objectives (see also pp. 32-34, 80-84, 112-15). Many of these occasions will involve goals already noted in the foregoing. My point here, however, is to build on the foregoing reflections about neighborly love and the stranger to suggest viewing interreligious dialogue as a practice of mutual transformation in these eschatological times of the now-and-not-yet, between the initial and final outpourings of the Spirit of God on all flesh. Reinhard Hütter, from whom we have already learned much about the works of the Spirit in the practices of the church (see above, pp. 59-62), suggests,

> Since truth is not produced but acknowledged, honoring the truth cannot be anything else than inviting others into the same acknowledgment ... In the most fundamental way, the practice of hospitality is itself a significant way to honor the truth; we tell the truth by giving ourselves as persons to other persons and by receiving others as persons. The practice of hospitality thus also points to the fact that truth is something in which we mutually participate as persons.[76]

For Christians who believe both that the truth is revealed in Jesus Christ and that the Holy Spirit will guide us into all truth, truth is not only propositionally or dogmatically formulated but is intersubjectively encountered, interpersonally inhabited, and intercommunally adjudicated. To be sure, Christians cannot receive religious others in exactly the same way as Christians receive other Christians—or else the differences between religious traditions will be ignored—but my point is that we can no longer ignore the fact that a multireligious, postmodern, and post-9/11 world and public sphere require that we learn how to receive one another across religious lines.

In these "between" times, then, interreligious dialogue, in whatever form it takes, is not an accidental luxury that we can take or leave but an essential practice that we must cultivate in order to live the truth and to grow in truth. Fidelity to the Son of God who went into a far country for

---

[75] Michael Barnes, *Theology and the Dialogue of Religions* (Cambridge: Cambridge University Press, 2002).

[76] Reinhard Hütter, "Hospitality and Truth: The Disclosure of Practices in Worship and Doctrine," in *Practicing Theology: Beliefs and Practices in Christian Life,* ed. Miroslav Volf and Dorothy C. Bass (Grand Rapids: Eerdmans, 2002), 206-27, quotation from pp. 217-18.

the sake of the world requires that we also take the journey into the far country of the lives of those in other faiths for the sake of our world, which includes us and them together. The result cannot but be mutually transformative, yet such transformation also cannot be a naïve syncretism because the identities of guests and hosts are not blurred but enriched. This is the paradox of the welcome and even the embrace that does not overwhelm the identity of the other but rather allows him or her to flourish.[77] It is also the paradox of the fact that the Spirit of truth leads us to the truth that sets us free—from ourselves, our fears, and our resistance to the alien, stranger, and foreigner—even as this same truth helps us to discern the voice and form of the devil from that of the Good Shepherd.

I suggest that in our postmodern and pluralistic world, Christians find themselves yet on the same journey as that launched on the Day of Pentecost, with the difference that whereas that initial outpouring took Christians to the ends of the earth, today's "latter rain" outpouring brings the ends of the earth to our doorsteps, wherever such may be. What has not changed is that the many tongues (dialogues) spoken and many practices (of hospitality) engaged by the earliest Christians are even more desperately needed today. From this (Day of) Pentecostal and pneumatological point of view, the Spirit's outpouring on all flesh is neither merely a historic curiosity (a past tense) nor a doctrine that needs to be believed (a settled fact). Rather, Pentecost is an eschatological experience between the then-and-the-not-yet manifest variously in the many tongues and practices that enable us to relate to and with strangers and those in other faiths, in the hermeneutics of charity that leads us to expect meeting the Spirit, even Jesus Christ, in and through the lives of people in other faiths, and in the posture of eschatological anticipation that believes all flesh might indeed be caught up in the radical, redemptive, and absolute hospitality of God. Is it possible that the promise of the outpouring of the Spirit on all flesh depends in part on whether or not we remain faithful followers of the hospitable God?

I have argued in this book for a pneumatological theology of hospitality as interreligious praxis that recognizes people of all faiths are aliens and strangers but also neighbors one to another. Hence Christian, Jews, Muslims, Buddhists, Hindus, and all other people of faith are potentially and increasingly guests and hosts to one another, according to the providential, hospitable, and redemptive economy of God. This Christian self-understanding affirms that there are many tongues through which the glory of God is made known and which are representative of the gifts of God to all people as mediated through the wisdom, cultural, and religious traditions of the world. At the same time, this belief is shaped by and borne out

---

[77] As brilliantly argued by Miroslav Volf, *Exclusion and Embrace: A Theological Exploration of Identity, Otherness, and Reconciliation* (Nashville, Tenn.: Abingdon, 1996).

through the many healing practices of the Spirit that cut across religious lines to bring about the reconciliation yearned for by the world in anticipation of the eschatological redemption of the hospitable God.

Hence, the end of this book is but another important starting point for the Christian journey in the postmodern, pluralistic, and multireligious world of the twenty-first century. This is a journey that Christians take more so alongside rather than over and against or in opposition to those in other faiths. It is also a journey that includes the kinds of interreligious conversations we have noted in this book and engaged in various depths of intensity and in different modes throughout this chapter. This is because Christian hospitality is empowered by the Spirit of the hospitable God. We have been graciously invited to participate in this divine hospitality and given many gifts, many tongues, and many practices through which to meet, interact with, and perhaps even bless religious others. Along the way, the Spirit of hospitality will transform us precisely through the interreligious encounter into the image of Jesus, even as we hope and pray—to the point of daring to believe—that as guests and hosts we can also be instruments of the hospitable God for the reconciliation, healing, and redemption of the world.

Select Bibliography

On the Relationship between Beliefs and Practices

Bartholomew, Craig, Colin Greene, and Karl Möller, eds. *After Pentecost: Language and Biblical Interpretation*. Grand Rapids: Zondervan, 2001.

Bass, Dorothy C. *Practicing Our Faith: A Way of Life for a Searching People*. San Francisco: Jossey-Bass, 1997.

Cartwright, Michael G. *Practices, Politics, and Performance: Toward a Communal Hermeneutic for Christian Ethics*. Eugene, Ore.: Wipf & Stock Publishers, 2006.

Chittister, Joan, Martin E. Marty, and Robert S. Bilheimer, eds. *Faith and Ferment: An Interdisciplinary Study of Christian Beliefs and Practices*. Minneapolis: Augsburg Publishing House; and Collegeville, Minn.: Liturgical Press, 1983.

Cunningham, David S. *These Three Are One: The Practice of Trinitarian Theology*. Malden, Mass.: Blackwell, 1997.

Dykstra, Craig R. *Growing in the Life of Faith: Education and Christian Practices*. Louisville, Ky.: Westminster John Knox Press, 2005.

Hauerwas, Stanley. *Performing the Faith: Bonhoeffer and the Practice of Nonviolence*. Grand Rapids: Brazos Press, 2004.

Hütter, Reinhard. *Suffering Divine Things: Theology as Church Practice*. Trans. Doug Scott. Grand Rapids, and Cambridge, U.K.: Eerdmans, 2000.

Jung, L. Shannon. *Sharing Food: Christian Practices for Enjoyment*. Minneapolis: Fortress Press, 2006.

Lacugna, Catherine Mowry. *God for Us: The Trinity and Christian Life*. New York: HarperCollins, 1991.

Lindbeck, George A. *The Nature of Doctrine: Religion and Theology in a Postliberal Age*. Philadelphia: Westminster, 1984.

Long, Thomas G. *Testimony: Talking Ourselves into Being Christian*. San Francisco: Jossey-Bass, 2004.

Marshall, Bruce D., ed. *Theology and Dialogue: Essays in Conversation with George Lindbeck*. Notre Dame, Ind.: University of Notre Dame Press, 1990.

Murphy, Nancey C., Brad J. Kallenberg, and Mark Nation, eds. *Virtues and Practices in the Christian Tradition: Christian Ethics after MacIntyre*. Harrisburg, Pa.: Trinity Press International, 1997.

Pickstock, Catherine. *After Writing: On the Liturgical Consummation of Philosophy*. Oxford, U.K., and Malden, Mass.: Blackwell, 1998.

Vanhoozer, Kevin J. *The Drama of Doctrine: A Canonical-Linguistic Approach to Christian Theology*. Louisville, Ky.: Westminster John Knox, 2005.

Volf, Miroslav, and Dorothy C. Bass, eds. *Practicing Theology: Beliefs and Practices in Christian Life*. Grand Rapids: Eerdmans, 2002.

Yoder, John Howard. *Body Politics: Five Practices of the Christian Community before the Watching World*. Scottdale, Pa.: Herald Press, 2001.

Yong, Amos. *Theology and Down Syndrome: Reimagining Disability in Late Modernity.* Waco, Tex.: Baylor University Press, 2007.
Zimmerman, Earl. *Practicing the Politics of Jesus: The Origin and Significance of John Howard Yoder's Social Ethics.* Telford, Pa.: Cascadia Publishing House; and Scottdale, Pa.: Herald Press, 2007.

ON THEOLOGY OF RELIGIONS

Barnes, Michael. *Theology and the Dialogue of Religions.* Cambridge, U.K., and New York: Cambridge University Press, 2002.
Cobb, John B., Jr., *Beyond Dialogue: Toward a Mutual Transformation of Christianity and Buddhism.* Philadelphia: Fortress, 1982.
Dhavamony, Mariasusai. *Christian Theology of Religions: A Systematic Reflection on the Christian Understanding of World Religions.* Bern and New York: Peter Lang, 2001.
———. *Ecumenical Theology of World Religions.* Rome: Editrice Pontificia Università Gregoriana, 2003.
Dupuis, Jacques. *Toward a Christian Theology of Religious Pluralism.* Maryknoll, N.Y.: Orbis Books, 1997.
Fredericks, James L. *Buddhists and Christians: Through Comparative Theology to Solidarity.* Maryknoll, N.Y.: Orbis Books, 2004.
Griffiths, Paul J. *An Apology for Apologetics: A Study in the Logic of Interreligious Dialogue.* Maryknoll, N.Y.: Orbis Books, 1991.
Heim, S. Mark. *The Depths of the Riches: A Trinitarian Theology of Religious Ends.* Grand Rapids, and Cambridge, U.K.: Eerdmans, 2001.
Jeanrond, Werner G., and Aasulv Lande, eds. *The Concept of God in Global Dialogue.* Maryknoll, N.Y.: Orbis Books, 2005.
Kärkkäinen, Veli-Matti. *An Introduction to the Theology of Religions: Biblical, Historical and Contemporary Perspectives.* Downers Grove, Ill.: InterVarsity Press, 2003.
———. *Trinity and Religious Pluralism: The Doctrine of the Trinity in Christian Theology of Religions.* Aldershot, U.K., and Burlington, Vt.: Ashgate, 2004.
Kiblinger, Kristin Beise. *Buddhist Inclusivism: Attitudes toward Religious Others.* Burlington, Vt., and Aldershot, U.K.: Ashgate, 2005.
Knitter, Paul F. *Introducing Theologies of Religions.* Maryknoll, N.Y.: Orbis Books, 2002.
McDermott, Gerald R. *God's Rivals: Why Has God Allowed Different Religions? Insights from the Bible and the Early Church.* Downers Grove, Ill.: IVP Academic, 2007.
Perry, Tim S. *Radical Difference: A Defence of Hendrik Kraemer's Theology of Religions.* Editions SR 27. Waterloo, Ont.: Wilfrid Laurier University Press, 2001.
Plantinga, Richard, ed. *Christianity and Plurality: Classic and Contemporary Readings.* Malden, Mass., and Oxford: Blackwell, 1999.
Sumner, George R. *The First and the Last: The Claim of Jesus Christ and the Claims of Other Religious Traditions.* Grand Rapids: Eerdmans, 2004.
Yong, Amos. *Beyond the Impasse: Toward a Pneumatological Theology of Religions.* Carlisle, Cumbria, U.K.: Paternoster Press; and Grand Rapids: Baker Academic, 2003.

―――. *Discerning the Spirit(s): A Pentecostal-charismatic Contribution to Christian Theology of Religions.* Journal of Pentecostal Theology Supplement Series 20. Sheffield: Sheffield Academic Press, 2000.

ON THEOLOGY OF HOSPITALITY

Arterbury, Andrew E. *Entertaining Angels: Early Christian Hospitality in Its Mediterranean Setting.* New Testament Monographs 8. Sheffield: Sheffield Phoenix, 2005.

de Béthune, Pierre-François. *By Faith and Hospitality: The Monastic Tradition as a Model for Interreligious Encounter.* Trans. Mary Groves. Leominster, U.K.: Gracewing, 2002.

Boersma, Hans. *Violence, Hospitality, and the Cross: Reappropriating the Atonement Tradition.* Grand Rapids: Baker Academic, 2004.

Bretherton, Luke. *Hospitality as Holiness: Christian Witness amid Moral Diversity.* Burlington, Vt., and Aldershot, UK: Ashgate, 2006.

Byrne, Brendan. *The Hospitality of God: A Reading of Luke's Gospel.* Collegeville, Minn.: Liturgical Press, 2000.

Derrida, Jacques, and Anne Dufourmantelle. *Of Hospitality.* Trans. Rachel Bowlby. Stanford, Calif.: Stanford University Press, 2000.

Geitz, Elizabeth Rankin. *Entertaining Angels: Hospitality Programs for the Caring Church.* Harrisburg, Pa.: Morehouse, 1993.

―――. *Fireweed Evangelism: Christian Hospitality in a Multi-faith World.* New York: Church Pub., 2004.

Homan, Daniel, O.S.B., and Lonni Collins Pratt. *Radical Hospitality: Benedict's Way of Love.* Brewster, Mass.: Paraclete Press, 2002.

Keifert, Patrick R. *Welcoming the Stranger: A Public Theology of Worship and Evangelism.* Minneapolis: Fortress Press, 1992.

Kessler, Diane C., ed. *Receive One Another: Hospitality in Ecumenical Perspective.* Geneva: WCC Publications, 2005.

Koenig, John. *New Testament Hospitality: Partnership with Strangers as Promise and Mission.* Philadelphia: Fortress, 1985.

Oden, Amy, ed. *And You Welcomed Me: A Sourcebook on Hospitality in Early Christianity.* Nashville, Tenn.: Abingdon, 2001.

Ogletree, Thomas W. *Hospitality to the Stranger: Dimensions of Moral Understanding.* Philadelphia: Fortress, 1985.

Pohl, Christine D. *Making Room: Recovering Hospitality as a Christian Tradition.* Grand Rapids: Eerdmans, 1999.

Richard, Lucien. *Living the Hospitality of God.* New York: Paulist Press, 2000.

Sutherland, Arthur. *I Was a Stranger: A Christian Theology of Hospitality.* Nashville: Abingdon, 2006.

Westerhoff, Caroline A. *Good Fences: The Boundaries of Hospitality.* Cambridge, Mass.: Cowley Publications, 1999.

Westfield, N. Lynne. *Dear Sisters: A Womanist Practice of Hospitality.* Cleveland, Ohio: Pilgrim Press, 2001.

Author Index

Subject Index

Other Titles in the Faith Meets Faith Series